# A VOICE WAS SOUNDING
## SELECTIONS FROM *THIS LAND* VOLUMES I & II

THIS LAND™
PRESS

Works appearing in this anthology were originally published between
May 2010 and December 2011 in *This Land*, Tulsa, OK.
Vincent LoVoi, Publisher; Michael Mason, Editor.

WWW.THISLANDPRESS.COM

Book design by Carlos Knight & Jeremy Luther.

First Edition, October 2012

ISBN-10: 0985848707
ISBN-13: 978-0-9858487-0-5

# TABLE OF CONTENTS

# TABLE OF CONTENTS

# CONVICTION AND TRANSFORMATION

# TABLE OF CONTENTS

## IMAGINARY OKLAHOMA

## POETRY

# TABLE OF CONTENTS

# TABLE OF CONTENTS

# TABLE OF CONTENTS

## PLAIN HUMOR

# A VOICE WAS SOUNDING

SELECTIONS FROM *THIS LAND* VOLUMES I & II

# INTRODUCTION

*By Michael Mason*

"I'M GOING TO CALL IT *THIS LAND*," I EXPLAINED to my friend Mark Brown in an email. It was February of 2009, a year after my first book was published. Newspapers were packed with stories of their impending demise, and you couldn't hear a television report about the journalism industry without a layoff being mentioned. In the industry implosion, I sensed opportunity. As an author and journalist, I had the good fortune of having worked under some of the best editors in the world, and I felt ready to try my own hand at publishing. Back then, I envisioned that This Land Press might operate as a family of websites, fueled by a co-op of writers and artists. I'd never started a business before and thought such a model might work. As a testing ground, a local author, Jeff Martin, and I started a podcast called *Goodbye Tulsa*, a sort of audio tribute to Tulsans who had died. We were both curious about whether our community would be interested in the kinds of stories we had to tell. The podcast gathered a large listenership and helped us develop our approach to local storytelling.

A year later, the ideas that began *This Land* evolved with the help of a friend of mine, Van Eden. Like me, Van loved good writing and he was frustrated with what he felt were shortages in the Oklahoma media market. But he was wise enough to understand that This Land Press needed some sort of patron or investor. Van eventually introduced me to a local businessman, Dean Williams, who operated a large auction company in Tulsa. Dean and I met on his patio and talked about our love for Oklahoma and our desire for stories that were relevant. I told him that I had an idea for a broadsheet publication called *This Land*, and I brought along McSweeney's famous publication, *Panorama*, to show him an example of the kind of creativity that the format allowed. It wasn't the broadsheet that sold him on the idea, though.

"You had me when you told me the title," Dean once told me. "*This Land* says it all: it's about our land and our connection to it."

I told Dean that I needed $5,000, and that I would deliver, in a month's time, 50 copies of the publication as a prototype.

We closed the first issue of *This Land* late one night in a tall building downtown. Carlos Knight and I sat shoulder-to-shoulder, bickering over hairlines and kerning. We had several great stories to work with—an original work by the fiction writer Rivka Galchen, a humorous bit about Tulsa's Skunk Whisperer, and a feature article by Randy Roberts Potts, the grandson of the televangelist Oral Roberts. Carlos and I went through each page of the issue together, with Carlos tweaking the size of fonts and changing colors here and there. In the same room, another friend, Dennis Leech, put the final touches on the cover he had designed. And then it was finished.

Instead of ordering just 50 copies of *This Land*, I used Dean's seed money to order 5,000 copies—and I had a little left over to pay my contributors.

When we circulated *This Land* around town, it was a gamble. I had a hunch that Oklahoma had a hole in its media industry, and I believed that it could be filled with stories that were longer and more in-depth—stories that could act as the literature of the community. I sensed that journalism was going local in the same way that food had gone local, and that a community might rise to support its local writers and artists just as they might support local farmers and restaurants. But there was still a lot I didn't know. I hadn't really done an in-depth analysis of the industry, and hadn't completely worked out how to make storytelling a viable business model. All I knew was that we were building great stories.

Shortly after the first issue came out, I met Vincent LoVoi at a friend's wedding. An attorney who no longer practices, Vince is a good-natured man, a real enthusiast of life and all its offerings. He calls himself a "boomeranger"; he returned to Oklahoma after years of living abroad. I had first met him a year before at a talk given by Malcolm Gladwell, and even then, we talked of newspapers. By the time I saw him at the wedding, he had already picked up a copy of *This Land* and immediately understood its aesthetic. He knew what I was hoping to accomplish from a content perspective, but he sensed I needed to develop a stronger business model to help propel the organization forward. While the entire industry of journalism was turning toward non-profit models, Vince believed that a for-profit enterprise might make a more sustainable business.

Vince and I began meeting for lunch on a regular basis—the pork belly summits, I like to think of them—and pushed ideas back and forth at each other. We wrestled with every aspect of a media operation: distribution models, subscription management, sales, content creation, and production. Vince's business acumen combined with his passion for journalism acted as a catalyst for the basic ideals upon which This Land Press, LLC was created. Sensing the timing was right, Vince encouraged me to put our ideas together into a business plan—one that he would ultimately decide to invest in.

In March of 2011, This Land Press became a full-fledged media company; Vince became our publisher and my business partner. We were able to bring on a dream team of talent. Unencumbered by the waste that saddles traditional media companies, we began producing astounding amounts of content in a variety of formats. By July, we were able to begin publishing the magazine on a semimonthly basis—the 1st and the 15th of each month—and we began releasing audio programs and short videos. Although our pace had increased exponentially, we were still able to maintain the quality of our content. Along with dozens of national and international media outlets, the *Columbia Journalism Review* noticed our work and called us "*The New Yorker* with balls," and "a rare example of literary journalism on the community level." We're proud of both descriptions.

Since our first print run, we've invested heavily in the editorial quality of our content, and I feel proud to say that several of our contributors have managed to build careers based on their reporting for us, while other more established writers have found in *This Land* a home for some of their best work. In this collection of stories, we've compiled selections from our first two volumes (calendar years 2010 and 2011) that we think communicate the broader story of life in the middle of the country. While most of the work here is non-fiction narrative journalism, we also publish fiction and poetry because they also help us understand who we are as a people.

*A Voice Was Sounding* is filled with stories of our history, investigations of our community, humorous takes on life in flyover country, and profiles of people who captivate us. Taken together, the works constitute an exciting new voice emerging from America's midlands.

Michael Mason, Editor
This Land Press

# EXAMINING OUR PAST,
# NEAR AND FAR

# THE NIGHTMARE OF DREAMLAND:

## TATE BRADY AND THE BATTLE FOR GREENWOOD

*by Lee Roy Chapman*

The seventeen men were terrified, and with good reason. They stood shivering in the November midnight air, their bare chests lit by the headlights of the parked cars surrounding them. In the dark, they could barely make out their captors, a group of about fifty men dressed in black hoods and robes.

Two hours earlier, during a special session of night court, Tulsa judge T.D. Evans had declared them all guilty of the crime of not owning a war bond—a conviction that smacked of political and ideological retaliation. All defendants but one were members of the Industrial Workers of the World (IWW), a worker's union. The "Wobblies," as they were commonly called, were opponents of the war effort and of capitalism. None of the men had a criminal record, but all men were fined a hundred dollars.[1]

They weren't expected to pay for their crimes, at least not in money.

Once the trial ended, policemen rounded up the seventeen and loaded them up in squad cars. Instead of jailing them, the police delivered the convicted men into the custody of the black-robed Knights of Liberty,[2] who were waiting for the Wobblies at the railroad tracks near Convention Hall.[3] The Knights kidnapped the Wobblies at gunpoint, tied them up, threw them into their cars, and drove them into the area west of town.[4]

"We were ordered out of the autos, told to get in line in front of these gunmen, and another bunch of men with automatics and pistols," Joe French, one of the Wobblies, would later testify.

One by one, they were pulled from the lineup and tied to a tree. A Knight then approached each man with a double piece of hemp rope and whipped the victim's back until blood draped his skin. Another man stepped forward and slathered boiling tar on the victim's back with a paint brush, coating him from head to seat. In a final act of humiliation, the Knight then padded the victim's back with feathers from a down pillow.[5]

"I've lived here for 18 years, and have raised a large family," pleaded an older man in the group. "I am not an IWW, I am as patriotic as any man here."

The man's cries were ignored; every man was whipped, tarred, and feathered. The incident became known "The Tulsa Outrage," and was reported in the national press. According to multiple interviews conducted by National Civil Liberties Bureau investigator L. A. Brown, two men were repeatedly identified as perpetrating the torture: Tulsa's Chief of Police, Ed Lucas, and W. Tate Brady, one of Tulsa's founders. That's Tate Brady, as in Brady Theater, Brady Arts District, and Brady Heights.[6]

The following day, November 10, 1917, the front page of the *Tulsa Daily World* would make an announcement to the city regarding the flogging of the Wobblies: "Modern Ku Klux Klan Comes into Being: Seventeen First Victims;[7] Black Robed 'Knights of Liberty' Take Prisoners from Police to Lonely Ravine."

## THE SEGREGATION OF HISTORY

According to the Oklahoma Historical Society's *Encyclopedia of Oklahoma*, Tate Brady was a "pioneer, entrepreneur, member of the Oklahoma Bar, politician, and early booster of Tulsa." The Brady Heights Historic District website calls him "a pioneer Tulsa developer and entrepreneur, who was a powerful political force in the state's early years. He was Oklahoma's first Democratic National committeeman, and he built the Cain's Ballroom and the now extinct Brady Hotel." *Tulsa World* wrote: "Brady, a pioneer merchant, was an incorporator of the city, as well as a political leader at the time of statehood."

All of these accounts exclude any direct mention of Brady's less-than-honorable traits: his violent behavior, his attempts to segregate Tulsa, his deep involvement with the Klan and affiliated organizations, and his abuse of power.

"Well, it's political," one employee of the Oklahoma Historical Society said, when asked about the gaps in Brady's biography.

Despite the widespread segregation of memory surrounding Brady, a rounder, more accurate portrait of the man emerges when all of the history is taken into account.

## THE MAKING OF COMRADE TATE

Wyatt Tate Brady was born in Forest City, Missouri, in 1870, and moved to Nevada, Missouri, when he was 12. By the time he was 17, he had taken up work at W.F. Lewis' shoe store, where he encountered his first brush with real terror—as a victim.

In the early morning hours of March 3, 1887, a customer unfamiliar to Brady entered the store. The stranger asked to see samples of shoes and offered to pay for them. Suspicious of the customer, Brady slipped his revolver from under the counter into his pocket. When Brady went to the safe for change, the stranger rushed Brady and shot at him, sending a bullet through Brady's left ear. Brady fired a shot back, missing the robber. A disoriented Brady was then pistol-whipped and the robber made his getaway.

Undeterred by the assault, Brady set out for a new frontier.

Three years later, in 1890, the young bachelor headed toward the Creek Nation, Indian Territory, to make his mark as a merchant, providing goods for the established cattle trade and railroad. By

Brady's arrival, Tulsa had a cemetery,[8] a Masonic Lodge, a post office, a lumberyard, and a coal mine.

Five years after his arrival in Tulsa, on April 18, 1895, Brady married Rachel Cassandra Davis, who came from a prominent Claremore family. She was 1/64th Cherokee, which gave her new husband special privileges among the Cherokee tribe.[9] Together, the Bradys had four children: Ruth, Bessie,[10] Henry, and John. Three years later, January 18, 1898, Brady and other prominent businessmen signed the charter that established Tulsa as an officially incorporated city. Tate Brady was now a founding father of Tulsa.

"Indian and white man, Jew and Gentile, Catholic and Protestant, we worked together side by side, and shoulder to shoulder, and under these conditions, the 'Tulsa Spirit'[11] was born, and has lived, and God grant that it never dies," Brady wrote in a *Tulsa Tribune* article.

Brady was operating a storefront by this point and preparing to expand his operation when an event occurred that would forever change Tulsa's history.

In 1901, the Red Fork oil field was discovered, which catapulted Tulsa onto the scene of world commerce. As the city began to swell with oil-minded entrepreneurs and workers, Brady saw an opportunity: the visitors needed a place to stay. In 1903, he opened the Brady Hotel, located at Archer and Main streets, just a short walk from the railroad tracks. It was the first hotel in Tulsa with baths. By 1905, with the discovery of more oil in the Glenn Pool south of town, the Brady Hotel found itself with a rush of clientele.[12]

With his hotel and mercantile businesses thriving, Brady began broadening his scope of influence. He lent financial support to an early paper called the *Tulsa Democrat*, and he began to buy and develop land near his businesses.[13] Along the way, Brady became a true Tulsa booster. In March of 1905, he, along with a hundred civic leaders, a 20-piece band, and "the Indian" Will Rogers, hired a train and toured the country to promote Tulsa as a city with unbound potential.

Brady's Confederate sympathies ran deep—sympathies that would steer his actions in later life. His father, H.H. Brady, had fought as a Confederate soldier in the Civil War. By 1912, Tate Brady's name had already appeared in Volume 20 of the *Confederate Veteran*. The magazine listed him as the commander of the Oklahoma division of the Sons of Confederate Veterans. In 1915, Nathan Bedford Forrest, General Secretary of the Sons of Confederate Veterans, visited Tulsa. In the *Confederate Veteran*, Forrest wrote that he consulted with "Comrade Tate Brady," and together they made plans for "an active campaign throughout Oklahoma."

Forrest, it should be noted, was the grandson of General Nathan Bedford Forrest, a pioneering leader of the Ku Klux Klan.

## THE TULSA OUTRAGE

Tulsa's oil was an important national resource during World War I. By 1917, the city was selling a tremendous amount of Liberty Bonds, a type of war bond that helped bolster the USA's financial position during the war. Because the war effort consumed so much oil, however, Tulsa stood to gain massive economic benefits. Any opposition to the war was viewed as a threat to personal prosperity and success.

To help support the war effort, the National Defense Act established the state Councils of Defense. In Tulsa, the Tulsa Chamber of Commerce fulfilled that role. Its members were asked to report any seditious activities, including statements of dissent, acts of industrial sabotage, or "slackerism" (the refusal to participate in work or war). In Tulsa, this essentially put business leaders in charge of finding and reporting anything or anyone they found threatening to the war effort.

No group was more hated or feared in Tulsa than the IWW. As individuals publicly opposed to the war effort, Wobblies felt compelled to dampen industrial productivity by encouraging workers to strike. If such a strike were to occur, it could impact oil production and threaten the supply of oil to the military campaign. Tulsa's economy was vulnerable to an act of worker sabotage.

On August 2, 1917, a sharecropper's uprising in southeastern Oklahoma resulted in the arrest of several hundred people. The Green Corn Rebellion, as it came to be called, essentially ended the socialist movement in Oklahoma. It also proved that anti-war sentiments had not only reached a wide level of social acceptance among working-class Oklahomans, but had escalated to the point that many were willing to take up arms in opposition to the war.

Brady held a particularly strong antipathy for the Wobblies. Just a few days before the Tulsa Outrage, on November 6, 1917, Brady saw a rival hotel owner, E. L. Fox standing at the corner of Main and Brady streets. A year prior, Fox had leased an office to the IWW, unaware of the Wobblies' mission. Their presence in the neighborhood infuriated Brady.

"When are you going to move those IWW out of your building?" Brady yelled at him.

"There's no North Side Improvement Association anymore," Fox replied, implying that Brady had no authority over Fox's business affairs.[14]

An aggravated Brady punched Fox, knocking him to the ground and beating him into the gutter. Dozens of people witnessed the assault, which was reported in the *Tulsa Daily World* the following day.

The Council of Defense had no better ally or mouthpiece than the *Tulsa Daily World*, Tulsa's largest newspaper. Historian Nigel Sellars called the *World* "the most pro-oil industry, pro-war, racist, anti-foreigner and anti-labor paper of them all."[15] Throughout 1917, most of the paper's vitriol was aimed at the IWW, whom the *World* accused of being a German-controlled organization.

In what is arguably one of the lowest points in the paper's history, *Tulsa Daily World* published an editorial titled, "Get Out the Hemp."[16] Glenn Condon, a managing editor for the *World*, wrote that "the first step in whipping Germany is to strangle the I.W.W.'s [sic]. Kill 'em as you would any other snake. Don't scotch 'em; kill 'em. And kill 'em dead."

The day after the article was published, the seventeen Wobblies were convicted of a minor charge and handed to the Knights of Liberty by Tulsa's own police. Brady was a ringleader in the kidnapping and ensuing torture in the woods west of town. Only two people in the mob were not robed—a reporter and his wife. The reporter was Glenn Condon,[17] who at the time was also serving as a member of the Council of Defense.

A month after the incident, in the December issue of their magazine *Tulsa Spirit*, the Tulsa Chamber of Commerce included this note:

"The Tulsa social event of November to attract the most national attention was the coming out party of the Knights of Liberty with about seventeen I.W.W. in the receiving line. As is usual in such social functions, a pleasant time was not had by some of those fortunate enough to be present."

## DIXIELAND

Terrible as it was, the Tulsa Outrage foreshadowed an event that would soon eclipse it in violence and notoriety. By 1918, extralegal violence, including lynchings, had spread throughout the state and had appeared to gain a quiet acceptance and collaboration among law enforcement, politicians, and business leaders. During this heated period of racial tension, Tate Brady and the Tulsa Chamber of Commerce brought the Sons of Confederate Veterans 28th Annual Reunion to town.[18]

Back then, the Sons of Confederate Veterans wasn't merely a benign Civil War re-enactment club, as it is so often portrayed in today's media. One of its organizing principles was, and remains, "the emulation of [the Confederate veteran's] virtues, and the perpetuation of those principles he loved."

As the largest gathering of Confederate veterans since the Civil War (more than 40,000 attended), the 1918 Tulsa convention celebrated Southern nostalgia and ideologies. Tulsa leaders banded together to raise over $100,000 to cover the cost of the event. Reunion visitors were treated to the best of Tulsa's marvels: tours to the oil fields, free trolley tickets, and lodging with modern-day heated quarters. Although Tate Brady was the primary organizer of the reunion, its committee members included judges, ministers, and influential names that are still widely recognized in Tulsa: R. M. McFarlin, S. R. Lewis, Earl P. Harwell, Charles Page, W. A. Vandever, Eugene Lorton, and J. H. McBirney.

The event was so popular that it took up several columns on the front pages of the *Tulsa Daily World*, which helped promote a number of other ancillary events happening across the city. While the reunion was largely received as an economic boost of civic pride, history won't excuse the darker attitudes that motivated the organization and its leaders. The reunion's figurehead, Nathan Bedford Forrest, served as the KKK's Grand Dragon of Georgia, and an "Imperial Klokann" for the National Klan.[19] The Klan actively recruited its members from the Sons of Confederate Veterans. A few years after the convention, Forrest served as the business manager of Lanier College, the first KKK college in Atlanta. "Our institution will teach pure, 100 percent Americanism," Forrest told the *New York Times*.

The 28th Annual Sons of Confederate Veterans Convention demonstrated that Tulsa's most powerful and influential leaders at the very least tolerated—and at the most promulgated—the beliefs and biases that primed Tulsa for its most violent display of racial tension, the Tulsa Race Riot of 1921. Publicly, there was no dissenting voice, no expressed opposition to the Tulsa Outrage or the reunion.

## BRADY AND THE RIOT

Tate Brady's prominence and wealth increased with each passing year. In their tenure, his retail stores sold some $5 million worth of goods ($60 million in today's dollars), and the Hotel Brady did $3 million in business. He began to invest in coal mining operations and farming interests. In the early twenties he began expanding his property holdings, spending $1 million in property acquisitions—some of which was in Greenwood.

In 1920, Brady built a mansion overlooking the city and modeled it after the Arlington, Virginia, home of one of his personal heroes, General Robert E. Lee. The home contained murals of famous Civil War battle scenes favorable to the Confederacy. Brady and his wife held galas celebrating Lee's birthday.

By 1921, Brady was a recognized city leader and a tireless booster of "Tulsa Spirit," a term he coined. Yet despite his position at the top of the town's social circles, he managed to find time to volunteer when civic duty called.

When the Tulsa Race Riot occurred on May 31, 1921, mayhem broke out in Greenwood, with buildings catching fire just two blocks from the Hotel Brady. During the early morning hours of June 1, white mobs numbering in the thousands were spotted on each major corner of the Brady district.[20] They headed eastward, invading Greenwood.

Brady and a number of other white men volunteered for guard duty on the night of May 31. During his watch, Brady reported "five dead negroes." One victim had been dragged behind a car through the business district, a rope tied around his neck.

The following week Brady was appointed to the Tulsa Real Estate Exchange Commission. The Exchange, created by the Tulsa Chamber of Commerce, was tasked with assessing the property damage.[21] The loss was estimated at $1.5 million. In conjunction with the City Commission, the Real Estate Exchange planned to relocate black Tulsans further north and east, and to expand the railroad's property over the damaged lands.

"We further believe that the two races being divided by an industrial section will draw more distinctive lines between them and thereby eliminate the intermingling of the lower elements of the two races," the Exchange told the *Tulsa Tribune*.

The Exchange then created new building requirements that made rebuilding in the area difficult. The Exchange reasoned that if residential property could be inhibited, commercial property would take its place, increasing its value by over three times its original cost. Greenwood's property value could skyrocket, and the races could be separated. To the Exchange commission, it must have seemed like an ideal plan.

Accusations of land-grabbing tormented Brady so much that he publicly issued a $1,000 reward to anyone who could prove that he benefitted from the Tulsa Race Riot. Brady, incidentally, owned rental properties that were destroyed in the riot, and tried to collect insurance on them, but did not succeed.

Despite the Exchange's efforts, Oklahoma's Supreme Court overruled the proposed ordinances, allowing Greenwood citizens to rebuild.[22] Black Tulsans were left to rebuild their homes without any aid from the city or from insurance companies.[23]

## BRADY'S CURSE

Following the riot, Klan activity increased. A large parade of Klansmen, women and youth was organized in the months following the riot. In 1923, the Klan, established as the Tulsa Benevolent Society, paid $200,000 for the construction of a large "Klavern" or gathering hall that could seat 3,000 members. Beno Hall, as it was known, was located at 503 N. Main St., on land owned by Brady.[24]

Brady's prominence in Oklahoma politics suffered a setback when Oklahoma Governor John C. Walton targeted the Klan. In August of 1923, Walton put Tulsa under martial law to investigate Klan activity.

During a related Oklahoma military tribunal in September 1923, Brady admitted his membership in the Klan.[25]

"I was a member of the Klan here at one time," Brady said, claiming he resigned his membership by October of 1922. "I have in my home the original records, some of my father's membership in the original Klan, and I think that you [the current Klan] are a disgrace." He didn't like the Klan telling him how to vote, he explained.[26]

Brady's testimony hinted at a larger social predicament. Oklahoma's Democratic Party was losing its dominance to the Republicans, putting Brady, a committed Democrat, in a weaker position politically. Nevertheless, he still appeared outwardly hopeful.

"As I look about me during this my thirty-fourth year in Tulsa, I see locks, once raven, sprinkled with snow, and life's fires burning low in the eyes of pioneers once bright," Brady wrote. "As we start this new year of 1924 may the spirit of the pioneer—the spirit that built Tulsa—prevail as of yore. Cursed be he, or they, who on any pretext try to divide our citizenship and destroy this spirit."

While he saw a sunny future for Tulsa, Brady's own situation did not appear as golden. By 1925, his considerable holdings had been reduced to about $600,000, according to a *Tulsa Daily World* estimation, which also suggested that he was indebted on those holdings.[27] In the spring of that year, his son John Davis Brady—a promising law student at the University of Virginia—died in a car accident.

Lacking the political power he once held through both the Democratic Party and his Klan affiliations, diminished in his fortune, and aggrieved by his son's death, Brady began to fall apart. Tulsans reported seeing him dining at his hotel alone, staring into space and leaving his meals untouched. Gone was the steeley-eyed entrepreneur. A portrait published in the *Tulsa Daily World* around this time shows an aged Brady looking weary and morose.

In the early morning hours of August 29, 1925, Brady walked into his kitchen and sat down at the breakfast table. He propped a pillow in the nook of one arm, and rested his head upon it. With his right arm, he took a .44 caliber pistol, pointed it at his temple, and pulled the trigger.[28] Brady, who worked to divide Tulsa along racial lines, died a victim of his own curse.

## THE BRADY DISTRICT TODAY

Today, the Brady Arts District is the focal point of multi-million dollar developments involving local organizations such as the George Kaiser Family Foundation, the Oklahoma Museum of Music and Popular Culture, the University of Tulsa, Gilcrease Museum, Philbrook Museum, and the Arts and Humanities Council of Tulsa. Local businesses also thrive in the district: numerous bars and restaurants,[29] the family-owned Cain's Ballroom (which once served as Brady's garage), and the Tulsa Violin Shop, to name a few. A large new ballpark separates the Brady District and the Greenwood area.[30]

In 2005, the National Park Service/US Department of Interior published *The Final 1921 Race Riot Reconnaissance Survey* commissioned in 2003 by the Oklahoma Historical Society and the 1921 Tulsa Race Riot Memorial of Reconciliation Design Committee. The purpose was to determine if Greenwood possessed enough "extant resources" to merit national significance. The survey concluded that the Tulsa Race Riot is significant because it is "an outstanding example of a particular type of resource," and "possesses exceptional value or quality in illustrating or interpreting the natural or cultural themes of our national heritage." In addition to the findings, the report explained Brady's role in segregating not only Tulsa, but Oklahoma.[31] Despite these findings, the Tulsa Race Riot area, including Greenwood, remains unregistered.

Preservation consultant Cathy Ambler stated, in a February 2010 PLANiTULSA proposal: "Today, there is a faction of Tulsans who take issue with some of the associations and choices that Tate Brady was involved with, but there is no denying that he was a huge supporter of Tulsa and played a very big part in its early development."

In September 2010, the Brady Arts District was placed on the National Register of Historic Places, owing to its significance as a place of commerce. It enjoys the full benefits allotted under the designation. ◢

## ENDNOTES:

1. Five men present were witnesses for the defense. Judge Evans convicted these men, along with the men charged, stating, "These are no ordinary times."

2. Referred to as a "faction" of the Klan, the Knights of Liberty were a short-lived secret order with cells throughout the nation. In Oklahoma, they carried out extralegal action on behalf of the Tulsa Chamber of Commerce and its Council of Defense, in the tradition of the Reconstruction-era Ku Klux Klan, the "Invisible Empire." After the end of the war, the Knights of Liberty, in some areas of the country, turned against the Klan.

3. The Convention Hall building is now known as the Brady Theater.

4. The area where the Tulsa Outrage tortures occurred was then known as Irving Place Editions, an area today understood as a combination of the Crosby Heights and Owen Park neighborhoods.

5. The act of tarring and feathering is a medieval form of torture, dating back to the 12th century. The application of hot tar burned the skin; the inclusion of the feathers added insult to injury. The most recent case of tarring and feathering occurred in 2007 in Ireland.

6. The L. A. Brown Papers were acquired by This Land Press from the New York State Archives. L. A. Brown was the investigator of the Tulsa Outrage for the National Civil Liberties Bureau (now the ACLU).

7. According to the Oklahoma Historical Society, the Klan did not officially arrive in Oklahoma until 1920 when the Invisible Knights of the Ku Klux Klan Inc. registered in the state. However, as far back as 1907 there were reported incidents of extralegal activities by "white cappers." The existence of a

Ku Klux Klan prior to 1920 is well-documented. For instance, Altus organized its own KKK in 1917, around the time of the Tulsa Outrage.

8. The cemetery was located at 2nd Street and Frisco Avenue—underneath the western half of the BOK Center.

9. Brady served as the General Chairman of the Executive Committee of the Cherokee Nation. According to Kiowa County's *Mountain Park Herald*, Brady sought to recover lands and money given to Cherokee Freedmen since 1866, which were then valued at $30 million dollars.

10. Bessie Brady would eventually marry Eugene Sloan Adkins, father of art collector Eugene Brady Adkins. Philbrook Museum of Art and the Fred Jones Jr. Museum of Art share the $50 million dollar Eugene Brady Adkins Collection.

11. This term was adopted by the Tulsa Chamber of Commerce and can be seen in use today on Tulsa Police Department patrol cars.

12. Not all of the clientele were oil-based. The Hotel Brady also served as a meeting place for Democrats. According to *A Century of African American Experience* (Don Ross, 2003), the hotel was "where Democrats headquartered, laid plans to control the Constitutional Convention leading to statehood that barred blacks, and also designed plots for segregation after statehood."

13. Around this time period, in 1908, Brady sustained a serious—perhaps life-threatening—injury when he fell from a streetcar. It's unknown whether he sustained any ongoing complications from that injury.

14. According to the *Tulsa Daily World*, Brady founded the North-Side Improvement Association, which "combined some of the functions of civic club and chamber of commerce on the north side." Brady wanted Tulsa to develop toward the north into the Cherokee Nation.

15. *Oil, Wheat, & Wobblies: the Industrial Workers of the World in Oklahoma, 1905–1930.*

16. The editorial "Get Out the Hemp" appeared without a byline on the op-ed pages. The managing editor at the time was Glenn Condon.

According to Sellars, the editorial may have been written by editor Eugene Lorton.

17. The year following the Outrage, Condon left Tulsa on a secret mission on behalf of the Council of Defense. He eventually settled in Tulsa in 1926, becoming a founder of the radio station KOME, "The Magic Empire." He was also a well-known radio personality for KAKC and later KRMG. Condon was an early member, then president of the Tulsa Press Club and Benevolent Association. He died in 1968.

18. Merritt Glass and Tate Brady founded the Tulsa Chapter of Sons of Confederate Veterans in 1908, at the Hotel Brady. During the convention of 1918, the Tulsa Chamber of Commerce provided meeting rooms for Forrest, who was headquartered at Convention Hall. Following the reunion, the Chamber of Commerce wrote that Tulsans had raised a considerable amount of money toward the event, and that it was "the best investment in friendship and hospitality ever made by any city in the South."

19. An "Imperial Klokann" was one of four positions known as an auditor; together with other administrators of the KKK, the Klokans acted as an advisory cabinet to the Klan. Grand Dragons were leaders of state Klan organizations that were supported by 11 cabinet members. At the time of Forrest's leadership, Georgia had about 156,000 members in the Klan, which earned Forrest an estimated $2.5 million annually in today's dollars.

20. The pogrom consisted of Oklahoma National Guard units, Tulsa Home Guard units under the command of Patrick J. Hurley, and various whites who were armed.

21. The Real Estate Exchange was established by the Tulsa Chamber of Commerce.

22. The ordinance was overturned by the efforts of B.C. Franklin, father of noted historian John Hope Franklin.

23. By the summer of 1922 an estimated 85 percent of the Greenwood area was rebuilt.

24. Today, the location is an empty lot owned by the Oklahoma State Department of Highways.

25. The Klan played a role in impeaching Walton.

26. John C. Walton Papers, Box 14, Folder 27, *Proceedings of the Oklahoma Military Commission in the Matter of Klan Activity of Tulsa, Oklahoma*, Western History Collections, University of Oklahoma Libraries, Norman, Oklahoma. A full transcript of Brady's testimony will appear online at thislandpress.com

27. A former owner of Brady's mansion, Tim Lannom, told *Tulsa World* that Brady "committed suicide so his wife could collect a million dollar insurance policy ... That was back in the days when you could get away with that." In a follow up editorial, Lannom apologized for the statement, writing that he had done research and could not substantiate the rumor, and added that he could not find any evidence linking Brady to the Klan. Lannom died in 2007, the victim of a gunshot wound to the neck.

28. Tate Brady was laid to rest in Oaklawn Cemetery. Dr. Clyde Snow, a forensic anthropologist who consulted for the Tulsa Race Riot Commission in 1999, believes that a mass grave of Race Riot victims is located at Oaklawn. The City of Tulsa prohibited the Commission from excavating the site.

29. Disclaimer: Vincent LoVoi, publisher of This Land Press, is a partner in the McNellie's Group, which operates The Brady Tavern restaurant.

30. The ballpark was originally to be located at 3rd Street and Greenwood Avenue, outside the areas identified in the report. It was relocated to its current location, which rests upon those lands designated as historically significant.

31. The report stated "A Tulsa city incorporator, and one of its first alderman, Brady built the first hotel in the city in 1903, where Democrats headquartered and laid plans to control the constitutional convention leading to statehood that provided the legal foundation for segregation."

# BENO HALL:

## TULSA'S DEN OF TERROR

*by Steve Gerkin*

The monstrous, three-story, steel reinforced, stucco building towered along the western edge of Greenwood. It dominated the landscape at the foot of Standpipe Hill, sporting a bright whitewash, the favorite color of its primary residents. Inside, its members vowed to protect their notion of "100% Americanism." To become a guardian of liberty, they reasoned, you had to swear to secrecy and seclusion. And you had to embrace intimidation and violence as a way to assert your values.

In January of 1922, the Tulsa Benevolent Association of Tulsa, Oklahoma was officially formed as a holding company for the Knights of the Ku Klux Klan, Incorporated. Among its founding members was Washington E. Hudson, the attorney for Dick Rowland—the young black man who was a scapegoat for the 1921 Tulsa Race Riot. They provided the financing and leadership to begin building their Klan temple, or Klavern, known as Beno Hall. Locals jokingly called it "Be No Hall," as in "Be No Nigger, Be No Jew, Be No Catholic, Be No Immigrant."

Six months after its inception and bolstered by a raffle of 13 Ford automobiles netting nearly half of the $60,000 purchase price, the Benevolent Association bought the Centenary Methodist Church, at Main and Easton streets. The organization quickly outgrew this facility and the church was razed, making way for the future monument of white supremacy. Beno Hall was built for $200,000

($1.5 million in today's currency). Financing of the construction was kept quiet, but the land for the building was owned by the entrepreneur, politician, and early booster of Tulsa, Tate Brady, and his wife Rachel Brady, who received a large parcel of land as a Cherokee allotment in 1910. When Beno Hall was completed, it was one of the largest auditoriums in the Southwest, holding 3,000 people. Its size alone provided Tulsa with a visual reminder of the Invisible Empire's power, passion and presence.

Abundant evidence points the finger at the Klan for fanning the sociological tinderbox that was 1920s Tulsa. Yearning for a spark, if even an invented one, a fired-up mob of whites took the bait and burned Greenwood to the ground in the Memorial Day, 1921 Race Riot. Two months later, a national Klan official, Caleb Ridley, who was also a Baptist minister, lectured at the Tulsa Convention Hall on the principles of the Klan, calling the Riot a complete success, adding that it "was the best thing to ever happen to Tulsa and that judging from the way strange Negroes were coming to Tulsa we might have to do it all over again."

Under the watchful eye of its Tulsa leader, the Exalted Cyclops William Shelley Rogers, membership grew to include all civic and social levels: from law enforcement to welders, bankers, dry cleaners, judges, commissioners, and oil field workers. All partook in the Beno Hall sessions that focused on increasing membership and efforts to keep Tulsa free from moral corruption and centered on family values.

Barely three months after the Riot, some 300 Tulsans, supported by a throng of 1,500 onlookers, were initiated as the first class of the Tulsa Klan No. 2. A year later, in a field north of Owasso, a nighttime "naturalization" ceremony initiated 1,020 Tulsa Klavern members before a fiery, 70-by-20 foot cross.

Recruiters known as Kleagles "capitalized upon the emotions in the wake of the race riot to propagandize the white community of Tulsa," writes Carter Blue Clark in his 1976 dissertation, *A History of the Ku Klux Klan in Oklahoma.*

While the Oklahoma Klan boasted over 150,000 hooded devotees in the early 1920s, the Tulsa Klavern—a reference to the smallest local unit of the organizational structure, wherein ritual ceremonies and Klan Khoral Klub rehearsals were held—swelled to 3,000 members. Hence the need for a permanent structure—a very large, secure structure.

Nestled near the two-year-old ashes of upper-class black homes that once sprawled up the slopes of Sunset and Standpipe hills, overlooking the industry that was Greenwood, Beno Hall towered over nearly 2,000 black Tulsans as they huddled in makeshift tents. They lived within earshot of the member revelry. From the halls of Beno sprung midnight parades, cross burnings along the boundaries of Greenwood, night-riding terrors, meetings determining political candidates' success or failure, plans to squash the proliferation of filthy people with filthy morals who bootlegged, gambled, consorted with whores, or were unfaithful husbands—all of which conflicted with the Klan's version of white, Protestant ideology.

The Klan loved parades. The most spectacular occurred in August of 1922, while the wounds of the 1921 riot were still fresh. The parade featured 1,741 white-robed members marching silently through downtown Tulsa before an estimated crowd of 15,000. The Women of the Klan provided extra pizzazz, carrying signs with various slogans such as, "Kiss the flag or cross the pond," a reminder that immigrants were not Americans, therefore, there should "Be None" on American soil, certainly not in Oklahoma.

The Knights had nothing against what they deemed "good niggers." They were also morally incensed by the behavior of white men—especially the oil field workers who used the trolley system to come to downtown Tulsa, where they spent their cash on booze, dames, and pounds of cocaine, morphine, and heroin. In *Tulsa!: Biography of the American City*, Danney Goble wrote, "Kluxers meted out rough justice to those that lived beyond the law's bounds"—justice that predominantly involved acts against white Protestants.

The Klan wasn't just for older white men, either. The Tulsa Klavern vigorously promoted the Women of the Klan society and an adolescent male branch called the Junior Ku Klux Klan, which recruited boys aged 12 to 18.

According to an invitation on Junior Ku Klux Klan stationery of the Tulsa Benevolent Association, a Junior KKK "Open Air Initiation" at the Lynch Farm north of Rose Hill Cemetery began at 7:30 p.m. Friday, September 18, 1924. It promised a ride to the event, if needed, and "lots of fireworks."

When the seasons turned chilly, Beno Hall became the Juniors' initiation site. On January 22, 1925, "All members were expected to be there, members received $.50 for each candidate they bring and new initiates must pay at least $2 on his initiation." Further, it announced the "Final Plans for the Big Weiner and Marshmallow Roast on Thursday night, January 29, when you can bring your girl." The attraction of the evening proved to be a talk by the assistant to the Exalted Cyclops and "ice cream sandwiches—O Boy!"

Beno Hall supplied new recruits with official Klan gear. For a premium price, reportedly pocketed by national officials, the home office in Atlanta regularly shipped cheap white sheets and pointed hats all with the tightly sewn-on patch of the organization. Yet, a Tulsa Knight's trappings were incomplete without the Klan weapon of choice, the official KKK whipping strap.

The strap was a piece of top-grain leather four inches wide and three feet long, the handle wrapped in industrial tape, its last six inches cut into ten slits, effective for slicing through skin. Hundreds of these prized weapons arrived in Tulsa.

During the Oklahoma Klan heyday years between 1921 and 1924, officials knew of 102 Klan floggings, three killings, three mutilations (including castrations), and numerous tar-and-featherings that, as a rule, followed whippings of the victims' backs. Official but incomplete tallies showed Tulsa County provided the most violations, with 74, Okmulgee County chalked up 20 while the rest of the state totaled 37.

At the time, lawlessness prevailed in Tulsa. A local reporter witnessed the flogging of J.E. Fletcher, an alleged car thief and bootlegger, on a remote Sand Springs road in September 1921. County Attorney John Seaver said no inquiry would be made, that Fletcher had gotten what he deserved and an investigation would just lead to criticism of the investigators. This gave carte blanche to extralegal marauding.

During that same month, a statement by H.O. McClure, president of the Tulsa Chamber of Commerce, put the writing on the wall in a *Tulsa World* article: "In Tulsa our courthouse and city hall are practically filled with Klan members, elected to office with Klan support." It wouldn't be long before an Oklahoma governor would step in to throttle the free hand of Tulsa's hooded fraternity.

After local Klansmen used their whipping straps to mutilate the genitalia of accused drug peddler Nathan Hantaman, the already unpopular Governor Jack Walton on August 14, 1923 declared martial law in the city and county of Tulsa. The results of the military court investigation drew statewide attention to the horror of the Oklahoma extremists as twelve locals were hauled away. The Oklahoma legislature passed an anti-mask bill hoping to stem vigilante violence.

The flamboyant Walton, aiming squarely at the Tulsa Klavern, even calling them by name, went on the attack, saying, "I don't care if you burst right into them with a double-barreled shot gun. I'll promise you a pardon in advance." Additional irresponsible statements, the suspension of the writ of habeas corpus, censorship of the press, an effective Klan defense and counter-attack, and the extension of military rule to include the entire state, further weakened public sentiment toward the state's leader.

Governor Walton's declaration of war on the Order exposed their reign of terror, but they would get the last laugh. The Klan influenced the impeachment of "Jazz Band Jack" Walton, who served but ten months as governor. The boys in white cheered the demise of their nemesis in their newly dedicated Beno Hall that had earlier been the site of the Tri-State Klan convention.

The next few years saw a healthy Klavern using their North Tulsa facility for holiday dances, ice cream socials, and political plotting. The outer foliage appeared robust, but inside, the society was withering from internal disagreements, greed and graft. By 1928, the Oklahoma Klan had negligible power.

The Tulsa Benevolent Association sold the storied building to the Temple Baptist Church in 1930. During the Depression, the building housed a speak-easy, then a skating rink, then a lumberyard, and finally a dance hall before radio evangelist Steve Pringle turned it into the Evangelistic Temple of the First Pentecostal Church. In his first revival meeting, Pringle introduced a little-known Enid preacher by the name of Oral Roberts, who worked his animated, faith-healing magic on the bare lot next door. Roberts impressed in the tent atmosphere and preached with his cohort inside the vast auditorium once known as Beno Hall. His fire and brimstone was a fitting bookend to the fiery crusades of the Klan.

Throughout the seventies, Beno Hall became a Main Street blight where vagrants gambled, drug transactions took place, and sex was exchanged for money. It was destroyed in 1976, and the empty lot now belongs to the Oklahoma Department of Highways. ◣

# A CONSPIRACY OF SILENCE:

## THE DEMISE OF BLACK WALL STREET

*by J. Kavin Ross*

T he Tulsa Race Riot of 1921 made national headlines on June 1 of this year, its 90th anniversary. Tulsa quietly commemorated the worst civil unrest on American soil since the Civil War with a candlelight vigil. A program titled "Greenwood Burned," located in the historic district, was poorly attended. The three-day conference of the John Hope Franklin Reconciliation Symposium included no riot survivors.

In the scorching summer of 1921, nearly 40 blocks of the black community of Greenwood were burned to the ground by a white mob. Thousands of Tulsans were forever affected by the destruction. Hundreds of lives were lost and many homes and businesses were destroyed. As the ashes cooled on America's "Black Wall Street," its citizens rebuilt Greenwood without the promised funds owed to them. Tulsa County commissioners denied all money from outside sources, vowing to take care of its own citizens, but never following through on their promise. The first commission had made plans to provide reparations to the riot victims but was quickly disbanded and reformed. The second commission sought to move blacks out of Greenwood entirely.

For decades, the events from those atrocities were kept dormant, but were tightly whispered from the lips of those who dared to tell.

The white community did not talk about race war because it left a stain on the fabric of the bustling oil capital. The black community did not talk about the massacre because those who committed the unpunished crime were still alive. Additionally, and unfortunately for the residents of Greenwood, the growth of Ku Klux Klan activity increased after the so-called riot.

In this environment, the conspiracy of silence was born.

In the 1830s, many African Americans journeyed to what would later be called Oklahoma, experiencing undesirable hardships along the Trail of Tears with the Five Civilized Tribes. Under President Andrew Jackson's administration, the Indian Removal Act relocated the tribes and their slaves to the established Twin Territories.

Of the 32 black townships that were established in America after the civil war, 28 of them were in Oklahoma before it became a state. O.W. Gurley, one of Tulsa's earliest pioneers, named the Greenwood district. An educator and entrepreneur who made his wealth as a landowner, Gurley purchased 40 acres in Tulsa to be sold to "coloreds only." Senate Bill Number 1, the state's first piece of legislation, prevented coloreds from residing, traveling and marrying outside their race. Gurley's property lines were Pine Street to the north, the Frisco rail tracks to the south, Lansing Avenue to the east and Cincinnati Avenue to the west. The still-unpaved streets would also serve as Tulsa's racial dividing lines.

After Gurley's purchase of the land, Tulsa began to grow. Black ownership was unheard of at that time, but under the state's Jim Crow laws, Greenwood was born out of necessity. The racial climate prevented coloreds from shopping anywhere but Greenwood. Among Gurley's first businesses was a boarding house located on a dirt road crossing the Frisco tracks, which would later be named Greenwood Avenue.

By 1913, more businesses followed, including law and doctors' offices of Buck Colbert Franklin and A.C. Jackson respectfully, Dunbar and Booker T. Washington schools, Vernon AME, and Mount Zion Baptist churches, Ricketts' Restaurant, The Williams' Dreamland Theater, Mann's Grocery Stores, Stradford Hotel, and a host of haberdasheries, drug stores, cafes, barbershops and beauty salons.

Famed educator Booker Taliaferro Washington visited Tulsa for a dedication of a small school named in his honor. Upon visiting the business district of Greenwood, he was amazed by the entrepreneurial spirit of the Greenwood residents. Washington would be credited for coining the phrase "the Negro Wall Street of America." In the turbulent era of civil rights, the tag became "Black Wall Street." The area thrived and was a source of pride in the black community—and a sore spot of envy across the tracks.

During the terrifying assault on Greenwood, many fled on foot, only to be rounded up and herded to internment camps around the city. Casualty counts varied; the dead were hastily buried in unmarked graves around the city. Funerals were forbidden. To date, the exact locations of the riot dead remain unconfirmed.

A now-legendary editorial in the June 4, 1921, editions of the *Tulsa Tribune* summed the up the sentiments of most Tulsans. "In this old Niggertown were a lot of bad niggers and a bad nigger is about the lowest thing that walks on two feet. Give a bad nigger his booze and his dope and a gun and he thinks he can shoot up the world. And all of these four things can be found in 'Niggertown'— booze, dope, bad niggers and guns. The Tulsa Tribune make no apology to the police commissioners or to the mayor of this city for having pled with them to clean up the cesspools in this city."

Through the heat of the summer and into winter's harshness, the survivors of Greenwood lived in tents and wooden shanties supplied by the American Red Cross while the city sorted through the rubble. The county commissioners at that time proposed to buy the land pennies on the dollar and sell the scorched lands to the highest bidders. Tulsa's power structure began to enforce various fire ordinances to prevent landowners from rebuilding. Those caught rebuilding would be arrested. Buck Colbert Franklin, father of noted historian Dr. John Hope Franklin, defended those arrested.

One such decree was that any new structure would have to be built from fireproof materials. The Acme Brick Company, located near the Booker T. Washington High School in the Greenwood District, was instructed not to sell its products, and nearby lumber yards also refused to sell to blacks. B. C. Franklin advised his clients to build with anything, even orange crates.

In an effort to expand the boundaries of downtown, the city proposed to move the Negro settlement further north and to the east of the Greenwood district. The county offered jobs to the now-unemployed black Tulsans. However, many refused to clean up the debris left by the mob. Commissioners Tate Brady, Jeff Archer, and others created another ordinance directly at the survivors: "Notice is hereby given that all men are ordered to either get a job and go to work or if you have no job work will be furnished you by applying at the Booker T. Washington Public School on Frankfort Street. All men who have no job and who refuse to work will be arrested as vagrants," the report read. This action prompted Franklin to take the city powers all the way to the Oklahoma Supreme Court, who sided with Franklin.

Riots were prevalent throughout the country during this era. In 1905, race riots occurred in Springfield, Illinois, the land of Lincoln, and 1919 was deemed the "red summer" for its outbreaks of race wars. Rosewood, a small rural community in Florida later depicted in a feature film, was destroyed in 1923. Each riot shared similarities: A white woman accused a black man of molestation. The white mob would react by terrorizing and destroying the black community.

Of all the uprisings, Greenwood is unique in that the razed community came back, bigger and better than before. Black residents of Greenwood during the 1940s and '50s enjoyed a peaceful but separate coexistence with the rest of the city. Separated schools were built to the north and east of the Greenwood district, including the new Booker T. Washington High School. The former BTW that survived the riot became Charles S. Johnson Elementary, which two decades later would become among the demolished inventory of Urban Renewal. The former grounds of that original BTW are now the Tulsa campus of Oklahoma State University.

The passage of the Civil Rights Bill in the 1960s allowed black dollars to be spent in white stores, and put a dent in the commerce and growth of the famed Black Wall Street. The end of an era began as Greenwood declined.

Once again, Greenwood was under attack. Not by the hands of an angry mob, but by the bulldozers of the federal government. Urban Renewal made it effects known Tulsa twenty years after the creation of the Housing Act and the Federal-Aid Highway Act of the 1950s. Highways divided neighborhoods and urban sprawl began. The removal of large populations of the city's minority was commonplace throughout large cities across the nation.

Tulsa was the first metropolis in Oklahoma to create an urban renewal authority. Opting not to bulldoze blocks of homes, Tulsa cleared problem properties while rehabilitating others. Homes and businesses that were rebuilt after the riot were bought and torn down, and Interstate 244—renamed the Martin Luther King Jr. Expressway in the 1980s—plowed through the heart of the remaining Greenwood Business District.

The University Center at Tulsa and the Greenwood Cultural Center were built in its place. Only Mount Zion Baptist Church and Vernon AME Church withstood the test of time. Also left behind was one block of buildings left standing in hopes that one day the once thriving and vibrant Negro Wall Street of America would be recognized.

In the early 1970s, a group of brothers—Robert, Ronnie and Charlie Wilson—formed The Greenwood, Archer and Pine Street Band, by doing overtly what Senate Bill No. 1 had done deceitfully, the brothers sought to honor the boundaries of their neighborhood.

Due to a lack of space on a poster, the promoter shortened the band's name to The Gap Band. The group went on to produce a string of hits in the 1980s.

Here and elsewhere, people are acknowledging the legacy of Greenwood. Underway in the nation's Capitol is the construction of a $500 million Smithsonian Institute Museum of African American History and Culture. The collection will include an exhibit titled, "Greenwood: Before, during and after the Tulsa Race Riot of 1921." Museum officials have made numerous visits to Tulsa to retrieve information and artifacts for the exhibit.

In Memphis, the National Civil Rights Museum is revamping its exhibits. At the Lorraine Motel—site of the assassination of civil rights leader Dr. Martin Luther King Jr.—a Greenwood exhibit will be among the highlights.

U.S. Representative John Sullivan (R) has authored a bill in the United States Congress to incorporate the Tulsa Race Riot Memorial/John Hope Franklin Reconciliation Park as a part of the inventory of the National Park Services. Also in progress is a grassroots effort to have the Greenwood district recognized on a National Preservation List of Historic Places.

With the creation of the new ONEOK Field, built on the former scorched lands of O.W. Gurley's Greenwood, the historic district is breathing new life as more patrons walk the same sidewalks from Greenwood's yesteryear. More construction in the area is planned in the future, including loft apartment.

In the spring of 2004, Bishop Desmond Tutu—who gained international attention for his role ending racial tensions and beginning the process of reconciliation in his homeland in South Africa—visited the former oil boomtown. "Tulsa is sitting on a powder keg. Because the city refuses to acknowledge and deal with its past," Tutu said. He continued to state if Tulsa ever deals with its race relations, this magic city could become a jewel to the world. ◣

# TIGRESS:

## THE LIFE AND TIMES
## OF KATHRYN KELLY

*by Laurence J. Yadon*

They were mostly dead by then, the girlfriends, mothers, and wives of the 1930s era gangsters who once dominated front pages. Their men put the once-obscure Federal Bureau of Investigation and its director J. Edgar Hoover in the headlines from coast to coast, during the largest crime wave in American history. Nearly all were gone, except Machine Gun Kelly's once-famous widow Kathryn, a favorite target of J. Edgar Hoover, who died May 28, 1985, in Tulsa with a contrived identity and no public notice of her passing.

Bonnie and Clyde had been ambushed in late May 1934 on a Louisiana back road the month after Clyde, or someone pretending to be him, dropped a letter to Henry Ford at the downtown Tulsa post office, praising his speedy cars. Ten months later, Ma Barker, a simple Missouri hillbilly whom J. Edgar Hoover reinvented as a criminal mastermind, was shot to death with her son Fred in Florida, eleven hundred miles away from their Tulsa shack on North Cincinnati. Gone too were doe-eyed Billy Frechette, the love of John Dillinger's life, who went to prison for him, and even Polly Hamilton, her replacement, who was with Dillinger when he was ambushed in Chicago. Ruby Floyd, former wife of Charles Arthur "Pretty Boy" Floyd died in Broken Arrow. Only Helen Gillis, the wife of Baby Face Nelson, outlived Kathryn Kelly, but she never had or wanted Kathryn's cunning, audacity, or ambition.

Kathryn was given the same birth name as Cleo Epps, queen of the Tulsa bootleggers, she who was pitched into the dank darkness of a west-side cistern after asking why she had to die. Cleo Mae Brooks didn't like that name and became Kathryn in eighth grade to seem more elegant.

And eventually, it worked.

But she started small in 1904 near Saltillo, Mississippi, eight years before Elvis Presley's mother was born there. After becoming Kathryn, she married at fifteen, divorced after her daughter Pauline was born and moved with her parents, James and Ora (Coleman) Brooks, from Mississippi to Oklahoma, where she was briefly married again.

Kathryn's mother Ora divorced Brooks, married Robert G. "Boss" Shannon, and moved with Kathryn and Pauline to his place near Palestine, Texas, north of Fort Worth. He was in the hospitality business, catering to gangsters; his rate was fifty dollars a night.

Kathryn's ticket out of that stark, weather-beaten farmhouse was her third marriage; this time the groom was Texas bootlegger Charlie Thorne. One evening after they quarreled, Charlie died of a gunshot wound. Despite Thorne's illiteracy, he left a perfectly typed note lamenting that he could not live with Kathryn, or for that matter without her. "Hence," Charlie announced, "I am departing this life." A coroner's jury shrugged and ruled him a suicide, despite rumors that Kathryn had threatened to kill Charlie. Soon Kathryn was convicted of robbery as "Dolores Whitney," but was released on a technicality without giving back the loot.

That stash and Thorne's money allowed the bereaved widow to improve her wardrobe and spend hours listening to jazz in Fort Worth clubs and bars. One of her suitors there later remembered that in the late 1920s, Kathryn "took me to more speakeasies ... bootleg dives [and] holes in the wall than I thought there were in all of Texas. She knows more bums than the Police Department. She can drink liquor like water. And she's got some of the toughest friends I ever laid eyes on."

•••

These qualities and Kathryn's striking looks appealed to yet another Texas bootlegger, who was doing business with a handsome, dark Irish southerner who called himself George R. Kelly, at least until George took his woman. They probably met in Fort Worth, as early as 1928 but perhaps later. Wherever and whenever Kathryn and George first locked eyes, they immediately began a torrid affair.

After the Kellys became famous, bootlegger R.L. "Little Steve" Stephens boasted to the Tulsa World in 1933 that he married Kvathryn and employed Barnes for five years, until his pedigreed bulldog disappeared. "I don't mind [Kelly] taking my wife and my car," Stevens quipped, "but I wish he'd left that dog."

Like Kathryn, George had a troubled past. He was born George Francis Barnes and grew up Catholic in an upper-middle class Memphis family. During his second and final college semester, he met and eloped with the daughter of a wealthy Memphis contractor. George worked for her father, later drove a cab, and even started a goat farm financed by his mother-in-law. But soon he turned his high-school bootlegging hobby into a full-time profession, causing his wife to file for divorce. After a few Memphis arrests, he changed his name to George R. Kelly, drifted west, and eventually landed in Santa Fe, where he was convicted of bootlegging March 14, 1927.

After several months in the New Mexico penitentiary at Santa Fe, George moved to a wide-open Oklahoma boom town that in its earliest years was overshadowed in booze, gambling and prostitution only by Catoosa, the hell-hole of Indian Territory. "The biggest mistake I ever made," he regretted later, "was leaving Tulsa."

George lived for a time at 1208 S. Quaker Ave., one block east of Peoria. "I got my start in '28," he recalled, perhaps off the mark a year. "I was the king of the rumrunners," crowed George, perhaps forgetting Little Steve. "I had the town, a good clientele [and] made a good living."

•••

Despite these late-life boasts of prosperity as a bootlegger, George did other things in Tulsa to make ends meet.

He became a prime suspect in a Saturday night robbery near Fourth and Main streets, July 23, 1927. The next evening, George was arrested for vagrancy, pending other charges, but was eventually released for lack of evidence. He was not so lucky the next year. In February 1928, he walked out of the Federal court at Third and Boulder convicted of bootlegging, bound for a Kansas lockup.

His Leavenworth stretch has often been described as a two–year tutorial in bank robbing, since many criminal luminaries of that age were also housed there. His mentors included Harvey Bailey, the "King of the Heist Men," and Frank "Jelly" Nash, who helped stage the last Oklahoma train robbery in August 1923 near Bartlesville.

George was released in 1930 and eventually traveled north to plan jobs with Bailey. A few years earlier, crooked law enforcement helped local gangsters create the Silicon Valley of America's criminal elite and a second home for several Tulsa gangsters.

"Of all the Midwest cities," reminisced sometime Tulsan Alvin "Creepy" Karpis, decades later, "the one I knew the best was St. Paul, and it was a crook's haven. Every criminal of any importance in the 1930s made his home [there] at one time or another."

George helped rob a bank at Willmar, some one hundred miles west of St. Paul, July 15, 1930, taking $70,000, in cash—worth about $900,000 in modern money—and as much in securities. The St. Paul Pioneer Press called it "one of the most daring bank holdups since the days of the Younger Brothers and Jesse James gangs." Even so, the James-Younger gang had been shot to pieces forty miles to the south in Northfield.

St. Paul homeboy Sammy Silverman grabbed an oversized share of the loot after the Willmar robbery. A month later, Silverman and two Kansas City racketeers were found dead high in the willow trees at White Bear Lake, fourteen miles northeast of St. Paul. The killings remained unsolved until George Kelly told authorities in 1934 that yet another Willmar accomplice had killed them all. George had used his own undersized share of the money dazzling Kathryn into marriage.

George later called this the turning point in his career. He should have just returned to bootlegging in Tulsa but, "No," George remembered, mixing up the timeline somewhat, "that wasn't enough. I had to go to Fort Worth and into that honky-tonk. [Kathryn] was pretty, the prettiest redhead I ever saw." A Minneapolis preacher married them in September 1930.

George helped steal $40,000 from the Central State Bank in Sherman, Texas, on April 3, 1931. Ten months later, he struck a bank nearby at Denton and scored almost another forty at a Tupelo, Mississippi, near Kathryn's birthplace on November 30, 1932. Since banks often ran out of cash during this, the third year of the Great Depression, Kathryn and George had begun to look for other opportunities.

•••

Kathryn always dreamed of better, brighter things and never-ending nightlife. George may have planned his first kidnapping during the 1931 Christmas season just to keep the peace. There is little or no evidence that Kathryn was involved.

George pulled young Howard Woolverton and his wife out of their car and into the cold evening air at South Bend, Indiana, the next January, demanding $50,000. Howard was the son of a local bank president who lived large, but was cash poor, due to Depression-era reversals. After three days, the young man gave his captors a face-saving yet totally worthless promissory note and was released. George and Kathryn sent notes demanding payment for months, but the family never even answered.

Kathryn knew what to do next.

She drove into Fort Worth, in February 1933, purchased a second-hand Thompson machine gun at a pawn shop and announced that from now on, the daily cocktail hour at the Shannon ranch would not begin until George finished target practice. She bragged about "the Big Guy" in Fort Worth dives, dumps, and hangouts, and soon began calling George "Machine Gun Kelly," even though George didn't care much for guns when he wasn't robbing banks.

Tulsa's Barker-Karpis gang abducted beer baron William A. Hamm at St. Paul, in June 1933. When they demanded a $100,000 ransom and got it, George, Kathryn, and their partner Albert Bates decided to try kidnapping again, despite a second failed effort.

Kathryn worked with George and Albert, planning the intricate details.

Silent, taciturn Charles Urschel started as an Ohio farm boy, served in the stateside Army during World War I, and put together enough cash to try his luck in the Oklahoma oil fields. He became the trusted business partner of Tom Slick, the wonder boy of Oklahoma wildcatters. Urschel married Slick's widow Berenice, and moved into her Oklahoma City mansion. Later, they fired their armed bodyguard because he slept too much.

On July 22, 1933, Urschel probably wished he'd found a replacement.

"Keep your seats, all of you," George demanded as he and Albert bolted through the screened porch door, interrupting a card game. The Urschels were entertaining Charles' business partner, Walter Jarrett and his wife, late that Saturday evening in the exclusive Heritage Hills district. When the foursome refused to identify Urschel, both men were shoved into the getaway car. Jarrett was later released with cab fare, but Urschel was driven blindfolded to the Shannon farm, sporting earplugs.

There were a few minor hitches during the first few hours of the abduction to be sure. Since the getaway driver forgot to fill the tank before the kidnapping, the party was stranded for an hour while someone went for gas. The driver also fell asleep, ran the car into a ditch and had to ask a farmer for directions to the hideout.

Urschel was treated well as the gang waited for the $200,000 ransom, larger than any paid previously in American history. Oilmen John G. Catlett of Tulsa and E.E. Kirkpatrick delivered the money to Kansas City on July 30. When the loot arrived at the hideout and the handshakes all around ended, Urschel was dumped on the north edge of Norman with just enough cash to catch a cab home.

•••

While Urschel was missing, former frontier lawman Charles Colcord offered a $10,000 reward for Machine Gun Kelly, dead or alive; the Kellys became the first major FBI targets under the new Lindbergh law, giving the FBI the lead in most American kidnappings.

The gang could not know that Urschel had a photographic memory. He mentally recorded all the sounds of dreary Depression-era farm life and peeked from beneath his blindfold at his captors until he was caught. Urschel also remembered the bitter taste of the water: the gang boasted about their bank robberies and described Bonnie and Clyde as small-time gas station bandits.

All this gave Urschel what the FBI needed to pinpoint the hideout more quickly than anyone expected. Urschel joined the August 12 raid on the Shannon place, carrying his own shotgun. The posse arrested the Shannons, but Kathryn and George Kelly were already on the run, sometimes together, sometimes separately. Harvey Bailey was found sleeping outside on a cot in the Texas heat with ransom money stuffed in his pockets, which did little to convince the jury he faced later that he was not a kidnapper. This was probably true.

Kathryn used Luther Arnold, a homeless farmer she picked up with his family along the road, to make an offer to federal prosecutors. She would surrender George and take a light sentence herself if her beloved mother Ora were released. When this didn't work, she had George write letters to prosecutors threatening "the extermination of the entire Urschel family." During the Shannon trial, a letter from Chicago smudged with George's fingerprints, addressed to "Ignorant Charles," told Urschel that "if the Shannons are convicted, you can get another rich wife in hell." These threats prompted E.E. Kirkpatrick to call Kathryn a "Human Tigress" fifteen years later, when she unsuccessfully applied for parole. But now, in late September 1933, the authorities were closing in on the Kellys, even as her Shannon relatives, Albert Bates and Harvey Bailey, were being tried in Oklahoma City.

"I've been waiting for you all night," George croaked, as he fidgeted with a pistol and nearly got himself shot before putting on his own handcuffs in a Memphis house, even as Kathryn screamed from the bedroom. He probably didn't leave the front door unlocked on purpose and definitely didn't say, "Don't shoot, G-men," either, despite stories that J. Edgar Hoover told for decades. The ashtray-strewn hideout was full of liquor bottles, but not a cent of the ransom was hidden in the trash and litter. About half of the $200,000 in ransom money has never been found.

The Kelly's fifty-six day run from Paradise to Omaha and Cleveland, from there to San Antonio, St. Paul, and finally Tennessee was over. Kathryn refused to put her street clothes on, faked an appendicitis attack at the Memphis jail, and claimed in a newspaper interview that she was only involved because George threatened to kill her.

•••

Ora, Boss, and his son Armon "Potatoes" Shannon, were found guilty of kidnapping with Albert Bates and Harvey Bailey September 30, 1933. They were sentenced the next day, but not until George and Kathryn were escorted into the same courtroom four days after their capture to plead not guilty in a separate case. During their jury trial later, Kathryn blamed George for everything, when she wasn't posing for newspaper photographers on the witness stand in black satin, as the gallery clucked. Kathryn's own relatives sealed her fate by describing her involvement in the smallest details of the abduction.

Thirteen days after their first appearance before Judge Vaught, he gave Kathryn and George life sentences. "Be a good boy," Kathryn said as George was led away. She never saw him again. Machine Gun Kelly died on his 59th birthday at Leavenworth in 1954. Charles Urschel, of all people, anonymously financed the college education of Kathryn's daughter Pauline, with Judge Vaught acting as intermediary, despite the many times the Kelly gang threatened to kill him.

Kathryn Kelly and her mother Ora were released from prison in mid-June 1958 when the FBI refused to release files revealing that George probably wrote certain Urschel threat letters that the government had attributed to Kathryn. That year Charles Bronson played the lead in Machine-Gun Kelly, his first starring role.

Elderly patients living at the county poor farm—the Oklahoma City nursing home of last resort a few years later—probably didn't know that kindly nurse Ora was a convicted big-time kidnapper. Perhaps she even gave shots and handed out pills. Kathryn worked there too, but as a bookkeeper.

When contacted in 1962, Kathryn was worried. "Why can't they just leave us alone? I'm afraid I'll lose this job if this constant barrage of publicity keeps up … I was just a young farm girl when I met Kelly back in 1930," she dissembled. "I wasn't used to all the money, cars and jewelry George offered me … Any farm girl would have been swept off her feet same as I was."

Despite this, Pulitzer Prize winning novelist Ace Atkins recently portrayed Kathryn as "the Lady Macbeth of Depression era America" in his historical novel *Infamous*, but she and her mother were long gone.

Ora died five years before Kathryn at the suburban Oklahoma City home they shared. Kathryn passed on in Tulsa as "Lera Cleo Kelly," a supposed Wisconsin native, who lived at a west Tulsa nursing home.

Kathryn spent her last, anonymous days at Oklahoma Osteopathic Hospital, in a building still perched high above the Arkansas River. She might have even seen the place near the 11th Street Bridge where Howard Hughes great-grandfather led captured Union Army wagons westward, down a hill and across the shallows during the Civil War. How Kathryn Kelly, the Human Tigress of 1933, would have marveled at the fabled million dollars in loot General Gano supposedly carried away that day, had she only known.

From Gano's crossing, you can see the place she died, her sleek, blue Cadillac, salad days of fame and sparkly diamonds long forgotten. ◥

# THE WHITE DOVE REVIEW:

## HOW A GROUP OF TULSA TEENAGERS CREATED A LITERARY LEGEND

*by Joshua Kline*

"Y ou can leave your contraband at the door," the woman tells me.

I've filled out and signed several forms and waited while my name, driver's license number and other personal information were filed away on a computer system. I've agreed that my camera, brought for personal reference, will not be used with a flash and will not at any time rest on a tripod. I've signed my life away in order to spend a single hour with a rare book, and now I'm emptying my pockets. I'm at the University of Tulsa, in the Special Collections department of McFarlin Library, and I'm here to view one of their most recent acquisitions.

I dig into my jeans and comb through change, keys, cigarettes, lighter, cell phone, loose ibuprofen tablets, a black Pilot ball-point. The woman—a friendly, if harried, librarian named Alison—motions to the table next to me. I toss the contraband onto the surface and follow her past the entrance.

We emerge into a magnificent reading room. The ceiling is high with an opulent crystal chandelier hanging from the center of it, and each wall is completely occupied by glass-encased floor-to-ceiling bookshelves filled with collections from greats like Robert Frost and Walt Whitman, plus the fourth largest James Joyce library in the world. Six very large desks lie before me in perfect symmetry. Each is identically furnished with a small lamp and a black, monolithic book rest. The light is perfectly dim, creating a glowing, otherworldly warmth.

She tells me to sit where I like. I slip into a seat at the nearest desk and wait. Earlier, I was told that a staff member would remain in the reading room to monitor my activity with the book, and, sure enough, an awkward student receptionist has taken a seat at the head of the room. I will not be alone with the *White Dove Review* for a moment.

"It's kind of hard to express what Special Collections does," department head Marc Carlson explained to me a few days earlier. A scholarly, bookish fellow, Carlson has run Special Collections for six years now, but even for him, the mystique of his department has not worn thin. As he struggles for the words to best explain the essence of that department, I realize that Carlson is really a gatekeeper to the significant puzzle pieces (historical artifacts, manuscripts, parchments) that compose the lost history of Tulsa— the parts that seem to be intentionally hidden by museums like Philbrook and Gilcrease.

Now, sitting in the reading room, I'm finally handed the aging black-bound text. The covers are unmarked; the spine reads "White Dove Review 1-5" in gold-embossed letters. The ripened paper is a deep yellow bordering on brown, but the ink seems fresh and vibrant, as if put to paper just moments before I arrived. I cautiously pull open the cover to the first page and my eyes widen: it contains wild, loose signatures and illustrations. The markings come from many of America's most renowned poets and painters.

A scrappy little literary journal published in 1959 and 1960, the *White Dove Review* contains in its brittle pages one of our city's best kept secrets: a clear, concrete link between Tulsa and the Beat Movement, America's most iconic literary scene of the twentieth century. It's also a telling portrait of Oklahoma's most important artists as young men, a small group who would go on to help define the New York School of the 1960s. The entire original five-issue publication is bound in this one guarded book.

"My understanding is this was a publication put out by, essentially at that point, a bunch of kids," Carlson told me. It's hard to believe that the ritualistic security protocol I've just gone through is for something created by a group of Central High students out of a house located just a few blocks from here.

## THE OUTSIDERS OF CENTRAL HIGH SCHOOL

In 1959, Ron Padgett was a working class teen, a misfit whose father was a bootlegger. He was a sensitive boy, intelligent and ambitious, an aspiring poet who was routinely drunk on Kerouac, Ginsberg, Camus and Rimbaud.

"Basically, I was an outsider on his way to becoming something of a bohemian," Padgett said of those early days, in an e-mail interview. "Fated to meet other outsiders, whether in Tulsa or New York."

While working at the Lewis Meyer bookstore on 37th and Peoria that year, Padgett had an idea. Taken with the work of the era's literary giants and New York-based "little mags" like the *Evergreen Review*, Padgett, barely 17 and still a junior at Central, decided that he would start his own avant-garde lit journal. He and his best friend Dick Gallup would be co-editors.

Gallup, who lived across the street from Padgett, had moved to Tulsa from Massachusetts in grade school.

"When I first met Dick (he was about 10, I was 9)," Padgett remembered, "he seemed rather exotic to me because he was from western Massachusetts and he spoke with that accent." The two meshed well. As children, they played basketball and baseball, watched television together and frequented local movie theaters like the Orpheum and the Majestic.

In junior high, the budding thinkers gravitated to more intellectual pursuits and pastimes, especially the quiet, observant Gallup.

"Dick was always coming up with rather abstruse and mysterious ideas about things such as anti-matter," Padgett recalled. "But inside he had a very good adolescent sense of humor, and if you knew him, you could sense that he was growing into his own person."

By high school, they were hanging out at Lewis Meyer Bookstore so often that Meyer offered Padgett a job. In addition to introducing the boys to a slew of edgy, contemporary authors, the store owner gave Padgett his first glimpse of what would lay the foundation for his concept: those avant-garde journals like *Evergreen*, *Yugen* and *Semina* that contained short-form work from the same Beat and Black Mountain writers he was then devouring.

With two enthusiastic editors, the ambitious concept was becoming a reality. The next step was to recruit art editors. Padgett was fascinated by the work of a classmate he didn't know named Joe Brainard. Instead of approaching him directly, Padgett sent the artist a Christmas card praising his talent. Soon after, he approached Brainard at school and revealed himself as the sender, and then pitched the idea of Brainard as the journal's art editor. Brainard agreed.

Padgett remembers the artist as being "shy, sweet, passive, soft-spoken—the epitome of a 'nice' kid," but also described Brainard's growth in high school as becoming increasingly aware of himself (Brainard was gay-- no easy burden for a teenager in '50s Tulsa) and "determined to take control of his life."

They invited fellow aesthete Michael Marsh, a classical pianist who introduced the growing team to the work of Debussy and Capote, to be Brainard's co-editor.

They called their magazine the *White Dove Review*, an homage to *Evergreen*, which featured on the cover of its sixth issue a striking black and white photograph of a young Asian woman holding a white dove. To fund its publication, they enlisted the help of Padgett's mother, who donated $20 of the first issue's $90 production cost. To typeset the journal, they borrowed the state-of-the-art IBM Presidential from their good friend and fellow classmate George Kaiser, who, Padgett said, "provided moral support for the magazine." Even then, the future billionaire philanthropist was indulging his altruistic tendencies, playing an arts patron through the simple loaning of a typewriter.

Though they didn't run in the same social circles, Padgett and Kaiser got to know each other through many shared classes.

"I liked him because he was smart and he had a good sense of humor," Padgett said. "We often had lunch together at Nelson's Buffeteria, or we'd hop in his car and speed out to Pennington's, then rush back to class, eating on the way."

They had their own poems, their own artwork, their own typewriter, and their own start-up funds. But then the White Dove editorial board took a bold step. Padgett and Gallup decided to fill the *White Dove*'s pages with work they solicited from their heroes.

"Dick and I made a list of the living writers we were excited by," Padgett explained. "Kerouac, Ginsberg, e.e. cummings, Malcolm Cowley, Paul Blackburn, etc. Then we wrote to them, care of their publishers, asking—begging, really—them for material. Our letter was rather immature, but in it we did confess to being in high school."

According to Padgett, "a surprising number of writers responded" to the solicitations, and with the submitted work he and Gallup were able to choose what best fit their vision. The crown jewel of Issue One is Jack Kerouac's "The Thrashing Doves," a poem submitted by the Beat godfather as a knowing salute to the *Review*'s avian imagery:

> *The thrashing doves in the dark, white fear,*
> *my eyes reflect that liquidly*
> *and I no understand Buddha-fear?*
> *awakener's fear? So I give warnings*
> *'bout midnight round about midnight*
>
> *And tell all the children the little otay*

*story of magic, multiple madness, maya*
*otay, magic trees- sitters and little girl*
*bitters, and littlest lil brothers*
*in crib made of clay (blue in the moon).*

*For the doves.*

## THE EDITORS ARE NOT HIPSTERS

Sitting in the grand reading room, I stare at the signatures on that first page: Padgett, Brainard, Gallup, Blackburn, Ted Berrigan, Fielding Dawson, among others. There's a handwritten date next to Peter Orlovsky's (the famous poet who was Allen Ginsberg's lifelong romantic partner) signature: December 14th, 1964. The autographs were likely collected in New York after the *White Dove* boys had already fled Tulsa. There's a goofily grotesque cartoon drawing of what looks like a half-elephant, half-man creature standing on a magic carpet. Resting under the drawing is the name "Lord Ganesh," and next to the drawing are the initials "AG" (later in the book I find Ginsberg's signature under his piece "My Sad Self"). Already, the camaraderie of the New York School and its inseparable connection to the *White Dove Review* is crystal clear.

I move on to the editors' introduction:

There has been sufficient criticism of materialistic, uncultured modern American society. The intention of this mag is not to add to this stockpile of criticism, but rather to present literature and art in a constructive light. Admittedly, The White Dove Review is a quiet complaint against the gaudy ideals of our society. Culture, along with some short-lived memories, is all a civilisation leaves behind it. We hope that the Schleimanns of the year 4000 do not find only beer cans and long cars in their excavations. (sic)

He adds in the next paragraph:

The editors are not hipsters, even tho they acknowledge certain beat ideas. But no one will ever find any 'organization' dogma within these covers.(sic)

Romanticized characterizations of the lusty city life pepper the contents of the *White Dove*—counterculture ruminations on jazz and drugs and sex and just barely scraping by—the kinds of images rampant in the seminal Beat offerings (*Howl, On the Road*) that Padgett and Gallup idolized, but were seldom, if ever, used to describe life in Tulsa.

Nevertheless, writings in the *White Dove* toggled freely between the earthy, Midwestern concerns found in poems like Marsha Meredith's "Streetlight in the Snow:"

*a candy candle*
*preening in the downy*
*dreamy*
*snowy*
*night*

and the freewheeling chaos of the Beat contributors and big city natives like Carl Larsen (who, in his poem "Crap and Cauliflower", paints a graphic portrait of loose sexuality culminating in rape and disillusionment) and Paul Blackburn's "Redhead:"

*you are the poor*
*slick-minded Madison*
*ave. man's*
*idea of a mistress*
*no serious thing at all.*

These peculiar juxtapositions of middle-American and coastal big-city musings cultivated a spiritual connection between Tulsa and New York City, a connection that would prove prescient for its creators in the years to follow.

## THE BEATS OF TULSA

Over the course of the *White Dove*'s five-issue run between '59 and '60, Padgett and company continued to showcase a distinguished mixture of lauded artists from New York and abroad (Ginsberg, Blackburn, Dawson, Major, LeRoi Jones, Simon Perchik, Ron Loewinsohn) along with a select core group of homegrown writers, painters and poets, including John Kennedy, Bob Bartholic, Dave Bearden, Paul England and Marsha Meredith.

Another Tulsa poet on board with the *White Dove* was Ted Berrigan. A patron of Lewis Meyer, Berrigan submitted work to the journal through the slot of an old cigar box that Padgett normally used to collect payment for the paper.

The coalescing, creative partnership between the three editors (Padgett, Gallup, Brainard) and Berrigan was particularly important during this period. Berrigan, whose work would eventually be considered "a fact of modern poetry" by Frank O'Hara, became a driving force behind the publication of the *Review*. At 25, the worldly TU student acted as an elder statesman and mentor to the fledgling editors behind the journal, and Padgett in particular was enamored with what he described during a speech at TU as Berrigan's "irresistibly romantic" and "glamorously outsiderish" persona.

"Even though he had not yet become 'Ted Berrigan,' he was already very different from Tulsans, more expansive and with a larger sense of humor," Padgett said.

The *White Dove Review* only ran for a year, but in that time the four young men became entrenched in Tulsa's art scene.

"There really weren't very many outsider poets and artists in Tulsa in the 1950s, which meant that we tended to huddle together, despite our differences," Padgett said. "The relationships tended to be intense, sometimes competitive."

They mixed with the student cutters of TU's *Nimrod* (of which Berrigan was an editor), hung out at coffeehouses, all-night diners, and the jazz club Rubiot (where a trembling Padgett gave his first public reading) and congregated at the house of John and Betty Kennedy on 6th and Peoria. The Kennedys were 30-something artists whose always-open home acted as an important point of convergence for a handful of Tulsa bohemians. They held frequent parties for their friends and transformed a wing of their home into a multi-purpose artist exhibition and work space dubbed Gallery 644.

The cover of Issue 3 is a portrait of Betty Kennedy's and Bob Bartholic's daughter Chrissie (by the girl's stepfather, John Kennedy), and the issue also features a moving piece by Padgett titled "Poem for Chrissie:"

*for now*
*stay warm and silent*
*and ten.*

By the time the younger of the *White Dove* graduated from high school, a mass exodus was underway. The Tulsa beatniks ran to New York, and Padgett, Gallup, Brainard and Berrigan followed closely behind. When they arrived in the Big Apple, they seamlessly integrated into the New York School, a loose collective of artists and performers who were radically re-defining the parameters of self-expression. Ultimately, the four *White Dove* boys carved out a niche of their own within the New York School, becoming known as The Tulsa School of Poets. The origin of this title is the subject of some debate, but it's generally agreed upon that poet John Ashbery first popularized the term. According to Terrence Diggory's *Encyclopedia of the New York School Poets*, the term "Tulsa School" was something of a running joke.

"To call them the '*soi disant* (self-proclaimed) Tulsa School,' as John Ashbery did, was to poke fun at the provinciality of Tulsa, from the perspective of New York," Diggory writes, "and to turn the tables on Berrigan, who jokingly authorized himself to enroll people in the New York School for a five-dollar fee."

Joke or not, the "Tulsa School" was a phrase that would forever be attached to the four T-town expatriates. The teenagers who started the *White Dove Review* eventually found recognition and acclaim in corners of the world spanning New York to Paris.

## A PRESENTATION OF YOUNG THOUGHT

An hour has passed. The student receptionist has graduated from awkward to bored, and I feel the onset of a lit hangover. I feel like I've been watching a peculiar, literary puppet show: trembling poets in smoky jazz clubs, rough-and-tumble hedonists, drunk writers, introverted painters, young intellectuals and innocents   s if Ginsberg's "best minds" were misplaced in Tulsa before finding their way back to Greenwich Village.

I flip back to the editors' introduction in Issue One and read again:

This is a presentation of young thought. We favor experimentation to traditionalism, but our judgments will be based on quality and message.

We sincerely hope you enjoy this review, because it is for you that we have put it together.

The White Dove flaps its wings.

The Editors. ◥

# THE WORLD IS YOURS:

## A PORTRAIT OF JOE BRAINARD

*by Holly Wall*

Joe Brainard made art the way some might obsess over a lover: in an all-consuming frenzy and for hours on end—sometimes all night. He once wrote of his amphetamine-fueled process in the summer of 1970 to his friend and fellow Tulsan, Ron Padgett.

"After oil painting all morning (I got up at 5:30!) I picked some green grass and did lots of green ink and brush drawings of it. Now I am cutting the grass out and then I am going to put it all together, in layers, to make a solid patch of grass ...

"It will be very pretty, I know. It can't miss. And it's a good thing to do (cutting out grass) when your head is tired but you are still sort of wound up. Just before a drink."

The cut-outs he was creating—collages of weeds and grass and flowers and paper painstakingly dissected with an X-acto knife and then arranged between multiple layers of Plexiglas— would soon become some of his best and most critically acclaimed work. But Joe would write, disappointed, "it doesn't give me that much satisfaction."

Years before, as a high-school student vacationing in Mexico with one of his early mentors and her family, Joe surprised them with his whirl.

"He never slept; he was on amphetamines," Nylajo Harvey remembered. "You could buy anything at the pharmacy that you could pronounce in Mexico. And so he was frantically working and he was working in tea and coffee so it was like a watercolor. He would paint or draw 10 or 20 hours a day."

Most of what Joe painted or drew in Mexico he discarded, considering them mere excercises, rather than "real art," but Nylajo, recognizing the beauty of his work, collected them and took them home to Tulsa with her.

Joe would continue that way for most of his 20-year career—working frantically, trashing what he didn't like, and criticizing what he did.

In the mid-1970s, he spent two years amassing 3,000 miniature drawings and collages, epic in their detail, half of which would be displayed at Manhattan's Fischbach Gallery in 1975.

The show was a success—critically because of immaculate caliber of Brainard's work; commercially because he sold the pieces cheap, some as low as $25. But, as he was prone to be, Joe was unhappy with his achievement. He had long doubted his inherent talent and was growing weary of the art world. He told People magazine, which featured him and his work in an article titled "Think Tiny," "The art scene has gotten too big, too serious, too sacred, too self-important, and too expensive."

But Joe Brainard was none of those things, and by the mid-1980s, he had put down his paintbrush and left the art world for good.

•••

Born in Salem, Arkansas in 1942, Brainard moved to Tulsa at a young age, but was never at home in Oklahoma. He grew up here, the second son of working-class parents, but he came of age in New York City, securing his identity as an artist—a contemporary of Alex Katz, Fairfield Porter, and Andy Warhol—and a writer and member of the New York School (composing, with his friends from Tulsa, what critics would come to call the "Tulsa School of Poetry"), alongside the likes of Frank O'Hara, Kenward Elmslie, James Schuyler, John Ashbery, and others.

As an artist, Brainard was perpetually critical of his work, never fully believing in its worth. As a man, he was perpetually kind. The most common and accurate word his friends, family, and eulogizers use to describe him is "nice," and he was a frequent bestower of gifts. In a memorial titled "Saint Joe" and published in the July 1997 issue of Art in America, writer and friend Edmund White writes: "Joe Brainard was both a collector and an antimaterialist. He loved beautiful objects and bought them, but he loved emptiness more and was always giving away his collections and restoring his loft to its primordial spareness."

That, and he liked making people happy.

Ron Padgett, Joe's closest friend, told me over the phone that "he was a superb gift-giver—not because his gifts were expensive, but they were just right for you."

And if there were anything in his possession that he thought someone else would do better with than he, he gave of that thing freely. He encouraged his friends to visit his miniatures at Fischbach and pick out "one you think would be nice to live with."

But for all his kindness and generosity, Joe was plagued by doubt, depression, and insecurity, heightened by speed and the frustration he felt with his work. A feverish and abundant creator for 15 years, it wasn't until he stopped making art that Joe seemed to find peace.

Joe's family was typical of those in Tulsa in the 1950s. His parents, Howard and Marie, were the working-class progenitors of four children: Jim, Joe, Becky and John. The three boys all grew up to be artists, and Becky dabbled in interior decoration and art gallery management.

"We all got along well and respected one another, but we weren't particularly close and didn't spend a lot of time together," said John Brainard, a painter who creates large, multimedia collages and lives in Paris.

Once the Brainard kids turned 18, they were free to leave the nest without much interference from their parents.

"It was kind of nice, in a way," John said. "Particularly for Joe it was nice because his lifestyle wasn't probably what was typical at that time for Tulsa parents. And my parents were good about not being intrusive in any way."

Marie supported the qualities that some might consider clues of his homosexuality. He fancied himself a fashion designer (until high school, when his friends chastised him for limiting his artistic potential with such a commercial endeavor), and his mother often put together her outfits by sewing frocks he had designed.

When he was 8, Joe designed a Grecian-inspired white gown, which his mother paired with gold accessories. When he was 14, the *Tulsa World* ran an article about Joe under the headline "Fair First is Budding Dior."

"A great many of my clothes are from Joe's original sketches," Marie told the reporter. "He sketches a dress, helps pick the material and then I get out the pinking shears and sewing machine and go to work. He always looks for the unusual in design and even helps me pick accessories which will go well with his design. There's only one area of disagreement between us and that is on shoes. Joe thinks it's terribly unfashionable when I wear anything other than spiked heels."

"It sounds to me that initially Marie and Joe's relationship was as much mother-daughter as mother-son," Ron Pagdett wrote in a memoir of his friend, titled *Joe*. "At the age of nine he began relinquishing the 'daughter' role to his newborn sister, Becky, whose gender was prized by Marie."

Marie was "in many ways an ideal 1950s housewife" who "always seemed to have just baked a pie," Padgett wrote. Howard worked for an oil field equipment manufacturer, graduating from the assembly line to a desk, and spent his evenings and weekends tinkering in his garage. But he harbored a secret: As a child, Howard had hoped to be an artist. As an adult, though, he probably didn't think a career as a landscape artist was an option for him—but when he recognized his sons' talent, he encouraged it. When Joe was 13, his youngest brother, John, was born. John was 5 when Joe moved to New York, seeking fortune and freedom as an artist, and John, once he was old enough to read the reviews of his brother's work, followed Joe's career closely and aspired to follow in his footsteps.

In high school, Joe spoke with a stutter and tended to be shy and soft-spoken. Tall and thin with black, wiry hair and thick glasses, he was not outgoing, but Padgett, his classmate at Central High School, picked him out of a crowd easily. He introduced himself to Joe by way of Christmas card and later in person, telling him, "I'm starting a magazine and I was wondering if you'd like to be the art editor."

Joe's answer—"Uh uh uh OK"—marked the beginning of a friendship that would last until Joe's death in 1994, and the magazine they started would prove as legendary as its creators.

•••

*The White Dove Review* was an ambitious five-issue effort by Ron, Joe, Dick Gallup, and Michael Marsh, who wrote to their favorite avant-garde authors of the time—Jack Kerouac, Alan Ginsberg, e.e. cummings, Malcolm Cowley, and others—asking them for work. Their writings were published by this group of 16-year-olds in their "little literary magazine." Joe would go on to collaborate with some of them in his adult years.

Joe and his high-school cohorts spent a lot of their free time absorbing the influence of older artists in Tulsa, who were happy to have them around but hesitant to encourage them to pursue careers in art, because they knew the difficulty that would come to them if they did.

One of Joe's earliest influences—though certainly not the most important; Bob Bartholic took credit for that—was Nylajo Harvey, who was once as distinguished by the fat, red braid that snaked down the length of her back as she was the oil portraits and landscapes she created so prolifically.

Harvey, who is 85 now, and lives in midtown—not too far from the home where Joe Brainard used to visit her—and remembers the boy fondly, though they lost touch after high school, after he left Tulsa.

In Harvey's downstairs bathroom, nestled in a mosaic of artwork, is a painting Brainard did in high school, representative of her favorite work of his. A girl, painted in shades of red, resembles an animal or insect—her eyes are dots, her nose narrow and pointed, her mouth pursed.

Upstairs, in a guest bedroom, are two more—one a blue version of the bathroom portrait and another an ink wash of a nude figure, the lines of her body blurred into the background, her face virtually featureless. It hangs beside a nearly identical portrait by Bob Bartholic, but his is obviously the work of an older, more mature painter. Seeing the works side by side is an excellent example of the homage Brainard often paid to those who inspired and influenced him.

When he moved to New York, his influences changed dramatically, and so did his aesthetic.

"In Tulsa, Joe was eager to absorb influences because he knew that's one way you develop as an artist," Padgett said.

When he and Ron arrived in New York, they immediately hit up the Museum of Modern Art and the Whitney Museum of American Art, taking in artists like Picasso, Vermeer, Matisse, Pollock, and de Kooning.

"It was staggering for Joe," Padgett said. "He and I arrived in New York together, and we went to the Museum of Modern Art, and Joe's eyes were as big as saucers, he was so happy to be there. It was like he had gone to heaven."

Joe's work began to take on a pop-art aesthetic; in 1962, he painted a large, colorful image of the 7-Up logo. It was the same year Andy Warhol debuted his first pop-art exhibit, which included the *Marilyn Monroe Diptych, 100 Soup Cans* and *100 Coke Bottles.*

He wrote of his work in a letter to Padgett. He wanted to paint things such as "an arrangment of modern Americanized bottled, wrapped, or boxed items especially prepared for our sterile and functional sense of the sanitary proper: 7-Up bottle, Pioneer instant coffee, and a Tareyton dual cigarette. Such items I often use in my paintings, because they are present, they are the ways of my country... "

Joe would come to admire Warhol's art, but he would abandon any effort that might suggest he was copying the artist. His friend and once-lover Joe LeSueur said: "I bought his painting *7-Up* for $14—but Joe gave up Pop art of that sort as soon as he saw Warhol's work later."

He would continue to paint everyday items, but he would do it in a way that set him apart from other pop artists. His 1977 oil-on-canvas painting of a butt-filled ash tray, titled *Cinzano*, is a good example. The image is duplicated 16 times, each one a different style of painting, all realistic, none of them reminiscent of Warhol.

In Joe, Padgett wrote: "His use of such iconography then and later was quite different than that of most pop artists, whose attitude toward the same images tended to be cool, distant, critical or ironic. Joe described himself as a realist, simply painting what was in front of him, but his depictions of pop images suggest that not only did he love seeing, he was in love with what he saw."

His kindness played a role as well.

John Ashbery wrote in the program for the retrospective exhibit of Joe's work: "Joe Brainard was one of the nicest artists I have ever known. Nice as a person, and nice as an artist. This may present a problem ... One can sincerely admire the chic and implicit nastiness of a Warhol soup can without ever wanting to cozy up to it, and perhaps that is as it should be, art being art, a rather distant thing.

"In the case of Joe, one wants to embrace the pansy, so to speak. Make it feel better about being itself, all alone, a silly kind of expression on its face, forced to bear the brunt of its name eternally."

The first time Warhol saw Brainard's work, it was the illustrated cover of a mimeographed journal of poetry by Brainard, Padgett, Ted Berrigan, and Dick Gallup titled *C Comics*.

In a letter to Padgett, Brainard wrote: "Andy Warhol says C cover (Joe designed the third one) is great. And he's to see me and some of my new work next weekend when I'll be in N.Y. Here's hoping he might pull a string for me. I've been doing great things. I can't believe it. Most of all I'm anxious for you all to see everything."

Warhol designed the cover of the fourth issue of *C Comics*, giving the screens he created, along with some black ink and a squeegee, to Berrigan to silk screen. On some that came out too faint, Joe painted and wrote—homages to Warhol.

•••

Brainard, like many who fear failure will be their destiny if they stay in their small, oppressive hometowns, left Tulsa for New York City, the only place he felt he could be a "serious" artist.

After stopping off in Dayton, Ohio, for a brief but paid-for stint at the Dayton Art Institute, Brainard joined his friends Ron Padgett and Ted Berrigan in Manhattan, sleeping and working in small, shanty apartments in the city's poorest neighborhoods. He didn't work, except as an artist, and money came neither quickly nor easily. He sold his blood on occasion, panhandled and picked up cigarette butts from the sidewalk, stuffing them into his pockets to later smoke or use in an assemblage. At times, he didn't eat.

"I spent the extra $2 you sent [Ron had sent him $10; $8 was spent on rent] immediately, and have been living off a loaf of bread for the past three days," he wrote to Padgett. "I'm not sorry, though. But today is Saturday late afternoon and I have left only two slices. And tomorrow is Sunday, so no mail. I put all my faith in Monday's mail."

When the mail arrived, though, there was no money in it, and Joe was forced to ask people on the street to spare their change. He earned 15 cents and he bought two candy bars and a five-cent stamp, which he used to mail the letter to his friend.

In 1962, he created a series of variations on the American flag, gluing them to white masonite, cutting and collaging them and collaborating with Berrigan to create flag-themed poetic collage.

He was supposed to exhibit the flag and other works in Tulsa at a small gallery owned by Bob Bartholic. Berrigan journaled: "My collaborative American flag with Joe was a Tulsa scandal. Bartholic didn't hang it, but he showed it. Another gallery cancelled Joe's show, partly because of the flag."

In 1963, Brainard moved to Boston for a while, and he was prolific in his creation of collage—or sculpture or assemblage, as he sometimes called it—gluing together ordinary things, like clocks, doll parts, birds, and cigarette butts.

Harvey prefers the work he created in high school and doesn't care too much for the work he did in New York.

"It wasn't art to me—old cigarette butts? Arms of little dolls?"

But Joe had never been happier with his work. He wrote to his friend Ron on several occasions, excited about the art and poetry he was creating:

"I'm truly a genius ... I feel super-good.

"I am doing work now which surpasses me. I watch myself work in total amazement."

He drew also, designing the cover of Padgett's self-published collection of poems Some Bombs , as well as *C Comics*. Brainard, Padgett, Berrigan, and Gallup began incorporating themselves into the New York School of Poetry, earning them the moniker, dubbed tongue-in-cheek by Ashbery, "the soi-disant Tulsa School of Poetry."

•••

Once he felt himself finished with his assemblages, Joe moved on to other projects—ironic imitations of Ernie Bushmiller's *Nancy* cartoon; gouache-on-paper collages of pansies, daisies, and irises; landscapes and still lifes in oil—

including some writing, the most acclaimed of which is his memoir *I Remember.*

His work, in terms of both style and medium, varied exponentially. He seemed to master a technique, to exhaust its every possibility, and then discard it, moving on to the next challenge. Some saw this as admirable; to others, it was the fatal flaw that prevented him from being remembered as a "great artist." He lacked a "signature style."

Like his art, his love life flourished. Free from the constraints of Tulsa, where he felt pressured to be someone (a heterosexual) he wasn't, Brainard embraced his sexuality, but not before some near-misses with a couple of women, one of whom would end up marrying his close friend.

Padgett writes that a giddy, tipsy Joe escorted Pat, Ron's wife, to her doorstep while he was out of town and nearly asked to stay the night, but something stopped him. Joe and Pat were always close, and Joe seemed to maintain a profound and prolonged crush on her, but it was more admiration than anything else, and nothing sexual ever happened between them.

Nothing sexual ever happened between Joe and any woman, but there were plenty of escapades with men.

"I've been sleeping around a lot but not getting much satisfaction from it," Joe once wrote to Ron. "I find myself just wanting to be in bed with people more than I really want to 'do' anything. (Sometimes.)"

In another letter he wrote: "What I really want to be is madly in love. (I do believe in it.)"

His most serious relationships were with writers Joe LeSueur, Frank O'Hara, Kenward Elmslie, and actor Keith McDermott. The love of his life was Elmslie, an author and playwright, though Brainard didn't always recognize him as such. They collaborated artistically, Joe designing covers and jackets for Elmslie's books and plays, and spent 30 years as off-and-on lovers but steady friends. Elmslie was with Joe when he died.

The pair spent summers in Calais, Vermont, where Joe would regularly abandon his erratic, Manhattan-inspired work schedule and in favor of leisure of the countryside. But he had a difficult time staying monogamous and enjoyed sex—especially anonymous sex with strangers. He didn't flaunt his homosexuality; upon seeing an overly flamboyant gay man, Joe once told Ron, "He's the kind that gives queers a bad name."

"I think he disapproved of the young man's aggressive behavior because what it amounted to was inverse machismo," Ron writes in *Joe*. "Joe felt that publicly flaunting your sexuality—gay or straight—was not only bad manners, it was probably an indication you had a problem with it." Joe's friends never had a problem with his sexuality, though they did sometimes disapprove of his promiscuousness, preferring he settle down with Kenward Elmslie.

Joe's homosexuality wasn't an issue for his brother John, who would join him in New York after attending art school at the University of Tulsa.

John had long looked up to his older brother, and Joe, sensing a kindred spirit—both because his brother was an artist and because he wrongly suspected John might also be gay—welcomed John to his new home in New York. Together, they began making regular visits to their parents back in Oklahoma. It had been 15 years since Joe had been to Tulsa.

Joe left Tulsa because he didn't think he could be a serious artist there; he didn't think anyone outside of New York understood his work. And he didn't think he could be himself in Tulsa.

"Everyone thought they understood him," Padgett said. "They treated him a certain way and expected him to behave a certain way, and he didn't feel that's who he was. He wanted freedom, a chance to figure out who he would become. He didn't think he could do that in Tulsa. He felt trapped there."

Harvey thinks he had a fear of being ordinary. "He felt his family was very ordinary, and he didn't want to be that way," she said.

Padgett says "conventional" is a better word. "Joe wasn't sure he wanted to be conventional ... He had a kind of revelation his senior year in high school that he might be able to develop and expand his talent so he could become an artist, rather than just, quote, a 'fashion designer.' It's such a small niche in art history, and he wanted to shoot higher than that, to see if he could be extraordinary."

And he was, for as long as he wanted to be.

"As he got a little older, I think he took a certain pleasure in life that took the place of the pleasure and pain of doing art," Padgett said. "Art seemed less important to him as he got older, and I think it was because he had done a lot of art and a lot of terrific people had absolutely loved it, and he made them incredibly happy and made a lot of friends who adored him.

"He confessed that he loved to make people happy, to please them, and he had accomplished that. His art had enabled him to do that. At the same time, I think he had come to know that art is not the most important thing in one's life. There are things that matter more. His life became his art."

•••

In the '80s, Joe Brainard's art career careened to a halt. He stopped showing new work, and eventually he stopped creating it. Though the critical acclaim and accolades bestowed upon his art never wavered, Joe's own confidence in his ability was fragile, to say the least.

"(H)e took an increasingly dim view of his work, seeing it as lightweight, facile, and lacking in the qualities of the high art of the oil painters he so admired, such as de Kooning, Manet, Goya, Katz, and Porter," Padgett writes in *Joe*. Though friends and critics raved (and rave) about his talent, that he never was able to paint faces undermined his success.

"Joe's still-lifes and landscapes in oil demonstrate how accomplished his technique was in that medium," Padgett writes.

"However, for him the ultimate challenge—and his nemesis—was oil portraiture. His friends sat for him, enjoying everything about it except his frustration with the results. Time and again, his sitter would be delighted by the day's work, only to learn that later Joe had scraped the face area with a pallet knife and rubbed it out with a turpentine rag ..."

Such was the result of portrait he attempted of Pat Padgett, Ron's wife, which he exhibited in its faceless, unfinished state in a show at the Fischbach Gallery in 1974.

"That he did so is a measure of his deep frustration," Ron wrote.

His constant self-criticism, coupled with a growing disdain for the art world, were motivation enough to leave it behind. Or, perhaps, as he did with each period of creation in his career, he felt he had mastered the technique and he was ready to move on to another.

Despite the warm reception his work received, it's largely unremembered in the annals of art history. Brainard purposely never created for himself a "signature style," perhaps to his detriment. His work varied and he never spent too much time on any one aesthetic, both of which make it difficult to immediately spot a "Brainard."

And this fact has opened up a debate among art critics as to whether Joe was a "major" artist or a "minor" one. It's a discussion Padgett addresses in his book, but he does so with some disdain.

"What difference does it make if the world thinks someone is a great artist or not?" he said when I asked him if he'd ever drawn any conclusions on the matter. "It matters in the marketplace, and in the museum world, but in actual intrinsic value, the urge to categorize artists as major or minor—and by the way, is there any in between?—that urge is very wrongheaded. It's erroneous thinking. It's a curious desire people have to rank everyone. But it's ridiculous.

"My conclusion is it's a question we shouldn't think about."

For Nylajo Harvey, who's produced more than 4,000 works in her 50-year career, Brainard's talents speaks for itself. Not much else matters. Padgett echoes her sentiments.

"Joe was gifted. Some people are. From childhood or birth, some kids can draw without being taught. It's a certain thing in their brain or their visual understanding of the world and the way that understanding communicates itself to the hand. Joe, by the time I met him, was clearly one of those special people. Not only did he have that inherent talent, but he was able to develop it, to nourish it, to challenge it. As a result, he made very beautiful things.

"But the distinctive part may be in his refusal of a signature style and the fact that he was able to do very superficially different types of art at the same time. He did highly realistic pencil portraits and, at the same time, he'd be doing collage paintings of flowers. If you examine the two, they don't look alike. Nonetheless, if you do look at the whole run of Joe's work, I get this sense of this one person behind it. To me, that's pretty distinctive."

•••

When he was 27, Joe wrote in his diary that he couldn't imagine living to old age.

"Can you imagine yourself 60 or 70 years old? I can't. I imagine, rather, that I will die young: 40 or 50. Not because I want to die young. But because I can't imagine being old. So there is nothing else to imagine. Except dying young."

He died in May of 1994 of AIDS-related pneumonia. He was 52.

Keith McDermott told Edmund White that Joe was surprised when he discovered he was HIV positive. "I thought he'd commit suicide, but no, he became very docile and just did whatever the doctors said."

Joe tested positive for HIV in 1990, after a bout with shingles led his friends to question his health. They encouraged him to get tested, and he did, but Ron and Pat Padgett wonder if he may have already known. In Joe, Ron wrote, "Pat has a gut feeling that Joe may have suspected or even learned of his HIV status as early as 1987. She can pinpoint a particular evening when he invited just the two of us out to dinner: his manner was unnaturally distant, his mood very odd. He might have just gotten bad test results, or he might have been on the verge of telling us. She also remembers that it was around then that he began to take superlative care of himself, joining the exclusive Crosby Street health club and buying nice clothes."

"We're not sure when he first learned of his diagnosis," Ron told me. "He didn't want to inflict pain on his friends by telling them," an obvious consequence of his ubiquitous niceness.

By the time John told his parents of Joe's illness, their mother's Alzheimer's made her "sort of out of it," but other than that, they accepted the news with stoic reserve, "typically not expressing much emotion," John said.

When Joe died, he "had been nearly forgotten, except by his legion of friends," White wrote in "Saint Joe." That legion went out of its way to ensure that Joe wouldn't be forgotten, organizing a series of events to honor the man and his work—work he had refused to show for the last 15 years. Among other efforts, they planned a 164-piece retrospective exhibit of Joe's work, organized by the Berkeley Art Museum, which traveled to the Donna Beam Fine Arts Gallery at the University of Nevada in Las Vegas, the Boulder Museum of Contemporary Art and P.S. 1 in New York City.

The exhibit was offered to Tulsa's Philbrook Museum of Art, which owns two of his works—one from 1959 and one from 1977—in its permanent collection, but Philbrook's leadership at the time sent Constance Lewallan, who curated the exhibit and wrote the accompanying program, a curt letter of rejection.

In 2004, Padgett published *Joe*, which is equal parts biography and memoir and paints an honest and touching picture of his friend. Next spring, the Library of America will publish *The Collected Works of Joe Brainard.*

"When someone we love dies, most of us do things to keep them from completely vanishing," Ron opens his text in the

Preface. "We summon up memories of them, we talk about them, we visit their graves, we treasure photographs of them, we dream about them, and we cry, and for those brief moments they are in some way with us. But when my friend Joe Brainard died, I knew I was going to have to do something beyond all these."

As someone who imagined death would come to him early, Joe Brainard accepted his fate with grace and what dignity he could muster. Padgett wrote that, when he died, he was wearing, beneath his hospital gown, pants and socks, "guarding these last vestiges of dignity to the end."

John Brainard told Edmund White that Joe "felt like he had enough time."

"Though he went through a lot of pain, he suffered it very bravely," John said.

"At his memorial ceremony, several speakers called him 'saintly,' " White wrote.

Ron Padgett remembers driving home from the hospital the day Joe died. "Just as we pulled up in front of our building, out of nowhere came a deafening machine-gun fire of hailstones that pummeled the roof of the car for fifteen seconds, then suddenly stopped." ◥◣

# SILKWOOD:
## THE MYSTERY OF KAREN SILKWOOD'S DEMISE LIVES ON

*by Sarah Denton*

Whien Richard Rashke's *The Killing of Karen Silkwood* was published in 1981, it was a groundbreaking, whistle-blowing work leveled at the nuclear industry. Overnight, it became a significant artifact for Oklahoma history. Despite the importance of Karen Silkwood and the events surrounding the now-defunct Oklahoma-based Kerr McGee plutonium plant, the discussion surrounding her death has grown quiet in the last three decades.

Yet there never was a solid conclusion as to what happened—not a believable one, anyway. There are still many contradictions and unanswered questions involved in Silkwood's death. Rashke's book keeps those questions alive, even 30 years later.

In 1970, Kerr-McGee opened a plutonium production plant near Crescent, in the heart of tornado alley, to make fuel rods for nuclear reactors. The corporation was a collaboration between Dean Anderson McGee, a lead geologist in the oil industry from Kansas, and Robert S. Kerr, 12th governor of Oklahoma and later U.S. Senator. While initially concentrated in oil-related endeavors, the corporation pursued a few ventures in the nuclear industry, including uranium mining and milling in Arizona and New Mexico, and uranium processing at plants in Gore and Crescent, not far from where the plutonium processing plant was later built. By 1974, Kerr-McGee was considered one of the most powerful energy corporations in the United States.

Beginning in August 1974, Karen Silkwood—lab technician

and member of the Oil, Chemical and Atomic Workers (OCAW) union at Kerr-McGee—began secretly collecting documents at the request of an OCAW legislator, Tony Mazzocchi, proving that quality-control tampering and other illicit activities were going on at the company's Cimarron Fuel Fabrication Site in Crescent. Three months later, on November 13, she left a union meeting at a Crescent restaurant with plans to deliver the documents to *New York Times* reporter David Burnham. She never made it. Silkwood's white Honda Civic was found in a ditch off Route 74. It was a fatal crash.

According to the report filed by the Oklahoma Highway Patrol, Silkwood fell asleep at the wheel under the inducement of drugs and alcohol use. A flask and some marijuana joints were retrieved from the crash. However, it was not determined that Silkwood was under the influence of marijuana at the time of the accident. Also, no one at the union meeting was drinking, including Silkwood, and the contents of her flask was later revealed to be tomato juice. Postmortem toxicology reports revealed a moderate amount of methaqualone in her bloodstream, for which she had a prescription. Lastly, and most importantly, neither Silkwood's notebook, nor her file folder, both containing evidence against Kerr-McGee, were retrieved from the crash site, even though a coworker who understood what those two items contained saw Silkwood leave the restaurant with them in hand.

OCAW hired A.O. Pipkin, a car crash expert who owned Accident Reconstruction Laboratories in Dallas, to conduct an investigation and analysis of Silkwood's crash. After studying the car and crash site, Pipkin determined that Silkwood did not fall asleep at the wheel; rather, she was chased by another vehicle (or vehicles) and was forced off the road, where her Civic collided with a cement wing wall.

Three months prior to her death, Silkwood met with OCAW legislator Tony Mazzocchi, who told her that plutonium was carcinogenic, which alarmed her. While it was known in the nuclear and mining industries that uranium (from which plutonium is obtained) was carcinogenic, it was not common knowledge, and the workers at Kerr-McGee's uranium and plutonium processing plants were not informed of the substances' carcinogenic properties. Like many employees of the Kerr-McGee facility, Silkwood had been contaminated on the job several times. According to nuclear and health physics experts who analyzed health and safety conditions at the Cimarron plant for Silkwood's trial, the working conditions at the plant were extremely unsafe. For one, some of the respirators that workers wore during their shifts were faulty. There was also a high turnover rate at the plant that led to a lot of untrained employees handling radioactive material. In fact, it was later disclosed that these workers—some of them only in their late teens—received little to no training for their highly hazardous jobs.

Mazzocchi, through his assistant Steve Wodka, secured Silkwood and two other Kerr-McGee employees and union members (Jack Tice and Jerry Brewer) a meeting with the Atomic Energy Commission (AEC). The AEC was in charge of investigating nuclear facilities, but also with promoting nuclear energy, a formula for inevitable partiality. Kerr-McGee had a high-dollar contract with the AEC, which created an ostensibly biased relationship.

It was in the time leading up to the meeting with the AEC that Silkwood began collecting evidence for reporter David Burnham at Mazzocchi's suggestion. Having worked in the Metallography Lab at the plant, where she conducted quality-control checks, and also having experience polishing fuel rod welds in accordance to acceptable standards, Silkwood had the knowledge and the access to records and the proof that quality-control records were being doctored. The doctoring allowed leaky, faulty rods to be used at the Westinghouse Fast Flux Test facility, a nuclear test reactor owned by the Department of Energy at the Hanford Site in Washington State, no longer in operation. She didn't know what would happen if faulty rods were used, but was smart enough to know that the results could not be good. In addition, Silkwood discovered that glove-box gaskets were leaking plutonium nitrate into the workplace. But, most importantly, Silkwood discovered that enough plutonium to make nearly three atomic bombs—approximately 40 pounds—was missing from the Cimarron plant, although it was never determined how she made this discovery or if she had documentation to prove it.

Furthermore, prior to April 1974, Kerr-McGee was not required to have security in place to guard from plutonium leaving the plant. As Rashke, and as Silkwood's lawyers suggested during her trial, such lax security made a plutonium-smuggling ring at the Kerr-McGee plant undoubtedly possible.

In early November, Silkwood was contaminated during her shift. She had 10,000 disintegrations per minute (d/m) on her right wrist—20 times greater than the amount declared safe by the AEC. Her nasal smear also tested positive (150 d/m). It was on her hands, neck, and face, and in her hair. An explanation for her contamination was never determined.

Two days later, on November 7, Silkwood was tested again. Results showed she had an astounding 45,015 d/m in her right nostril and 44,988 d/m in her left nostril (despite the fact that she had a blocked nasal passage in her left nostril). This indicated that she was most likely *exhaling* plutonium from her lungs and that her exposure, in this particular case, had not occurred at the plant.

Two Kerr-McGee employees investigated Silkwood's house after her contamination results. Her kitchen stove tested positive for 25,000 d/m, the refrigerator door, 20,000 d/m, and inside the refrigerator, an astonishing 400,000 d/m. The bologna inside the refrigerator was contaminated, as well as frozen strawberries, vegetables, and other items within the home, including cereal, Q-tips, a bicycle and bath oil and cologne.

Her roommate, Sherri Ellis, who also worked as a lab technician at Kerr-McGee at the time (although not a union member) mysteriously suffered minimal contamination. Silkwood alone appeared to be seriously affected.

As Rashke points out, the contamination within Silkwood's home was no accident. The likelihood that Silkwood would intentionally contaminate herself to make a point on behalf of the OCAW union, as Kerr-McGee suggested, was not plausible, since she understood plutonium's carcinogenic properties. Silkwood also told a coworker that someone contaminated her and told her sister during a phone call that someone was trying to harm her but that she couldn't discuss the details over the phone.

The results of the AEC investigation of the Kerr-McGee Cimarron facility following Silkwood's crash determined that she had inhaled and eaten plutonium, among other details. However, the AEC investigation did nothing to resolve *who* was responsible for contaminating Silkwood, nor did they look very far into why quality control negatives were being doctored, or why workers were receiving such little training at the plant.

As Rashke points out, both Kerr-McGee and the AEC benefited from the Crescent plant's existence. The coziness of the relationship was threatened by the union.

On December 29, 1974, the *New York Times* published Burnham's report that thousands of pounds of nuclear materials were missing from 15 nuclear processing plants in the United States, including Kerr-McGee. The missing plutonium, according to the AEC, was the result of accounting and inventory mistakes. Barbara Newman reported in a 1976 article in *The Nation*, "Some of Our Plutonium is Missing," that in 1974 the Kerr-McGee plant closed down on two occasions to conduct inventory because of missing plutonium—plutonium that was "found" on both occasions. The inventory was conducted by Kerr-McGee and did not provide any objective proof that the plutonium was actually accounted for. Furthermore, Kerr-McGee was licensed to produce 1,000 kilograms of plutonium, even though the average amount recorded in their inventory was approximately 360 kilograms.

But despite all the question marks hovering over the Kerr-McGee plant, its relationship with the AEC, Silkwood's contamination and, most importantly, the missing plutonium, the FBI investigated for only five months before closing the Silkwood file.

It should be noted that the events leading up to and surrounding Silkwood's death only take up the first *third* of Rashke's book. The remainder of the pages follows the bizarre quandaries and threats encountered by investigators and lawyers involved in the congressional subcommittee investigation (focused on proving poor working conditions at the Cimarron plant) and the civil suits filed by Silkwood's father.

For starters, it was verified by an anonymous source within the FBI that Silkwood's union-related activities and investigations were being monitored. There was strong speculation that Silkwood's home was bugged. Furthermore, the same source also divulged to a private investigator involved in the Silkwood lawsuit investigation that the CIA was diverting plutonium from U.S. nuclear plants and delivering it to international political allies. This information suggests that Kerr-McGee was up to no good from the start and that whatever was going on at the plant in small-town Crescent involved the FBI and a potential collaboration between the FBI, the Intelligence Department of the Oklahoma City Police, the CIA, the NSA, and the U.S. Navy.

And, Rashke suggests, that a 28-year-old union laborer stumbled onto it and paid the ultimate price.

In 1977, while working on another story, Rashke met with attorney Dan Sheehan, who would go on to represent Silkwood's family in her civil trial. During their meeting, Rashke caught a glimpse of the Silkwood lawsuit sitting on Sheehan's desk and asked to look at it. He was instantly intrigued.

"I'm addicted to David and Goliath stories," said Rashke during a phone interview. "What struck me immediately was that if Silkwood had been a man, this would not have happened. She was a woman. She wasn't married at the time. She was very vulnerable. She didn't have a lot of money, so it was easy to squash her.

"I never believed [it] when I heard that she fell asleep at the wheel on the way to Oklahoma City to deliver evidence to *New York Times* reporter David Burnham. I laughed and said, 'Tell me another one.'"

Rashke worked closely alongside Sheehan and private investigator Bill Taylor, hired by Sheehan to help build the Silkwood case. There were times when potential risks to Rashke's safety arose. He had a hideout in Oklahoma City, a church where he was to go if he ever felt threatened. If necessary, Taylor could provide him a haven on an island off of Florida. It never came to that, although there were times when Rashke admits he grew anxious.

"The stakes were high in terms of life and death with Silkwood," says Rashke. "The stakes were very, very high on the level of the health of the workers ... [and] the stakes were high for the government, in terms of terrorism, and also in terms of diverting plutonium, if that's what they did."

When asked what matters to him today about the book, Rashke said: "No one in all those years, including Kerr-McGee, was able to come back to me and say, 'You made a serious mistake here.' Not a single person."

For Rashke, the subject is not dead, nor has it lost importance.

"Silkwood," he says, "will always be close to my heart." ◥

# PRIVATE MANNING AND THE MAKING OF WIKILEAKS:

## THE INSIDE STORY OF THE OKLAHOMAN BEHIND THE BIGGEST MILITARY INTELLIGENCE LEAK EVER

*by Denver Nicks*

Midnight, May 22nd, 2010. Army intelligence analyst Private First Class Bradley E. Manning is sitting at a computer at Contingency Operating Station Hammer, east of Baghdad. He is online, chatting with Adrian Lamo, an ex-hacker and sometimes-journalist based in San Francisco.

"Hypothetical question," he asks Lamo. "If you had free reign over classified networks for long periods of time... say, 8-9 months... and you saw incredible things, awful things... things that belonged in the public domain, and not on some server stored in a dark room in Washington DC... what would you do?"

Manning, 22, is probing Lamo for guidance–and approval.

"I can't believe what I'm confessing to you," he types.

Outside of the chats, little is known about Bradley Manning. We know that he grew up in Crescent, Oklahoma, a town made famous by one of the biggest whistleblowing events in American history a decade before Bradley was born. Currently, he's in solitary confinement at Marine Corps Base Quantico in Virginia, awaiting trial, and unable to speak to the press. His family and many of his close friends have been advised not to talk to the media. If the allegations against Private Manning are true, the 22-year-old from

Oklahoma is responsible for the biggest leak of military secrets in American history.

Records of the chats, which continued over several days, portray a dejected, disillusioned soldier. His long-distance relationship has ended, he's been demoted from Specialist to Private First Class after he struck another soldier and the Army has removed the bolt from his rifle out of concern for his mental state.

"I'm a total fucking wreck right now," he tells Lamo.

Brad feels alone, invisible, like his career and his relationship–the life he had finally built after years of drifting–is falling apart. For months, he'd been disenchanted with the wars in Iraq and Afghanistan. He points to a specific instance, in which, investigating 15 detainees for printing "anti-Iraqi literature" he found that the paper in question was merely a scholarly critique of corruption in the government and brought the revelation to an officer.

"He didn't want to hear any of it," he types. "He told me to shut up and explain how we could assist the FPs in finding *MORE* detainees."

Brad had lost faith in the American military as a force for good in the world.

"I don't believe in good guys versus bad guys anymore," he tells Lamo. "Only a plethora of states acting in self interest."

In further chats with Lamo, Brad describes how he used his security clearance and computer skills to access confidential government networks and download classified material, including video of American soldiers killing civilians, hundreds of thousands of internal military reports and more than 260,000 diplomatic cables. Disclosure of the classified material, he says, will have implications of "global scope, and breathtaking depth." He tells Lamo he's been delivering the classified information to Julian Assange, the quixotic founder of the shadowy whistleblowers website Wikileaks, which is releasing it publicly for the world to see.

The information he allegedly unleashed into cyberspace reverberated across the globe. The anti-war Left seized upon the leaks as evidence that the wars in Afghanistan and Iraq are unjust and unwinnable. The Taliban promised to kill those Afghans who, the documents reveal, have collaborated with the Americans. President Obama said the leaks endanger the lives of American troops. Supreme Court Justice Sandra Sotomayor predicted the leaks will lead to a new free-speech ruling in the supreme court, which could overturn the precedent set in the Pentagon Papers case, the foundation of modern-day jurisprudence on questions of national security and freedom of speech.

•••

Crescent, Oklahoma is stamped out in a one-square-mile rectangular grid and bisected by Highway 74, which becomes Grand Avenue in town. On this main thoroughfare is "the stop sign," a frequently referenced landmark when locals give directions. There is the gas station, where men gather in the mornings to talk and drink coffee; the Baptist church – one of 15 churches in town – an unadorned, rectangular block, with a plain white spire and beige metal siding; Kelly's Café, where locals fill the dining room to capacity at lunchtime. A towering, white grain elevator looms over the skyline. There are a few empty shells of buildings on Grand Avenue, but Crescent lacks the bombed-out look of crumbling decay visible in so many small Oklahoma towns. The cliché is unavoidable–Crescent, by all appearances, is a happy, healthy little town.

Crescent's favorite son is Geese Ausbie, the "Crown Prince of the Harlem Globetrotters," but there's another character who isn't as cherished, a 28-year-old woman who spoke up in 1974 and got the world's attention.

Several miles south of town, on the Cimarron River, a decommissioned Kerr-McGee plutonium plant sleeps in quiet, conspicuous retirement. The plant was closed in 1975, a year after plant employee Karen Silkwood was last seen alive at a union meeting at the Hub Café (now closed, across the street from Kelly's). After the meeting, Silkwood drove south on Highway 74 toward Oklahoma City to meet with a reporter from the *New York Times* allegedly carrying documentation of gross safety violations at the plant. Silkwood's car was discovered crumpled in the embankment, its driver dead. The documents were never found.

An Oscar-nominated film was made about the incident, and the name Silkwood became a rallying cry for union organizers. But, for Crescent locals, the story is more than lore. Many in Crescent know someone who worked at the plant with Karen Silkwood, and for years the town's residents shared an association with whistleblowing and martyrdom.

Perry's Roadhouse is several miles south of town and effectively Crescent's bar. Bumper stickers decorate a back wall: "Don't steal, the government hates competition," and "U.S. Government Philosophy: If it ain't broke, fix it till it is."

Perry's isn't far from where Silkwood died on the same highway, and a few questions from a reporter still get locals speculating. An acquaintance says Silkwood was a drug addict. Perry heard that Kerr-McGee got the state to resurface the road, covering the skid marks before they could be analyzed. A friend of a friend says she backed into a telephone pole, putting the dent in her back bumper that, some believe, is evidence she was run off the road. Invariably, someone will add that Karen Silkwood was not from Crescent and lived in Oklahoma City.

The memory of the Silkwood incident lurks far in the background of life in Crescent–for the most part people don't particularly care to talk about it, and, polite that Crescent locals are, when they do, most don't have much to say. Still, the story remains unsettled. When Bradley Manning was growing up it was 20 years less settled.

Several miles north of Crescent, on Highway 74, a paved county road turns off the highway and into the countryside. The Manning family lived out here, in a two-story house in the country, near the end of a gravel road before it turns to dirt. Trees obscured the view of the house from the street and cast shadows over the property. There was an above ground swimming pool and a bountiful garden that produced what one neighbor called the biggest asparagus stalks he'd ever seen. The house was isolated and quaint. Neighbors were a quarter mile and more away. Brad grew up here with his older sister, Casey, his mother, Susan, and his father, Brian.

Brian Manning spent five years in the navy in the late 1970s, working with the high tech naval systems of the day. He studied computer science in California, and went to work for Hertz Rent-a-Car as an Information Technology manager. While in the Navy he spent time at Cawdor Barracks, in Wales. He married a Welsh woman, Susan, and moved with his family to Crescent, from where he could commute to the Hertz office in Oklahoma City.

By all appearances, according to people who knew the family, Brian Manning, who did not respond to interview requests, was a difficult man to live with.

"He was just real demeaning," said Rhonda Curtis, a neighbor. Another neighbor, who asked to be called James, put it more bluntly.

"Brian's a dick."

Brian Manning's own words, however, contradict the image of a domineering jerk. While his son was in Iraq, in December of 2009, Brian posted on Brad's Facebook wall:

"Happy Birthday Son!...Did your gift arrive? I sent it yonks ago."

When Bradley returned home briefly on leave, in January 2011, his dad posted again, "Welcome back son!"

Less than a minute later, apparently after reading that his son's profile listed Potomac, Maryland as his hometown, Brian added, "and your hometown is Crescent, Oklahoma."

•••

As a little boy, Brad was high-strung and abnormally intelligent. Like his parents, he has always been smallish.

"We used to think of him kind of like a cocker spaniel," said Rhonda Curtis.

"He was just a little nerd," said Danielle, Rhonda's daughter, and a childhood friend of Brad's. As kids, she and Brad rode bikes around the neighborhood, swam in his pool, played Super Mario Brothers at her house and Donkey Kong at his.

Bring up Bradley Manning in Crescent, and you're likely to hear that he was, "too smart for his own good." He was a promising saxophonist in the middle school band, always excelled in the science fair, and starred on the quiz bowl team. On bus trips to quiz bowl competitions around Oklahoma, he and a small group of friends passed the time talking about ideas and big picture questions of right and wrong.

"We'd talk about stuff that, for that age, was pretty deep," said Shanée Watson, who recently graduated from the Massachusetts Institute of Technology. "We discussed morality and philosophy a lot—I know that sounds weird, but that's what we did."

He was polite and obedient in class, with no disciplinary record at all from his elementary and middle school years. He did not, however, shy away from confrontation.

"You would say something, and he would have an opinion, which was a little unusual for a middle school kid," said Rick McCombs, currently the school principal, who was a high school history teacher and coach when Brad was in school. "Don't get me wrong, we had the cut-ups and the clowns and the mean ones and the bullies and those kinds of things, but this young man actually kind of thought on his own."

While still in elementary school, Brad first expressed an interest in joining the U.S. military.

"He was basically really into America," said his friend Jordan Davis, in an email. "He wanted to serve his country."

Brad's school bus ride home was an hour long, and acquaintances say he spent most of the trip quietly doing his homework, while other kids had paper ball and spit wad fights.

Johnny Thompson, whose bus stop was last on the route, just after Brad's, recalls a quiet but not exactly anti-social kid. "After everyone else was gone I'd actually go over there and talk with him a little bit," Thompson said. "He was pretty nice if you were nice to him."

As Brad got older his playfulness receded. He stopped playing with neighborhood kids, spending more time on the top floor of his home where he had his computer–this was the late 1990s, just as the Internet was becoming a truly global phenomenon, with, literally, a world of opportunity for a young man who felt increasingly alienated from the community he lived in.

Events in Brad's life collided to put tremendous stress on the boy. As his peers were confronting their own sexuality in a context that was, at worst, prudish and ambivalent towards it, Brad was shouldering an added burden.

While Brad was in middle school, Brian Manning came home one day and announced he was leaving Susan. He moved out abruptly. Eventually, Susan and Brad moved into town, to a small rental house near the Baptist church. Brad's grades dropped. Amidst the disintegration of his family, pubescent Brad was coming to terms with his own sexuality. Shanée Watson recalls Brad gathering she and Jordan Davis near a tree at Jordan's grandmother's house to give them important news. Brad told them that he would very shortly be moving with his mom to Wales for high school. He also told his two best friends he was gay.

This moment warrants pause. Bradley Manning, still effectively a boy, had few friends, and his family had all but fallen apart. In a time before Facebook and sustained long-distance friendships, he was leaving his two best friends for what could easily have been the last time (for Shanée Watson, it was). He didn't need to tell them he was gay in order to confess a hidden affection, to explain a behavior or even to allow his friends to know him better—in a short time he would be gone. And yet, presumably for no other reason than that he was who he was and wanted to live honestly in his own skin, he felt compelled, in a conservative, religious town, to confide in his friends that he was a homosexual. Not only must it have taken tremendous courage for such a young man, it displays a crucial aspect of Brad's personality. As his Facebook profile still says today, "Take me for who I am, or face the consequences!"

•••

Brad moved to Wales with his mother to a much bigger small town, Haverfordwest, population 13,367, where he attended high school. He was teased for being effeminate but was not, apparently, open about his homosexuality. Friends say he was quiet, and kept his personal life to himself. He'd stopped playing the saxophone, got into electronic music and spent a lot of time on the computer. Though small and provincial itself, Haverfordwest must have been an exotic metropolis compared to Crescent.

After finishing high school, he returned to the United States, moved in with his dad in Oklahoma City and went to work for Zoto, a software company. Brad's strained relationship with his father cut that living arrangement short—the situation turned toxic, at least in part because of his homosexuality, and his dad kicked him out. He was homeless, moved to Tulsa and stayed with his friend Jordan Davis. He eventually moved into a south Tulsa apartment near Davis', lived alone, and worked low wage jobs at F.Y.E., a retail entertainment chain, and Incredible Pizza.

Brad drifted from Tulsa to Chicago to Potomac, Maryland, in the outer suburbs of Washington, D.C. He moved in with an aunt and began to get a steadier footing. He had jobs at Starbucks and Abercrombie and Fitch, took classes at a Community College, and had enough money and stability to take a trip back to Chicago for the Lollapalooza music festival.

Not long after his trip to Lollapalooza, in the late summer of 2007, Brad joined the Army. He'd long expressed interest in serving, and the Army was a natural next step for an unsettled but talented and ambitious young man.

"I think he thought it would be incredibly interesting, and exciting," Jordan Davis told me in an email. "He was proud of our successes as a country. He valued our freedom, but probably our economic freedom the most. I think he saw the US as a force for good in the world."

Brad did basic training at Fort Leonard, in Missouri, but he sustained a nerve injury in his left arm, and his future in the Army was put on hold. That Christmas on Facebook he posted cheerful pictures of a visit with his family in Oklahoma, including pictures of his father. After the holidays, Brad returned to basic training in Missouri. He graduated in April 2008 and moved to Fort Huachuca, in southern Arizona, excited to be back in contact with the civilian world. "Hit me up on the phonezors if you can!" he posted.

While at Fort Huachuca, Brad was reprimanded for putting mundane video messages to friends on YouTube that carelessly revealed sensitive information. The infraction must not have been serious, because by August he'd graduated from training as an intelligence analyst with a security clearance.

After Fort Huachuca, Brad was stationed at Fort Drum in upstate New York. It was an election year, and Brad was pulling for the celebrity freshman senator from Illinois, Barack Obama. Also on the ballot that year was California's Proposition 8, which, in a significant setback for the gay rights movement, banned gay marriage in the state when it passed on Election Day.

Just days later, Brad went to a rally against Proposition 8 in front of city hall in Syracuse, New York, and an hour and a half from Ft. Drum. At the rally, a soldier was interviewed anonymously by high school senior Phim Her for Syracuse.com, a local news website. The soldier was Bradley Manning.

"I was kicked out of my home, and I once lost my job [because I am gay]," he told her. "The world is not moving fast enough for us at home, work, or the battlefield." Brad told her that, for him, the Don't Ask, Don't Tell policy is the worst thing about being in the military. "I've been living a double life," he said.

After Proposition 8 passed, Brad's Facebook wall becomes a flurry of activity, much of it related to the gay rights movement, though most updates were ordinary messages from a happy young man, newly in love. He spent the holiday season in the Washington, D.C. area, and just before Christmas announced a relationship with a new boyfriend. He began posting more often than ever. "Bradley Manning is a happy bunny." "Bradley Manning is cuddling in bed tonight." For an active duty soldier, he was remarkably transparent about his sexuality on his Facebook wall. After returning to base: "Bradley Manning is in the barracks, alone. I miss you Tyler!" And, "Bradley Manning is glad he is working and active again, yet heartbroken being so far away from hubby."

Over the next several months Brad's posts are nearly all related to progressive politics or his boyfriend. He seems happy and confident, comfortable in his life and positive about the future.

In September 2009, his relationship status changed to single, and posts between he and Tyler tapered off, though they maintained friendly communication. This was likely a safety measure in light of the Don't Ask, Don't Tell policy. A month later he deployed to Iraq.

Brad arrived in Iraq in late October 2009. His infrequent status updates are mostly mundane: "Bradley Manning has soft sheets, a comforter, and a plush pillow... however, the war against dust has begun," and "Bradley Manning is starting to get used to living in Groundhog Day."

After gay marriage failed on the ballot in Maine, he posted, "Bradley Manning feels betrayed...again." In late November he posted, "Bradley Manning feels forgotten already," but for the most part he remained positive. The holidays brought a flood of well-wishers, but Brad was notably quiet. Considering what was to follow, Brad's wall posts from this period are strikingly boring.

At the end of January 2010, Brad returned to the U.S. for a brief visit. He landed in D.C. just as a massive blizzard blanketed the city, and his plans were partly derailed. But as he left he wasn't dispirited: "Bradley Manning is hopefully returning to his place of duty over the next few days. Hope I don't get caught up in this next storm," he posted on February 8.

This is the period in which Brad is accused of having leaked at least some documents to Wikileaks. Bradley Manning is officially charged with leaking classified information between November 19, 2009, and May 27, 2010. In his chats with Adrian Lamo, Brad references a "test" document he leaked to Julian Assange (presumably to verify Assange's identity), a classified diplomatic cable from the U.S. Embassy in Reykjavik, sent January 13, 2010. Wikileaks posted the document on February 18, 2010.

If Brad was indeed the source of Reykjavik13, as the document has come to be known, he had to have leaked it sometime before mid-February, and Wikileaks tends to take time to analyze and verify the authenticity of leaked documents, if possible. Brad didn't return to Baghdad from his visit home until February 11, and he left for home on January 21. If Brad leaked Reykjavik13, he almost certainly did so sometime over the eight-day period from January 13, 2010, when the cable originated, and January 21, 2010, when he left Baghdad for the United States.

The timing debunks the overarching narrative in the media that Brad was an anti-social outcast lashing out at the world and crying for attention when he decided to leak military secrets. On January 14, 2010, the day after Reykjavik13 originated, Brad posted, "Bradley Manning feels so alone," to his Facebook wall—perhaps this is the period when he decided to become a leaker. He appears distraught, there is no doubt, but hardly the emotional wreck portrayed in the Lamo chats that took place months later.

Over the next several months, when Brad may have leaked most of the documents, he appears happy and carefree. His posts are peppered with smiley emoticons. On March 14, he "wishes everyone a Happy Pi Day!" Not until April 30, after a change in his boyfriend's relationship status does his emotional state seem to deteriorate. That day he posts that he "is now left with the sinking feeling that he doesn't have anything left..." Days later, on May 5, 2010, he says he "is beyond frustrated with people and society at large," and the next day he "is not a piece of equipment."

This is Brad's last Facebook post. Later that month he apparently initiated a chat with Adrian Lamo, who had recently been profiled in *Wired Magazine*. Brad, it seems, broke down to Lamo and over a series of days confessed his shocking breach of U.S. military security.

The magnitude of classified material Brad is suspected to have leaked is astounding. He appears to have leaked the Collateral Murder video, in which American soldiers in an Apache helicopter gleefully gun down a group of innocent men, including a Reuters photojournalist and his driver, killing 16 and sending two children to the hospital, a video of the 2009 Granai airstrike in Afghanistan, in which as many as 140 civilians, including women and children, were killed in a U.S. attack on a suspected military compound, a cache of nearly 100,000 field reports from Afghanistan, known popularly as the Afghan War logs, about 260,000 diplomatic cables and a set of as many as half a million documents relating to the Iraq war that, even on their own, likely constitute the biggest leak of military secrets in history.

Lamo notified the authorities.

Brad's Facebook status, on June 5, 2010, probably posted by someone else, reads: "Some of you may have heard that I have been arrested for disclosure of classified information to unauthorized persons. See [link to the Collateral Murder video]." He'd been arrested days before, and was then being held in Kuwait, before being transferred to the brig at Quantico.

Brad currently faces three counts of unlawfully transferring confidential material to a non-secure computer—military jargon for leaking state secrets. If convicted, he could spend a half a century in prison. U.S. Rep. Mike Rogers (R-Mich.) has called for his execution.

•••

On July 25th, 2010, Wikileaks released the Afghan War Logs. The documents reveal hundreds of civilian deaths in unreported incidents, rapidly escalating Taliban attacks, and indications that the Pakistani intelligence service, ostensibly a U.S. ally, works intimately and supportively with the Taliban and Al-Qaeda. *The Guardian* called the logs "a devastating portrait of the failing war." *The New York Times* called them "an unvarnished, ground-level picture of the war in Afghanistan that is in many respects more grim than the official portrayal."

Critics of Wikileaks accused the group of publishing documents that included the names of Afghan informants, putting their lives in danger. Wikileaks withheld publication of 15,000 documents to redact the names of others to whom the leaks could bring harm, and claims to have invited the Pentagon to help—though the Pentagon denies this. The Pentagon has said that it will not cooperate with Wikileaks under any circumstances, has called on the group to stop publishing leaks and demanded that it immediately return all classified material. *The Daily Beast* has reported that the Pentagon now has a 120-person strong "Wikileaks War Room" to minimize harm from the leaks, to try to preempt them and to collect information to be used, at some indeterminate future date, in prosecuting Julian Assange for espionage.

Wikileaks anticipated becoming an enemy of the state. Quietly and without fanfare, with threats to its existence rising, Wikileaks uploaded to its website an encrypted document called "Insurance file", which has been downloaded more than 100,000 times to date.

The file is about 20-times bigger than the Afghan War Logs. If– or when–Wikileaks releases the password for the file, the whole world will know what it contains. In Wikileaks, the Pentagon is confronting a challenge like none before. The agent was Assange, but the raw material likely came from Bradley Manning.

Since its debut on the world stage in 2006, Wikileaks has posted a document leaked from Somalia's Islamist rebels, the contents of Sarah Palin's email account, documents temporarily discrediting now-vindicated climate change scientists, internal papers from the Church of Scientology, the membership list of the pseudo-fascist British National Party and more. Big scoops all, but not until Collateral Murder and the Afghan War Logs did the American government initiate a concerted effort to shut the website down. Once a source of newsworthy if mostly innocuous revelations, Wikileaks has officially become a threat to national security. If the allegations against him are true, Brad made Wikileaks what it is today.

•••

The last day I spent in Crescent was a bright Sunday morning. I sat on a bench not far from the Hub Café, where Karen Silkwood spent some of her last moments. As trucks lumbered down Grand Avenue and drivers waved hello, the town came to life.

I went to Sunday school at the Baptist Church. In the class for young adults I attended, we discussed the familiar troubles of jobs, children and romance–troubles Bradley Manning is unlikely to experience for many, many years, if ever again. Toward the end of class we bowed our heads, and Rick McCombs, the principal of Crescent schools, led a prayer for Bradley Manning and his family.

After church, I spoke with Johnny Thompson, Brad's old buddy from the long bus ride home. We met up at a gas station and talked about his life growing up in Crescent: the boredom, the tragedy of the closing of the arcade in the laundromat, the ridicule from kids in bigger cities, the independent streak instilled in him by being a social outcast in a small town. At the end of the interview, I turned my recorder off and started to stand. Thompson asked me to turn it back on.

"Just one last thing," he said. "No matter what he did, every memory I have of him is just a little kid I talked with on the bus. It don't even really seem right that he's some big criminal right now."

Thompson, a stonemason, has the hulking look of an overgrown boy soon to become a man. His dark, smoky eyes are fidgety and uncertain, betraying a humble, earnest sensitivity.

"I was worried that they might execute him."

Thompson had caught my eye days earlier, when he mentioned in passing that he was reading the classic subversive novel written by Oklahoma City native Ralph Ellison, *Invisible Man*. I asked if I could interview him later. He said sure, then walked away. As I too walked toward my car, he turned and added, "Not everyone in Crescent's a bunch of rednecks." ◥

# ASHES TO ASHES, DUST TO DUST

*by Gene Perry*

J ust outside Bokoshe, Oklahoma, is a winding stretch of properties known as "the loop." The land is heavily wooded and sparsely populated—a place where you'd likelier see a bull snake crossing the road than a person. It's hardly anyone's idea of a center of pollution and disease.

But as Tim Tanksley drove the loop, he pointed left and right and left again, indicating nearly every home we passed.

"Someone there has cancer," he said.

At the next house, "There's cancer in that one."

And the house after that, "A woman there is on oxygen."

A grandfather with a trimmed gray mustache, cowboy hat, patient demeanor, and heavy Oklahoma drawl, Tanksley is not the typical image of an activist or environmentalist. But he and other residents of Bokoshe have spent years battling a coal ash dump near their town. They believe the ash is causing serious health problems in the 450-person community.

The ash comes on trucks out of the AES Shady Point coal plant, seven miles east of Bokoshe. AES Shady Point stands out against the green of rural Le Flore County—a pale, sprawling complex with one long smokestack pointing at the sky. If you live in central Oklahoma, Shady Point's electricity likely lights your home. You might have sipped on carbon dioxide that was scrubbed out of its smokestack to make its way into your soft drink. You've also paid with your tax dollars to keep it burning Oklahoma coal.

And for the Oklahomans living nearby—in small towns with memorable names like Spiro, Panama, and Bokoshe—the impact is impossible to miss.

Not everyone in Bokoshe and nearby communities is convinced that the coal ash is dangerous. They defend the economic benefits of the plant, from those directly employed by AES to retailers who get regular business from the ash truck drivers.

The dumpsite near Bokoshe is owned by the five Jackson brothers: Ken, Kevin, Chad, Daryl, and Mark. They run a company formerly known as Making Money, Having Fun, LLC. After getting negative publicity, they changed the name to Clean Hydro Reclamation.

"We are a hard working family," Chad Jackson told a local newspaper. "We go to work every day, try to make an honest living and have some fun at it. That's why the company was formerly named MMHF."

One of the Jackson brothers lives in a house adjacent to the dump site, where he is exposed to the ash as much as anyone. But according to a count by Bokoshe residents, 14 out of the 20 households near the site have someone with cancer or severe respiratory problems. Bokoshe elementary school teacher Diane Reece said 9 out of 17 students in her sixth grade science class have asthma. That compares to about 1 out of 10 children with asthma nationwide. The school is 1.5 miles from the coal ash pit. Reece was diagnosed with colon cancer in 2002 and breast cancer in 2007.

•••

Kenneth Self is a former coal ash worker who knows the dangers first hand. Today he lives near Panama, Oklahoma, in a trailer home that as we talked in the yard was exited by more people and dogs than it seemed could comfortably fit inside.

He rolled up a sleeve to reveal an arm speckled with white. The spots are remnants of alkali burns, from when coal ash reacted with his sweat to form a blister.

"It gets hot anytime it contacts moisture," he said.

Alkali burns are a common ailment for people who work with wet concrete, to which coal ash is commonly added. The ash is under our feet everywhere in streets and sidewalks. Locked away in pavement, it is unlikely to pose a health threat, but before it gets there is another matter.

In the early 1990s, Self worked at a coal ash dumpsite operated by the P&K Coal Company. P&K was one of numerous small companies with brief lives that have overseen coal ash disposal over the years. AES Shady Point may be their only customer, but the liability is one step removed.

Self operated a bulldozer at the P&K site, tamping down mounds of ash after they were dumped from trucks. Self said he and the other workers were "young, dumb, and making good money." He didn't think about the dangers of inhaling the ash.

"Like my daddy said, they can kill you, son, but they can't eat you," he said.

After 2½ years on the job, he began to have trouble breathing. One day he woke up hyperventilating. He rushed to the hospital, where doctors found a mass in his lungs that they at first thought was cancer. It turned out to be a clump of coal ash.

Eventually he was diagnosed with "small airway disease due to chemical accumulation." After a year of legal battles, Self settled out of court with P&K for $7,624.50. After attorney fees and other expenses, he received a little over $5,000.

Self said he still experiences breathing problems that make it hard for him to work, and today he lives on full disability.

The pit where Self worked is no longer in use. A sign warns visitors, "Private Property: Keep Out," but the gate sits torn off its hinges and buried in weeds. Past the gate and up a small hill is the coal ash mound. A couple days after heavy rains, it looks like black mud but quickly turns to a gray powder as it dries on the skin. The mound is criss crossed with tire tracks from local kids' dirt bikes and 4-wheelers. Back at AES Shady Point, 3,000 tons of coal arrive every day by train. The coal is sent to one of four boilers where it's floated on jets of air as it burns in a bubbling mixture of gas and solids. The smokestack sends up no visible emissions because filter bags catch most of the particulate matter. But the particles have to go somewhere, so they end up in the ash. Then the ash is sent to Bokoshe at a rate of about 80 truckloads per day.

This year Shady Point celebrated its twentieth anniversary. Members of the media, politicians, and current and former employees gathered to praise the plant. They spoke of its contributions to the area, like building a new elementary school in Panama and funding patrol cars for the Le Flore County Sheriff's Office.

Others are more skeptical.

"AES Shady Point should have never been built," said Harlan Hentges, an Oklahoma lawyer and director of the Center for Energy Matters. "And it was only built because of government interference."

The plant is a subsidiary of the multi-billion dollar AES Corporation, which goes by the slogan, "the power of being global." But the history of Shady Point, why it was built and whom it touches, is an Oklahoma story.

When the plant began operating, the peak of Oklahoma coal production was a decade gone. In 1981, 5.7 million tons of coal were taken from Oklahoma mines. Ten years later, production had dropped more than two-thirds.

Some Oklahoma lawmakers took it on themselves to revive the industry. The legendary Gene Stipe (the longest serving member of the legislature until he resigned amid a campaign finance scandal in 2003) traveled to Virginia to lobby AES corporate leaders to build a plant especially designed for Oklahoma coal.

•••

The effort was successful, and AES Shady Point opened in 1990. Demand for Oklahoma coal had fallen away partly because it is high in sulfur, which is restricted by the Clean Air Act, but Shady Point came with the latest technology for reducing sulfur-dioxide emissions. It was also the first U.S. coal-fired plant to extract from its emissions food-grade carbon dioxide, which is then used for dry ice, flash-freezing chicken, and carbonated drinks.

In its first years, the plant used 100 percent Oklahoma coal. In some years, it has used 65 percent of all the coal produced in Oklahoma.

But sulfur was not the only problem for the industry. Coal is nearer to the surface and much cheaper to mine in Wyoming. After transportation improved and the prices diverged, AES began preparing to move away from Oklahoma coal.

The legislature again stepped in, passing a mandate that all utilities in the state use at least 10 percent Oklahoma coal. This was overturned by the U.S. Supreme Court in 1992, after Wyoming sued. So in 1993, they created a tax credit. AES Shady Point would get $2 for every ton of Oklahoma coal that it buys. In 1997, the credit was increased to $5 per ton.

The coal credit was also made transferable. That means AES can sell it to any Oklahoma business or individual, who can then deduct the full amount from their own taxes. AES receives more in credits than they owe in taxes, so they sell the surplus for a profit. That's how most of the coal credit ends up going to insurance companies. In 2009, it paid out about $6 million.

AES spokesman Lundy Kiger said the transferability is needed to keep Shady Point buying Oklahoma coal and supporting Oklahoma mines. Their contract with the mining company, Georges Colliers Inc., is void if the credits expire.

Kiger argues that the credit has paid for itself and created 1,500 to 2,000 direct and indirect jobs in the area. "We're talking about coal miners, their families, and others," Kiger said.

AES Shady Point employs about 90 people, with a payroll of $15 million. The plant sells enough electricity to Oklahoma Gas & Electric to power 230,000 homes and businesses. Coal mines directly employ about 180 workers statewide, down from more than 400 in the early 1990s.

The jobs are certainly needed. In 1991, Le Flore County saw almost 14 percent unemployment. The unemployment rate gradually fell through the '90s, and by 2000 it was as low as 4 percent, though in the current recession it has gone back up to nearly 10 percent.

Today, AES Shady Point uses about 40 percent Oklahoma coal. Kiger said they would prefer to use all Oklahoma coal, but a Chinese company called Dragon Energy bought exclusive rights to the coal from one of their suppliers. Dragon Energy took over a coal seam that stretches across the Oklahoma-Arkansas border to make a substance called coke, formed by burning coal in an airless furnace at temperatures as high as 2,000 degrees Celsius to drive out almost everything but the carbon. Although China has plenty of its own coal, a building boom created enormous demand for coke, which is used to make steel. Between 2009 and 2010, American coal exports to China increased more than tenfold.

Oklahoma's coal credit was suspended along with several others in 2010 due to state budget shortfalls. However, it is scheduled to go back into effect on July 1, 2012, and will continue through 2014. Kiger said AES advocates extending the credit beyond that year.

The extension to 2014 aroused some controversy. Representative David Dank, chair of the House Taxation and Revenue Committee, wrote in an Oklahoman op-ed piece that lawmakers "extended a multimillion-dollar coal industry tax credit through 2014, despite a total lack of evidence that the coal industry needed or deserved such special treatment. [It was] passed by both houses of the Legislature in the final 30 minutes of the session, with no House debate, questions or discussion allowed."

As Kiger describes it, he approached legislative leaders and the governor with a proposal that AES would pay the mining company the equivalent of the credit to keep them in business over the two years suspension if it was extended another two years after that.

"We'll do this, if you'll do this," he said.

•••

The mound of coal ash outside Bokoshe keeps growing. It was originally proposed as a reclamation project for an abandoned strip mine, but the ash filled the mine years ago. Today it rises more than fifty feet high across an area larger than 15 football fields. When the wind picks up, residents say they've watched clouds of ash entering the air.

For some Bokoshe residents, the coal ash is a constant specter. After spending years in the shadow of the coal ash pit and what they believe it is doing to their health, they begin to see ash everywhere—in attics, air conditioner filters, even the dust on top of ceiling fan blades. Some of their concerns may be more justifiable than others, but their experience with AES, state regulators, and politicians have done little to assuage the fears.

Kiger said that to ease concerns from Bokoshe citizens, AES bought new trucks began sending them through a wash station before they leave the plant. However, AES still denies that coal ash poses any health threat.

•••

After years of no action from state agencies, last year the EPA cited Clean Hydro Reclamation for dumping oil and gas wastewater into a nearby creek, a violation of the Clean Water Act. The EPA has referred the case to the Department of Justice. Even if the water pollution ends, coal ash dumping would likely be allowed to continue. There are currently no federal regulations for coal ash, and state oversight falls under three different agencies: the Oklahoma Corporation Commission, the Department of Mines, and the Department of Environmental Quality. On paper, it is DEQ's responsibility to monitor air quality at the site, the Corporation Commission's responsibility to regulate water quality, and the Department of Mines' job to monitor the coal ash itself. Until the EPA stepped in, none of these agencies had identified any problems with the dumping.

•••

The Environmental Protection Agency (EPA) began to consider classifying coal ash as a hazardous waste in 2008, after a ruptured dike spilled 1.1 billion gallons of coal ash slurry into tributaries of the Tennessee River. The ash contains trace amounts of mercury, lead, arsenic and other dangerous heavy metals.

In a series of hearings on proposed regulations, the agency received more than 450,000 public comments. They are currently reviewing those comments, and EPA Administrator Lisa Jackson said she doesn't expect any new rules to be ready this year. Congressional Republicans have repeatedly proposed bills that would prohibit the EPA from taking any action regarding coal ash.

At EPA hearings in Dallas last September, Tanksley spoke about the land his family has lived on since before statehood.

"[Our home] is a legacy that's been passed down to me through my family generations, and it's a legacy that I would like to pass on to my children and grandchildren," he said. "But I'm afraid it will not happen. If they continue to dump the ash around Bokoshe, it's not going to be a safe place for them to live." ◀

# MISCONDUCT CITY:

## THE ASSAULT OF ARTHUR BRADLEY
## REVEALS A CULTURE OF CHAOS

*BY JOSHUA KLINE*

The white '75 Buick Regal races through the red light at 51st Street and careens left onto 129th East Avenue. Tulsa Police Officer Quentin Houck pursues closely behind, the lights and sirens of his patrol car piercing the night. It's nearly 4 a.m. on May 20, 2000, and Houck's dashboard video camera documents the high-speed chase that began with the robbery of a Git 'n' Go store at 16th and Memorial.

The Buick glides through the deserted streets of Tulsa with Houck in pursuit. The wide road narrows to two lanes; the distant flashes of patrol cars approaching from the opposite direction signal the end of the line for the rogue Regal. The driver brakes and swerves right into a residential entrance. The car stops. Suddenly, the driver's door flies open and James Ezell, 27, jumps out and bolts into the neighborhood. Several patrol cars arrive as another passenger, 17-year-old Willson Duckett, makes a run for it.

As officers sprint after the two men, the Buick's passenger door opens and two raised arms emerge. A third man, 20 year-old Arthur Bradley, does not run. Instead, he lowers himself onto the pavement, arms above his head, clearly indicating surrender.

Officer Houck is out of his car, his gun raised. Without hesitation, he approaches Bradley and kicks him hard in the upper chest, barely missing his jaw. Houck screams, thrusting the full weight of his hulking body toward Bradley. Houck is a big man. Oklahoma big. Bradley, skinny and diminutive, remains on his stomach, his feet still resting just inside the car. Houck boots Bradley hard, then boots him again. Bradley's feet go limp. Houck screams and Bradley responds—the words are inaudible. Houck then yells "SHUT UP! SHUT UP!" He holsters his gun and steps onto Bradley. With his leg pinning the suspect and his arms victoriously angled to his waist, the officer poses like a hunter and his prized buck. After a few moments, Houck wraps his arm around Bradley's and drags the young man off the ground and into his patrol car.

Officer Houck is now Sergeant Houck. Ezell and Duckett were both sentenced for their crimes, but not Bradley. His story took a completely different path, one that illuminates a growing public safety concern. In the past decade, Tulsa has become one of America's worst cities for police misconduct—outranking places famous for their out-of-control officers. Does the Tulsa Police Department (TPD) allow violent acts of misconduct to bypass public scrutiny? How did this happen, and who, if anyone, is responsible?

The answers begin with a small-time crack dealer.

•••

Arthur Bradley sits in Conner Correctional Center, his second stint in the medium security prison located on the edge of Hominy, 45 minutes northwest of Tulsa, for a charge unrelated to the robbery. The visitor's room, thick with the acrid stench of body odor, has the stifling aura of a run-down public school cafeteria.

Bradley grew up under the care of an overworked single mother in the violent, gang-infested neighborhood of 56th Street North and Peoria Avenue. His two brothers are incarcerated, a third is dead. His sister has three children and lives in Houston.

When Bradley speaks, he reveals a jagged, haphazard set of teeth.

"I joined a gang at a young age, a really young age," he says. He was 10 when an older cousin introduced him to the notorious 57 Hoover Crips. As a teenager, he learned to hustle the streets and avoid the law. At 14, he was sent to Shadow Mountain for "behavioral problems," but the treatment didn't take, and Bradley eventually dropped out of McLain High School to nurture his blossoming gift as a crack dealer ("I had one hobby: makin' money"). At 16, he was arrested for possession of a controlled substance and given probation, and, just before his 19th birthday, Bradley was sent to prison—the same one he sits in now—for the first time.

On May 19, the day before his encounter with Officer Houck, Bradley was still stretching his legs as a newly freed man. He'd been released from Conner less than three months earlier and was living with his mother, who'd since relocated to West Tulsa.

By his own admission, Bradley's recollection of this particular day is foggy and somewhat contradictory.

"I prefer not to dwell on it," he says.

He remembers that he ended up in the Comanche Park Apartments, a gritty public housing complex known for its drugs and guns, on 37th Street North and Quaker Avenue, where he met James Ezell, Willson Duckett and Tyree Walker. The extent of Bradley's prior relationship with the three men is unclear (Bradley claims he didn't know them), but that afternoon, the 20 year-old ex-con found himself lounging around with the men, smoking weed laced with PCP. It was his first experience with the powerful hallucinogen, and as evening turned into night, Bradley was ready to get back to his mother's. He offered gas money for a ride west; Ezell agreed. With Duckett and Walker tagging along, the group set out to get Bradley home. According to Bradley, at some point near the beginning of the car ride, he passed out. (The more likely explanation is that the dissociative effects of PCP caused him to black out).

Bradley did not make it back to his mother's. Instead, he sat in a white Buick while his new friends robbed a gas station.

•••

Around 3:30 a.m., Ezell, Duckett and Walker entered the Git 'n' Go at 16th and Memorial. Ezell locked the doors. The armed men then approached Assistant Manager Martin Hawkins and took his wallet and personal cash. They forced Hawkins to strip, bound him with duct tape (including his eyes and mouth) and tossed him in the bathroom. Walker donned Hawkins' Git 'n' Go shirt for the benefit of curious passersby, and the men cleaned out the register.

When Hawkins could no longer hear the robbers, he managed to break free and trigger the silent alarm.

Officer Houck happened to be nearby when the call went out.

•••

A new law enforcement watchdog group, dubbed The National Police Misconduct Statistics and Reporting Project (NPMSRP), recently released its 2010 numbers on police misconduct tracked across the United States. For a department its size (between 500 and 999 officers sworn), Tulsa ranked 3rd in the nation for police misconduct complaints. On a per capita basis, however, Tulsa far surpasses cities notorious for misconduct, such as Los Angeles, New York, Detroit and Philadelphia. The national average of credible misconduct complaints is around 977 per 100,000 officers, or less than one percent. Tulsa's number was 42 credible complaints against 812 sworn officers—5,172 per 100,000, over five times the national average.

TPD has yet to release their own 2010 report, but NPMSRP's 2009 numbers nearly match TPD's findings in the same year. On a national level, the vast majority of these complaints fall under

"Excessive Use of Force" (other complaint categories include sexual misconduct, fraud/theft, drugs, civil rights violation, and murder). Within the Excessive Force category, 57 percent of these complaints are said to be "physical" (as opposed to "firearm," "taser" and "chemical").*

Bradley is quick to excuse Houck's excessive use of force, which he matter-of-factly describes as an "assault" and then proceeds to defend.

"I don't think it was out of line," he offers. "We was on a high-speed chase, my adrenaline would be pumping too if I was the driver trying to chase somebody down."

After ditching the Buick, Duckett and Ezell were apprehended and, along with Bradley, taken back to the Git 'n' Go for Hawkins to identify. Traumatized, the clerk—a military veteran with a history of medical problems—mistakenly identified Bradley as being in the store at the time of the robbery. The three men were taken in for questioning.

The next day, Walker was apprehended. On May 26, District Attorney Tim Harris filed charges against the four men. Bradley was charged with three counts—robbing Hawkins, robbing the Git 'n' Go and, oddly, obstructing justice by claiming to be a victim of the three robbers.

After barely 50 days of freedom, Bradley was back behind bars, nursing the bruises caused by a police officer's boot and awaiting trial for a robbery he allegedly slept through.

Bradley never reported the beating.

•••

The videotape from Officer Houck's patrol car first emerged in pre-trial discovery as simple evidence of the chase. On Aug. 10, 2000, Judge Clancy Smith held a preliminary hearing. Notably, during the hearing, the videotape was referenced by prosecution and witnesses for the state, but had not yet been provided to the defense.

Assigned to prosecute on behalf of the state was Assistant District Attorney Bill Musseman, an aggressive 29–year-old just three years out of OU's law school who came from a law enforcement legacy (his father was an ex-cop who also served as ADA in the late '70s). With sandy brown hair, piercing blue eyes and a lean, athletic build, Musseman had the kind of All-American, "I Believe in Harvey Dent" demeanor that could win elections.

A litany of problems emerged during the hearing. By now, the security footage from the Git 'n' Go had been reviewed and it was clear that Bradley was never in the store, despite Hawkins's positive ID. Detective Bob Little, who initially interrogated the defendants the night of the robbery, testified that Bradley had confessed to discussing the crime with his co-defendants beforehand and to being awake while the robbery went down. But Little also testified that, during questioning, Duckett confirmed that Bradley had been asleep in the car the whole time.

Musseman could not get a consistent positive ID out of Hawkins—in open court, the traumatized clerk once again mistakenly identified Bradley as Ezell. The transcript of Hawkins's testimony reads like a tragic version of the old Abbott and Costello "Who's on first?" routine, with a frustrated Musseman playing the role of straight-man, trying desperately to get a consistent answer out of the befuddled witness.

John Harris, Bradley's attorney, argued to Judge Smith that the evidence was clear: Bradley was not in the store and did not participate in the robbery. His argument was compelling, but based on Bradley's initial confession, Smith determined he would stand trial.

•••

Tulsa District Judge Linda Morrissey was about to preside over the jury trial against Bradley when she first saw the videotape of the assault. Although several people had seen the videotape already, including Musseman, nobody had bothered to report what appeared to be a case of violent police misconduct.

"Once I saw the video tape, I felt like I had an ethical duty to apprise the chief of police about it," Morrissey told me.

Morrissey took the videotape and personally walked it over to the city municipal building, where she presented it to Chief Palmer and an Internal Affairs investigator.

"My concern was the physical actions taken by the police officer," she explained. "When that defendant was removed from the car and placed on the ground, the police officer proceeded to take some physical action that I felt should be made known to the chief of police, because it was pretty aggressive."

Sometime in September, Bradley received a visit from two Internal Affairs investigators who questioned him about the incident.

"They asked me a few questions about the officer," Bradley remembered. "Was I assaulted ... I said I was roughed up a little bit."

The investigators came and went and, for a while, it looked as if the video was a non-factor in the case against Bradley. Bradley's attorney certainly wasn't making it an issue, and the defendant himself seemed to hold no ill will against Houck's aggression.

In October, John Harris filed a motion to dismiss charges against his client for lack of evidence. On Oct. 24, Musseman countered the motion, saying, "There is enough evidence to bind this defendant over and survive this motion ... Argument can clearly be made this defendant served a role as a lookout."

Two days later, five months before trial was set to begin, Musseman inexplicably backpedaled. He moved to dismiss all charges against Bradley.

What caused Musseman to change his mind so abruptly?

•••

There's a warehouse in North Tulsa that contains the hard copies of every court case filed in Tulsa County before 2009.

Though well-hidden—it's tucked away just off Apache, between Lewis and Harvard, disguised as an extension of the John Crane mechanical seal factory—its doors are open to the public. A small side door bears the name, "Sally Howe Smith – County Clerk."

When you enter, you'll likely wait at least a minute before a government employee slinks out of the obscured, back-office space to take your order. Offer a case number and the clerk will write it down and retrieve it for you. Depending on the day and the particular clerk, you may or may not be required to document evidence of your visit. If you are required, you'll simply write your first and last name on a pink slip of paper. No identification will be requested to verify the information. You'll receive the file, and you'll sit down at one of two large tables available in the front area. The clerk will retreat to the back and you will be left alone, save for the occasional coming-and-going of an attorney or courier. You will not be monitored by cameras. You will not be required to check large bags. When you return the file, the clerk will likely barely acknowledge your presence. You will be able to leave with a potentially large number of documents from the case—hearing transcripts, filed motions, police reports, even physical evidence—leaving the clerk happily clueless. The case file will be returned to its proper place of storage.

Decades worth of Tulsa court records are completely unpoliced and up for grabs. Anyone, for any reason, can simply walk in and walk out with original copies of some of the most important case files in our city's history. Missing material will not be noticed until days, months or years down the line, when the random attorney or reporter complains of the absence of a vital document.

The case of Arthur Bradley is stored here. Over the course of several visits, I pored over the entire file in an effort to find Musseman's dismissal of charges against Bradley. There was no documentation of any kind, no evidence that the case had been dismissed except for Bradley's complete absence in the jury trial transcript and an invoice dated in November from John Harris to the State, requesting payment for his representation of Bradley.

On the Oklahoma State Courts Network (oscn.net), the docket history for the case against Bradley briefly lists Musseman's initial response to Harris's motion as well as the prosecutor's own dismissal several days later. The website does not provide details, only the most barebones summary of what went on in court. I called the County Clerk's office and requested that they pull the information missing in the physical file from their computer database.

Amazingly, the information was missing from the computer as well. The clerk chalked it up to mis-filing and told me that system is run by "flawed human beings" who occasionally invert a number or two when filing. Unfortunately, she said, there's no way to retrieve the information once the mistake is made.

•••

Bill Musseman now sits as an elected district judge, presiding over criminal cases he would have prosecuted as an ADA. On this particular day, he's devoted his lunch recess from a jury trial to explain to me his reasons for dropping charges against Bradley. He's an energetic 39, warm and friendly, and eager to accommodate. Though he's only given the 11 year-old case a cursory glance in preparation for this interview, his memory is remarkable.

"At no time in the motion, nowhere anywhere else that I can remember, did I ever make the argument that the decision with Bradley could survive trial muster or survive beyond a reasonable doubt. So there wasn't much of a difference in opinion from the time I filed the motion—the motion was responding to a question of, on a legal basis, would the state survive to fight another day?"

In other words, Musseman doesn't see the move to dismiss as a contradiction of his response to Bradley's motion. "There wasn't really a turnaround, at least in my mind, as far as the position I held when I filed the reply to a legal question, and the final decision that I didn't have enough evidence to take it to trial, to win at trial beyond a reasonable doubt. So I made the decision I made."

Musseman goes on to explain with remarkable nuance the reasons a case against Arthur Bradley was more or less doomed from the beginning. He covers Hawkins's mistaken identification of Bradley and the fact that Bradley's prior criminal history would not be available to the jury. He even illuminates the problem with Bradley's supposed "confession" (not available in the case file) which, based on Musseman's description, was somewhat misrepresented by the detective during his testimony at the preliminary hearing. "You have statements that (Bradley) had made that they had talked about (the robbery) before and he knew that they were thinking about it," Musseman explains. "But my recollection is that he never admitted that they said, 'We're going to do it this day, this is when we're doing it, here's your role.' "

According to Musseman, Ezell was the obvious ringleader and the one he wanted to convict. In order to assure that his case against Ezell was ironclad, he made a tactical decision to shed the weakest link, the least culpable suspect.

"One of the big things that made it difficult is they chased this car, and it was a long chase," says Musseman. "It ended up in East Tulsa, 145th East Avenue or something. I forget who was driving, but I think Ezell. Bradley, I believe, is in the back seat. Well, they all get out and disperse. And Bradley doesn't move. He sits there. So that's significant in the sense that you really don't even have an argument of consciousness of guilt."

Musseman doesn't mention the kicking incident, and our conversation moves on to Bradley's criminal record. A few minutes later, I bring the conversation back to the chase.

"It's actually videotaped from the officer's dash-cam," I volunteer. Musseman's body shifts, he leans back in his seat and moves his hand to his chin as if deep in thought. His eyes narrow ever so slightly; he's either deeply curious or extremely annoyed with where I'm leading the conversation.

I describe the events caught on camera.

"What I'm curious about, since the tape had already been viewed by the time of the preliminary hearing, did that play into your decision (to dismiss charges)?"

"I wanna be careful how I answer, because the answer is, 'Yes,' " says Musseman. "I don't want to give you the impression that I gave it undue weight. It was in a situation where the arrest seemed to have been a bit excessive in force and which I think was later disciplined as excessive force. I don't want to give you the impression that since that happened, everything's lost. But yes, it was a factor to be considered with others."

But after having seen the video himself, was Musseman under any obligation to report it? Our legal system incentivizes people to keep quiet. If Musseman reported the incident himself, he would've likely lost the case against Bradley immediately. If he kept quiet about the assault, and nobody outside of the defense discovered the incident, it would strengthen his chances of convicting Bradley. But someone else did notice the tape.

I ask Musseman if Judge Morrissey might've told him to report the tape to the proper authorities. Musseman is well-versed in legalese; he knows the right answer.

"I don't recall," he says. "I don't remember."

I ask what his initial thoughts were upon first viewing the video tape.

"I don't remember."

But according to Morrissey, Musseman presumably saw the tape before she did. Then they, along with other attorneys, had a meeting about it.

"I did express real concern about the level of physical force used on the codefendant, and that the videotape should be submitted to IA [Internal Affairs]," Morrissey said. "I felt it was incumbent upon me to report it."

Morrissey implied that she had an ethical duty to report the tape; I asked Musseman if he felt a moral obligation to make sure that the videotape was investigated.

"Well, luckily in our system we have open discovery which really provides everything to the defense. Everything is inspectable, viewable … That pressure is not so great because everyone knows what happened."

In other words, Musseman believes it should've been up to the defense to report Houck's assault, and he was under no obligation to report it. Musseman's situation—in which a private individual acting as a prosecuting attorney is at odds with the responsibility of a public official—suggests the complicated ethical waters the Bradley case stirs. Is a public official obligated to report the misconduct of a public servant, even if it means having to turn a known felon loose?

•••

Sergeant Quentin Houck now patrols out of the Riverside Division (South Tulsa). He's married, lives in Broken Arrow, and, according to his Facebook page, is a big fan of Las Vegas casinos and luxury cruise lines. He also serves on the Board of Trustees for the Fraternal Order of Police.

The Houck/Bradley incident occurred at a time when IA's protocol was much more flexible and complaints often went undocumented. Still, at the behest of Judge Morrissey, the incident was investigated and Houck was ultimately disciplined—suspended for two days, according to TPD Public Information Officer Jason Willingham. The suspension was absorbed into Houck's vacation time.

Houck's record as an officer shows that from 2004-2010 he's had at least three incidents involving a use of force, but no complaints. He has a respectable record. Houck declined to be interviewed for this story, as did Chief Chuck Jordan.

The assault of Arthur Bradley represents the most prevalent form of police misconduct reported in Tulsa, but is TPD's misconduct record the result of an out-of-control police force, or an uncommonly effective and transparent Internal Affairs department?

Tulsa Police Captain Luther Breashears would prefer to believe the latter. The 45-year-old has been with TPD for almost 20 years, the last four of those spent as Unit Commander of Internal Affairs. According to him, the majority of misconduct complaints are "public relations issues"—an officer's harsh tone or aggressive body language can just as easily result in a misconduct complaint as a kick to the ribs. In defense of IA, Breashears cites changes brought about by 2003's Consent Decree, a legal truce of sorts that ended nine years of litigation between a group of black TPD officers and the City of Tulsa and directly affected how IA and the department at large conducted and policed itself.

"The biggest change that the Consent Decree brought about for the entire department was some sort of consistency in the way we do business," Breashears told me. That new consistency included, for the first time, holding the department accountable to the standards of the Commission on Accreditation for Law Enforcement Agencies (CALEA). A new complaint investigation process was coupled with a Data Collection policy—complaints in every form, anonymous or not, would now be documented ("I've investigated a complaint written on the side of a shopping bag," said Breashears), investigated and archived for data reporting purposes. It's this data collection that has since allowed organizations like NPMSRP to reveal police misconduct trends.

"Most complaints are bullshit," a TPD officer, speaking anonymously, offered me. "They stem from a misunderstanding of what an officer has to deal with on a moment-to-moment basis." Other officers I spoke with expressed similar opinions.

Breashears was surprised by Tulsa's high ranking on NPMSRP's misconduct list, even in light of the recent federal corruption probe that's resulted in five officers being indicted and two more pleading guilty for crimes far graver than excessive use of force.

"We average around 200 complaints a year, but the majority of those are public relations issues," Breashears said. "We've had a few demotions, we've had some suspensions and some terminations, so I think whatever we come across in Internal Affairs, the chain of command is responsive to what the appropriate discipline is for our city, for our officers, for our department personnel. I can't comment on an outside entity and how they collect their information, but I think our public, in a recent survey that was done by the city, (said they) are very satisfied with their police department."

Unfortunately, most of the data collected by TPD's Internal Affairs is not readily available to the public through its own website.

•••

"Karma is a motherfucker." Back at Conner, Arthur Bradley explained to me how robbery is not his "thing."

"People choose to do what they wanna do and it ain't one of my choices, robbing somebody. And the Tulsa police know that. The 36th precinct knows the type of situation I've been in, what department I work in. (Robbery) ain't my behavior profile."

ADA Musseman got his big fish in Ezell, who is currently serving time at Davis Correctional Facility in Holdenville. He won't be eligible for parole until 2047. Willson Duckett and Tyree Walker both served less than five years for their roles in the robbery. With the charges against him dropped in October 2000, Bradley was once again a free man. He continued to sell and use drugs, and just three months after his release he found himself pleading guilty to a possession charge. He served a year-and-a-half of a four-year sentence. Upon release, he went to a halfway house and found a job in a mechanic's shop, but the allure of easy money was too much, and soon he was back in the game, selling crack on the street. A year later he was convicted of drug trafficking and false impersonation. He's seven years into a 20-year sentence and is currently eligible for parole.

Right now, he passes the time in Hominy by playing pinochle with fellow inmates and reading paperback thrillers by Vince Flynn and James Patterson. He goes on walks when allowed.

"I've been in and out of this place all my life," Bradley acknowledged. "I'm 30 now, I'm tryin' to finish school." He hopes to be approved for transfer to a lower security facility where he can take classes and prepare for life on the outside. Once released, he plans to develop a trade, maybe learn welding, "something simple."

"I gotta figure something out, 'cause this ain't it." ◤

# CONVICTION AND
# TRANSFORMATION

# SOMETHING GOOD IS GOING TO HAPPEN TO YOU

*by Randy Roberts Potts*

I was twelve years old when it happened, in the 7th grade, attending Victory Christian School on 71st Street in South Tulsa. My grandfather, Oral Roberts, climbed up into a tower and began telling the world on national television that God had commanded him to bring in eight million dollars to further his work on Earth. If he didn't come up with the cash, the Lord, my grandfather said, would take him home.

I was twelve years old and, in the world I was living in, this wasn't as unusual as you might expect. There was a rhyme and reason to everything in God's world–if you had a question, the Bible always had the answer. So when my grandfather climbed into that tower, I randomly opened the Bible for guidance and my fingers landed on this passage from the book of Isaiah:

*Behold, I have given him for a witness to the people, a leader and commander to the people. Behold, thou shalt call a nation that thou knowest not, and nations that knew not thee shall run unto thee because of the Lord thy God, and for the Holy One of Israel; for he hath glorified thee.*

*I was twelve years old, and this tower business didn't really make sense, but then again, there was that passage from Isaiah, with God seeming to speak directly to me.*

At night I had dreams that the eight million dollars in donations wouldn't come in, and my grandfather would be taken up to heaven in a fiery chariot like Ezekiel, another Old Testament favorite of mine. Once at school I overheard two teachers talking about how Oral was a Cherokee Indian, and how it was a longstanding tradition among Indian chiefs to declare the day of their death as a way to get the tribe to do something drastic it didn't want to do, and the teachers said that if the tribe didn't cooperate, the chief literally fell over and died on the promised day. Turns out there is no such tradition, but even so, I imagined my grandfather, who at 70 years of age, with his long-hanging ears and bulbous, impressive nose really did look the part of an Indian chief, sitting up there in the Prayer Tower one day and suddenly expiring on his prayer rug. I imagined a lot of things, all far-fetched seeming now, but at the time completely in line with the culture I lived in, a culture in many ways shaped by the teachings of my grandfather.

Oral began "preaching the Word" in the late 1930s as a nineteen-year-old during the Great Depression—my grandmother Evelyn told me that food was often scarce, and Oral would sometimes go out and shoot "swamp rabbits" which she would then dutifully clean and bring downtown where you could rent communal freezer space. Oral's ministry grew slowly, reaching its prime in the sixties and seventies when he built Oral Roberts University and pioneered the "electric church," becoming the first television evangelist. His television programs came out of studios in Burbank, California, and his message was simple, and contrary, to what priests and preachers had been telling us for thousands of years: God, according to Oral, wasn't very interested in punishing us. In fact, God was just dying to heal us. All we needed to do was stretch out our hands in faith and believe, and God would bring healing. Healing to our bodies, healing to our marriage, healing to our loved ones and, yup, healing to our pocketbooks. It was a revolutionary message and one that hadn't really been heard before in quite the same way.

"God is a GOOD God," Oral intoned on national television. "Something GOOD is GOING to HAPPEN to YOU!"

By January of 1987, when Oral climbed into that tower, donations had been falling off for years. The fall of Jim Bakker, the fall of Jimmy Swaggart, and the failure of the City of Faith, Oral's 60-story hospital complex (much of it still sits empty today, 23 years later) were all part of the reason for the decline in revenue, as well as an ebb in popularity for the brand of televangelism Oral helped create. His efforts to bring in the money to keep his empire afloat became more and more ridiculous, but he continued using that feel-good phrase, "Something GOOD is GOING to HAPPEN to YOU!"

Even now, as a 35-year-old gay man whose church and family has rejected him, I can see the appeal in those words. "Hope is the thing with feathers," Emily Dickinson once wrote, "that perches in the soul, and sings the tune–without the words, and never stops at all." These days selling hope is a well-worn path, and Barack Obama, for whom my grandfather voted, inspired the nation by blanketing walls and subway stations and billboards with this one powerful word. It's surprising, I'm sure, that Oral voted for Obama, but given a choice between a man selling fear—fear of nuclear weapons, fear of the black man, fear of change, fear of Muslims, fear of a bright, sunny future–and a man who simply said "Yes, We Can," it must have been an easy choice for Granville Oral Roberts, who grew up in a shotgun shack in an impoverished corner of Oklahoma. He ended up building a 500-acre kingdom on the banks of the Arkansas River, a kingdom funded by faith, and faith alone. "Something GOOD is GOING to HAPPEN to YOU!"

But I digress. I'm not 35, an out-of-the-closet gay writer happily raising his kids in Dallas, Texas; nope, I'm just twelve years old, and my grandfather just climbed into a 200-foot-tall tower, and the whole city of Tulsa, Oklahoma, and the evangelical reaches of the entire world (which numbers, perhaps, in the hundreds of millions) were holding their collective breath awaiting the outcome. And me? I wasn't so worried about Oral. I figured either he would get the money and come down, or he wouldn't and God would take him to Heaven—either way, if you believed the hype, it was a win-win situation. When you're twelve, you buy just about everything your family tells you, so I really didn't worry much at all. About Oral, that is.

What I did worry about, and continued to worry about for at least the next 15 years, was the condition of my soul. While everybody else was worrying about Oral, I was worried that Jesus would come down, perched on a cloud in the sky, and whisk all the Christians up to Heaven in "the twinkling of an eye," as the Bible says. Like the title of the popular evangelical novel blares loudly from its cover, I was worried about being *Left Behind*.

Why choose 1987 to start worrying about the rapture? It wasn't, after all, until 1989 that Oral first said Jesus was coming back and the world was going to end, when I was in ninth grade attending Jenks High School. Nineteen eighty-seven made sense because Oral was up in that tower, and that tower, for me, was a symbol of the Second Coming of Christ, and this is exactly how Oral planned it. The Prayer Tower was built, along with most of the other buildings on the Oral Roberts University campus, in the late 1960s as a symbol of hope. At that time, on college campuses across the nation, students were sitting in groups by the thousands, smoking pot, drinking, swearing, having sex, wearing their hair long, and spending a lot of time saying "No!" to The Man.

Parents were scared, and Oral had an idea: why not build an evangelical university, where the students keep their hair short, their faces shaved, and their skirts long, and rather than saying "No!" are instead taught to say "Yes!" to the calling of God on their hearts? And in the middle of this campus, why not build a tower, constructed in such a way that, from any angle, it represents the image of the cross? In this tower he installed two things: a phone bank manned by faithful, little old ladies who would answer your call, day or night and pray with you on a toll-free number; and a gas flame, installed on the top of the tower, manned at all times, day and night, by a born-again Christian whose heart was "right with God."

This tower became the focus of my fear of the rapture. In 1987 I had a dog, a scruffy, old, monstrously-huge Irish Wolfhound, the kind of dog you see in movies about medieval England sitting calmly at the foot of the king in his castle. His name was Samson, and because he was such a big dog, I had to take him on a long walk every day or he would go stir-crazy and eat the cushions off our couch. We were living on the Oral Roberts compound off of 75th Street, in South Tulsa, just north of Lewis Avenue, a three-acre piece of land surrounded by an eight-foot stockade fence and a chain-link topped with barbed wire and electrified. I would walk down my 50-yard-long driveway, out the first gate, and out the second gate (always waving to the security guard in his little hut) and across 75th Street to the campus of ORU. There was another gate, and as soon as Samson and I went through, there was the Prayer Tower in the distance, that gas flame shining brightly on the top.

Or, at least, I hoped it was. On bright, sunny days it was almost impossible to tell, and that's where the fear crept in. The whole point of having that gas flame manned by a born-again Christian whose heart was "right with God" was this: if Jesus were to come down, perched on a cloud, and whisk away all the born-again Christians (the Catholics, and probably even the Episcopalians, were not really included in this group), that gas-flame operator would also be whisked away, and the flame would go out. That flame, perched on top of a 200-foot tower at the center of campus was both a promise and a threat—Jesus is coming back, but he's not here yet, so if you've sinned, get your heart right with God, because He might come at any moment.

Well, how do you know if your heart is right with God? Even at 35, I still haven't figured that one out.

So while everyone else was worried about Oral in that tower, I was worried about that gas-flame operator, looking every day to see if the flame was still there. On weekends, the campus could be awfully still and quiet, and if the sun was at just the right angle and I couldn't quite tell if the flame was still lit, chills would go down my spine. In fact, sitting here writing this, they still do. Some things just don't go away. I'm not scared of the rapture anymore, or the boogie man, or going to hell because I'm gay, but some nights when the house is too quiet I almost wish there were a tower across the street to remind me that all is well.

I was twelve, my grandfather was in a tower, and I was worried about the rapture, but I was also a seventh-grade gay kid in an evangelical Christian middle school, trying my best to develop crushes on girls. There was one girl I asked out every single day for a month and she said no every time, until it became a sort of joke and I asked her the way I scratched my nose, that is, quickly and sharply. And why did I ask her every day? Because my best friend at the time, a boy I haven't seen since 1988 but still remember his full name and telephone number (918-528-0897), had kissed this girl. I think I was hoping that, if I kissed her too, I would somehow get some of his germs. Or something like that. None of this was conscious, but looking back it's the only way I can make sense of it. Because, looking back, while I romanced the girls I ended up being nothing but a pest, stealing their lunch bags, undoing their bra as a joke, etc.—all I was really interested in were boys.

In seventh grade, I went through a series of crushes on boys, five of them to be exact, each one more painful than the one before. I would fall for them, spend a lot of time around them, and then, realizing eventually that they would never feel for me the way I felt for them, would suddenly stop talking to them. The last of the five, in April of 1987, called me up, mad as a hornet, asking why I wouldn't talk to him anymore. "You just go through boys like Kleenex," he said, "you blow your nose on them and throw them away." Neither of us understood what the hell he was talking about, not literally, but we both knew he was right. I swallowed, hard, and quickly hung up. I swore off boys then and there, and didn't really have close friends (other than girls) for a long, long time.

When I was 18, I met a girl the first week I arrived at the University of Oklahoma, and she reminded me of my grandmother Evelyn–graceful, witty, intelligent, and always free to say exactly what was on her mind. I told her I liked men, but that I didn't want to be with one, which was exactly how I felt about things at the time. Two years later we were married. Six years later we had our first daughter on Father's Day, and five years after that, after having three kids and trying our best to build the perfect little picket-fence family, we were divorced after 11 years of marriage. I cried, for at least a year and a half, at this great, great loss. There was nothing I wanted more on earth than to give my children a loving, happy, stable home comprised of a Mommy and a Daddy and a dog and a garden and the whole nine yards. But like in Toni Morrison's novel *Beloved*, sometimes in a relationship between two people a ghost from the past intervenes, and starts shaking things up, and sometimes in the aftermath there's nothing left but a wrecked marriage and a chance to start all over again.

There were several ghosts that wrecked our marriage, things that happened in the Pentecostal compound I grew up in that came back to haunt me, and one of them was the ghost of a man who shot himself in 1982. That ghost would be the presence, in my mind, of my uncle, Ronald David Roberts, Oral's eldest son, and at one time the man Oral had hoped would inherit his kingdom. "Ronnie" to the family, he was, by all accounts, one of the most brilliant men anyone who came across his path had ever met; at Booker T. Washington High School he taught English as well as Russian and Chinese. Nancy McDonald, who worked with him at the time, told me he was not only one of the brightest teachers she had ever met but also one of the most loved by his students. In his mid-thirties, Uncle Ronnie was divorced and committed suicide soon thereafter, six months after coming out to Troy Perry, founder of the first gay-friendly congregation in Los Angeles, and four months after he was arraigned in court on prescription drug charges–leaving his two children, ex-wife, and extended family to bear an unbearable burden.

Growing up, I didn't know any of this about my uncle, but I always wanted to be like him. Every time my mother mentioned him I noted two things: one, that she had loved him more than she had ever loved anybody else; and two, that the memory of his path brought more pain to her than any other memory.

I suppose it makes sense I wanted to be like him. I didn't know, when I was a kid, that the "path" my mother said brought him down consisted of being gay, intellectual, and godless. All I knew was, I wanted my mother's eyes to light up like that when she talked about me. Having ended up on this same "path" (gay, intellectual, godless), her eyes don't light up anymore, and haven't in years—for the last five, at least. And that's a shame, because I really do think that if she got along with Uncle Ronnie she could find a way to get along with me. But we were talking about ghosts. The first time the ghost of my Uncle Ronnie entered my life was in the Spring of 2002, at Mayflower United Church of Christ in Oklahoma City, Oklahoma.

My wife and I were in transition–having both rejected our Evangelical past, we were trying to find a way to still be Christian but also true to our intellect, and we found ourselves attending Robin Meyers' church, Mayflower. We were there when Carlton Pearson, founder of Higher Dimensions (at one time one of the largest evangelical churches in the nation), came to speak to our liberal, almost-Unitarian Christian church. My family and I had attended Carlton's church in middle school and high school and, in fact, my parents went to Oral Roberts University with him in the early 1970s. At one time, Oral had publicly referred to Carlton as his son, so you might say he felt like an uncle to me, even though I hadn't seen him in years.

Carlton preached an amazing sermon that day, one that brought me to tears. Hearing him was like hearing my grandfather all over again. Here was a man who, instead of preaching that

God was sending gays, and communists, and Catholics to Hell, said there was no Hell, and no mean, angry God dying to punish us. He might as well have said "GOD is a GOOD GOD" or "Something GOOD is GOING to HAPPEN to YOU!" I had finally admitted to myself a year before that I was homosexual, but being gay, Christian, and married with children does not give you many good options. During that year I had often wished I would die, but Carlton's message gave me hope.

After the sermon, my wife and I waited in line to get a chance to talk to Carlton. It had been a long time since we'd seen each other – I probably hadn't been to his church since I was 15 or 16, and here I was a full-grown man of 28 with his own children in tow. We waited about ten minutes as Carlton greeted each person who wanted to tell him how much his sermon moved him, and finally there we were, my wife and I, standing about three feet directly in front of Carlton. I smiled, big, and moved as if to hug him, but his face darkened immediately, and I hung back, and a chill passed through my spine. We might have only stood there for 20 seconds, but it felt like an hour – me looking at Carlton with a silly grin pasted on my face, and him looking back at me like he'd seen a ghost. He clutched his Bible tightly and his face went white, as white, anyway, as a black man's face can go.

"Which one are you?" he finally asked, barely breathing, still looking scared. After another long pause, he said "You're Ron and Roberta's son, aren't you?" and I nodded, "I'm Randy," I said. He nodded back. "I thought you were Ronnie," he said. And we both stared at each other, and then, finally, hugged. It was a big bear hug, a reunion of sorts, and we were both misty-eyed as we talked that day.

Sometimes, a particular mantle is thrust upon you, whether you like it or not. My grandfather, with all his faults, was at heart a man who wanted to spread a message of hope. While it's likely that many of the decisions he made later in life were motivated by money or at least the desire to keep his ministry afloat, it's not my impression that's what he was thinking when he was 20, 21, 22 years old and standing in healing lines and touching, for hours upon hours, people with tuberculosis and cerebral palsy and cancer. It's not my impression that he started out to make a quick buck. Oral started out as a preacher, in tiny towns in southeastern Oklahoma, convinced that the mantle thrust upon him was to encourage the poor Pentecostals around him that God was a good God, that God did not want them to be poor, that God did not bring on diseases (as some evangelicals have suggested that God brought HIV to kill off gay men). Oral's mantle was one he felt thrust upon him, and his message of hope transformed the evangelical church.

A year ago I took my children to Los Angeles for Spring Break; for them it was a chance to go to Disney World, to Universal Studios, and to see movie stars, but for me it was a chance to pay my last respects to a man who had overshadowed almost every memory from my childhood. Oral spent the last 20 years of his life living in a home on a golf course in Newport Beach, California, and while this sounds ostentatious, his home was fairly simple, a 1,000 square-foot condominium, the dining room table covered in water rings, the living room small and cramped, and the sixty-year-old home smelling vaguely of mold. I hadn't spent more than five minutes with him in the previous ten years, and a man changes a lot from 81 to 91. I felt sorry for him. Without my grandmother by his side, he seemed lonely.

Oral never could remember my name when I was growing up; even though I lived just down the hill from him and ran up to see my grandmother several times a week, "boy" and "son" were the only things he ever called me, if he called me at all. But in the Spring of 2009 he eagerly played at great-grandfather, showing off that he had done his homework by greeting each of my three children by name, and, because he was no longer the scary grandfather I remembered but, instead, a 91-year-old man barely able to hear and completely unable to leave his chair without assistance, I gladly played along. Although we never spoke of it, Oral knew I was gay, and yet that day, it didn't seem to matter—he signed a copy of his newest book for my children and gave them each a twenty dollar bill, and our hour-long visit passed quickly.

•••

I'm grateful for that afternoon with my grandfather because, frankly, the man I grew up with in the compound was not a kind, warm grandfather. He was a driven man, one who slept four hours a night and the other twenty working. Even while "relaxing" on the golf course, Oral would be processing his next sermon in his mind or networking with business partners who might be able to help keep his ministry alive. There was always another tower to build, or another tower to climb up into; that mantle burdened his soul and there was never any time for children. But this day was different. Oral seemed at peace, happy to sit in his armchair and play great-grandfather.

He looked at me several times during that visit and sighed, and I almost felt that he was looking right through me. Before we left he asked me to come over to his chair; the children were watching a cartoon in the spare bedroom and the living room was quiet as I knelt down beside him and held his hand. Oral had large hands—the 60-foot bronze sculpture of hands clasped in prayer which stands at the entrance to the university are modeled after his—and I noticed that day that they also looked a lot like mine. I was a little shaken up–we both knew this was likely to be our last visit. As I stood up to leave, he held my hand tightly, looked up from his chair with that characteristic twinkle in his eye, and said "Son, something GOOD is GOING to HAPPEN to YOU!" ◥

# THE GOSPEL OF JOHN:

## LENNON'S LOST LETTER TO ORAL ROBERTS

*by Lindsey Neal*

I n the early 1970s, Oral Roberts' evangelical TV program was at a peak, with an estimated 37 million viewers. After each show, the ministry commonly received upwards of 500,000 letters. One of those letters in particular has since caught the world's attention.

On Friday, January 26, 1973, Roberts stood behind the podium at the Mabee Center and held up a sheet of paper to an audience comprised of his university students and faculty. Nobody could have expected the claim Roberts was about to make.

"I hold in my hand probably one of the most unique letters or documents that I've ever shared with anybody in the world," Roberts said. "It happens to be from one of the Beatles, John Lennon, who was probably the most gifted song writer of the group. And he wrote it by hand."

Sitting in the audience that day was Scott Aycock, who remembers the chapel service vividly.

"The majority of students at that time were converted hippies. We called ourselves Jesus Freaks," recalls Aycock. "When John Lennon writes to Oral Roberts, you can believe it had a huge impact. There was hardly a dry eye in the place."

The most commonly cited source for the letter is David Edwin Harrell Jr.'s 1985 biography *Oral Roberts: An American Life*. It appears to offer the full text of Lennon's letter and cites an audiotaped transcript as its source. The actual transcript, however, is different. Harrell Jr.'s book contains some telling omissions—

omissions that add new intrigue and dimension to one of the most trying phases in Lennon's life.

In the version below, Lennon admits to his disenchantment with being a Beatle. Although he claims to be under the influence of pills while writing the letter, Lennon openly discloses his police record involving drug use and check forgery, and he confesses to prompting the break-up of The Beatles. Additionally, we learn that Lennon's marriage to Yoko Ono created a major barrier in his relationship with his son Julian, and that Ono is "going crazy" over the disappearance of her daughter.

In this reprinted transcript of the audiotaped sermon, Oral Roberts' asides appear in italics and any text in bold indicates phrases that were omitted from Harrell Jr.'s biography.

This is what Oral Roberts said that day:

Rev. Roberts, this is ex-Beatle, John Lennon.

*Aside: And it's a little hard for me to read, so I had it typed. I don't mean that in a bad way, don't misunderstand me. I just don't always get every word, as people don't always get every word I write by hand, too. Are you ready? This is quite a letter.*

Rev. Roberts, this is ex-Beatle, John Lennon. I've been wanting to write you but I guess I didn't really want to face reality. I never do this, this is why I take drugs. Reality frightens me and paranoids me. True, I have a lot of money, being a Beatle, been all around the world, but basically I'm afraid to face the problems of life. Let me begin to say, I regret that I said the Beatles were more popular than Jesus. I don't even like myself anymore, guilt. My cousin, Marilyn McCabe has tried to help me. She told me you were praying for me.

**Here's my life.**

*Aside: In his letter he said it like so many do over there, here's 'me' life.*

Here's me life.

Born in Liverpool, my mom died when I was little. My father left me at three. It was rough because just my aunt raised me. I never really liked her. I had an unhappy childhood, depressed a lot. Always missing my mom. Maybe if I'd had a father like you, I would have been a better person. My own father I hate with a passion because he left my mom and me, came to me after we found *A Hard Day's Night* and asked for some money. It made me so mad, Paul had to hold me down. I was going to kill him. I was under the influence of pills at that time.

Married Cynthia, had a son John. I had to marry her, I really never loved her. She always embarrassed me walking around pregnant, not married, so I married her. Only one regret, John has had to suffer a lot because recently she's been married again. He and me never get to see each other **because she refuses because I'm married to Yoko.**

*Aside: I hope I'm pronouncing the name right, Yoko.*

**So life as a Beatle hasn't been all that great[1.]**

**I came out and told them I wanted a divorce[2]** because Paul and me never got along anymore and that's how the four ended. **Since 1967 I've had a police record for dope and forging 12 checks to America. My wife Yoko and I have searched all over for her daughter, we can find[3]. Her ex-husband took her away, Yoko is going crazy.**

As the song we wrote is that we wrote, Paul and me, "Money Can't Buy Me Love," it's true.

The point is this, I want happiness. I don't want to keep up with drugs. Paul told me once, "You made fun of me for not taking drugs, but you will regret it in the end."

*Aside: He doesn't mean me personally.*

Explain to me what Christianity can do for me? Is it phoney? Can He love me? I want out of hell.

P.S. This address staying at the cousin's house. Rev. Roberts, also, I did watch your show until Channel 6 took if off the air. Please try to get it back on. A lot of people I know loved your show. I especially like the World Action Singers, your son Richard is a real good singer. George told me he met you and them when he was at the studio.

*Aside: This was George Harrison, isn't it? I didn't get to meet George, but the singers did at NBC.*

Sincerely, John

P.S. I am, I hate to say, under the influence of pills now. I can't stop. I only wish I could thank you for caring.

After reading the letter, Roberts said, "This handwritten letter of his was three pages and I wrote him four or five back. Would you like to hear a little of what I'm saying to him? The second time, I'm writing to him again because the urge just wouldn't leave me."

Roberts went on to read the students a letter he had addressed to both John and Yoko. He said there may have been "some truth" in Lennon's infamous "more popular than Jesus" statement at the time, but that "Jesus is the only reality." He then asks John to keep writing him and expresses his hope that God will save his soul.

"I never dreamed that someone like John Lennon would have been watching the television program," Roberts said later in the chapel sermon. "Is that the way you feel? It never would have entered your mind and we never know what we are doing for the Lord."

In addition to writing back to Lennon personally, Roberts also orchestrated a return message from the students of Oral Roberts University.

"Oral asked all of the students to come to the cafeteria where they had a huge roll of butcher paper," recalls Aycock. "They rolled it out on several tables and asked all of the students that wished to, to write a note to John Lennon, in response to his letter. Of course, being young and a fan, I participated in writing a note to John."

Lennon's letter received a tremendous amount of fanfare, both at the time of the reading and since then. It has been mentioned in several books, numerous blog posts, a *Christianity Today* article, and was even referenced in Roberts' obituary in *The New York Times*. However, every reference to the letter cites the incomplete version in the Harrell Jr. biography. And all of these references may actually be wrong. Why?

"We have looked for the original for years, but it is nowhere to be found," explains Roger Rydin, curator of the Oral Roberts University (ORU) archive. "We have done a good job over the years of keeping up with these kind of items, but this one got away. We had a researcher here in 1985, and it was 'lost' then, and has not been found since."

Without the original letter, it's impossible to verify whether it was actually Lennon who wrote it. When Roberts read the letter at the chapel, he was reading a typed version of the letter, and when he read it out loud, he frequently interrupted the letter and altered the words. The most accurate record of the letter is Roberts' audiotaped sermon, but representatives from ORU are oddly skittish about allowing access to the audiotape; their public relations director ignored repeated requests for permission to hear the tape.

While we may never know for certain if Lennon actually penned the letter, there's an interesting allusion Lennon left for us to consider—and we have audio of John Lennon singing it.

On November 14, 1980, less than a month from his murder, Lennon recorded a song he had written to Yoko called, "You Saved My Soul." It exists only as a rough demo of the very last recording he ever sang on, passed around as a bootleg copy.

The lyrics read:

When I was lonely and scared, I nearly fell for a TV preacher in a hotel room in Tokyo. Remember the time I went to jump right out the apartment window on the west side of town of old New York. You saved me from that suicide and…I wanna thank you, thank you, thank you for saving my soul with your true love.

It appears that Lennon had found the savior he was seeking.

"I know personally, my heart went out to him, and I thought of him often after that and wondered if he was happier later in life," says Aycock, speaking of Lennon.

"It certainly seemed he was happier in the few years leading up to his death." ◼

## ENDNOTES:

1 From the transcript, it is uncertain whether this line is an aside from Roberts or a portion of Lennon's letter.

2 In 2009, a lost interview of John Lennon surfaced, indicating that indeed Lennon had asked Paul McCartney for a 'divorce.' Prior to 2009, it was widely believed that McCartney was responsible for the Beatles disbanding. "At the meeting Paul just kept mithering on about what we were going to do," says Lennon. "So in the end I just said, 'I think you're daft. I want a divorce.'

3 Possible transcription error; the sentence may more accurately state "We can't find." Ono was reunited with her daughter Kyoko Cox in 1994.

# ASYLUM

*by Jennie Lloyd*

*EDITOR'S NOTE:*
SOME NAMES AND IDENTIFYING DETAILS HAVE BEEN
CHANGED TO PROTECT PATIENT PRIVACY.

I wrote this all down to keep myself alive.

For six days and five nights, I was a mental patient in total lockdown at one of Oklahoma's fifteen publicly-funded mental hospitals, the Oklahoma County Crisis Intervention Center (OCCIC) in Oklahoma City. I was a Catch-22 mess of a woman: on the outside a silent, complacent patient, but on the inside a survivor overwhelmed and maddened by the conditions of a state-run mental hospital.

I didn't check myself voluntarily into OCCIC. No, in my mind, I could've solved my mental illness pretty simply: with a plan and a gun. This was the second lock-up in two months; I'd attempted suicide by an overdose of Xanax and rum only five weeks before. After a six-hour IV-drip and a vomiting episode at OSU Medical Center, I spent a mere 12 hours at the Tulsa Center for Behavioral Health (TCBH). I told the psychiatrist I wasn't suicidal anymore, so she signed discharge papers and sent me home before the double-vision and shadows in my eyes cleared (that would take another three days). The next few weeks, I wandered around like a ghost. I passed through the long lines at Family & Children's

Services, got new meds, quit my job. But I wasn't better.

The summer before the overdose was normal. We celebrated my birthday at the creek—my two boys, one tween and one toddler, splashed in a bright kiddie pool in the backyard. We ate grilled hot dogs and bought sparklers. The problem was me–I was changing. Panic attacks stalked me wherever I went, and I felt nauseated constantly. I left my coffee bar job early because of stomach ailments and bolted from summer classes after anxiety attacks drove me from my seat. I began to think, obsessively, that I was no longer the healthy and sane mom my sons deserved. Instead, my intelligent and beloved boys were stuck with *me*. The guilt and despair pounded inside my head, day in and day out, over and over again: *These boys deserve a mom whose moods don't snap like twigs, a mom who isn't drowning in life's battering waves, who isn't choking on its foam.* I found evidence of my failure everywhere I looked–in laundry piles and dust bunnies, in weeds and my drained bank account.

I did the only thing I could think of: I made an appointment with my family physician to switch anti-depressants. I was on Zoloft for ten years, during which that little blue pill had curbed my panic attacks side effect-free and held back the curtain of despair so I could step into my life. But over the summer it abruptly stopped working, even at a higher dosage.

In my experience, family doctors don't know much about anti-depressants except that they can prescribe them. So my doc, who actually specializes in sports medicine, suggested I "just pick another one."

"So, you just want me to pick another anti-depressant?" I asked to make sure I heard him correctly.

"Yes," he said, unabashed, then waited patiently for an answer.

I picked the first one that popped into my head–Prozac, because it's similar to Zoloft and cheaper–and I started taking it the next day. I developed strange woozy-brain feelings every afternoon, but wrote it off as part of an adjustment period. But my depression didn't lift, and when the dust settled, I found myself in a dark ravine of despair and anxiety. I could no longer see the stars in the sky for the black vacuum of space.

So five weeks later, I gingerly slipped my boyfriend's loaded, snub-nosed .38 out of its hiding spot. It was cold and heavier than expected. I placed it on the smooth, dark wood of my computer desk, and I felt a jolt in my stomach at the metal clang it made. I snatched sideways looks at its brass-topped bullets and its lethal, black bulk as I typed a sort of exploratory surgery on my brain with cold fingers, an attempt to understand the exact nature of this new illness. My rapidly-changing rounds of antidepressants–Zoloft, Prozac, Celexa, double Celexa–shot through my body like bullets into a fire.

When I finished writing, I quietly walked out into the navy night, unlocked my car door and slipped the gun under my front seat. *Tomorrow night would be the night*, I thought. I was afraid of the gun, but maybe even more afraid of being alive.

Part of what I wrote that night was this:

I feel so fenced in by these walls; these steel-beamed, 100-year-old walls. One hundred years of entrapment, of misery, of loneliness bend toward me each day. Each day I wake up and wonder, How many pills can I take, and how soon?

… I feel like a monumental asshole for not getting any better. I feel rage at every morning I wake up to a multitude of my failures. The price [for my failures] has been steep. I don't have the heart for that kind of gore [suicide by handgun]. It's just too awful and disgusting. But I don't know if I have the heart to go on anymore, either.

The next morning, Sept. 29, 2010, all hell broke loose when I called Blake and admitted to taking his gun. I wanted to die, but I'd made him a promise after the first attempt—that I would tell him if I was going to try again. So I did. Suicidal minds embrace contradiction: yes, I wanted to die, but I wasn't dead yet and as a living being I had to abide by this promise I'd made. He immediately called a mental health help number, which sent over two Tulsa police officers and a pair of crisis therapists from Family & Children's Services within an hour. After an officer retrieved the gun, and I talked briefly to one of the counselors, I was deemed unsafe to stay at home.

I panicked as the officers and therapists closed in, ready to take me into protective custody. I hadn't spent much time at TCBH after the overdose, but I knew I didn't want to stay there again. The facility is a plain, one-story place off Harvard, stripped-down, with beefy psychiatric technicians positioned throughout the hallway to tamp down any violent outbursts. Last time I was there, Aug. 20, 2010, I counted at least four techs, but only half as many nurses. Inside, haunted, wide-eyed patients pace the hallways like zombies. I didn't want to go, but I didn't have a choice anymore.

The officers drove me to TCBH, where I was interviewed by two different intake workers only to learn there were no empty beds.

A sad-eyed, middle-aged man sat behind a yellowing computer in a little room and asked me a familiar round of questions, to determine the severity of my condition. I pitched the answers in as few words as possible:

"No, I don't sleep much."

"Yeah, I eat fine."

"I always take my meds."

"Yes, I had a plan. I stole his gun. Five weeks ago I overdosed."

"Too many reasons to explain."

All the private hospitals in Tulsa said they were full, he explained. There was no room at the inn, so to speak. As I waited to see what would happen next, I eavesdropped on two psych techs talking in the hall. They complained loudly about a local private psychiatric hospital that only seems to have available beds when a person has insurance.

*Oh shit*, I thought, *I don't have insurance.* Anxiety sparked like lightning through the thunderheads of depression in my mind. Little did I know at the time that for all of Oklahoma's 77 counties, there are only 15 publicly-supported Community Mental Health Centers to serve our state's mentally ill.

Faced with at least a budget shortfall of $800 million for the fiscal year 2012, cuts to Oklahoma's mental health programs are slicing services down to the bone. Already the last year and a half has seen mental health funding cut by more than $25 million, over 200 employees laid off, and a Norman substance abuse treatment center close down. Forty mental health beds for children are gone. A men's treatment center in Tahlequah is now shuttered and dark.1 And that leaves Oklahoma with a rising number of calls made to the state's suicide hotline, as well as an increase in suicides. It's an increase Oklahoma can't afford, according to Mental Health America's ranking system. Our state ranked 46th, near rock bottom, for cases of depression each year. Oklahoma's suicide rate ranks only slightly better, 39th.[2]

So, there I was—an uninsured, suicidal patient—stuck inside the claustrophobic process of finding a bed at on? of the publicly-funded facilities that treat all the uninsured, in-crisis, or severely ill mental patients in Oklahoma.

TCBH issued an emergency order of detention (EOD), I was "ED'd" as mental health workers say, and, because all the beds in Tulsa were full, I was transferred to Oklahoma City, 100 miles away.[2]

On the hour-and-a-half police cruiser ride, I stared out the windows in silence and tried not to think about the metal handcuffs cutting into my wrists, which were "for my own safety." Occasionally, one of the Tulsa police officers tried to cheer me up with a snack or a compliment about my looks. Once we arrived at OCCIC, a rundown little center in a rough area of Oklahoma City, I was led inside, still handcuffed, by the officers. Before they left, each officer gave me a long, purse-lipped stare and said, "Good luck."

Throughout the entire day nothing had really punctured my black mood until about 10 minutes after I sat down in the partitioned triage area. An Oklahoma City police officer corralled a freshly-handcuffed guy into the small area with me. He was wild and ferocious and looked about 16, though I overheard him say he was 20. He grabbed one of the wall phones, dialed a number in a frenzy, and started screaming at his mother, alternately calling her a bitch and begging her to come get him. When she hung up on him, the boy started to bash his head against the thin wall that separated us, rattling the chair I sat in. *Bang, rattle. Bang, rattle.* When he had enough of hurting himself, he began to verbally abuse everyone within hearing distance. He screamed every vile, racist utterance he could conjure, directing his anger toward the OCCIC workers, who were a majority African American. His arresting officer finally shouted, "Son, I'm gonna Taser you if you don't shut up!"

I stuck my fingers in my ears like a scared kid, but I could still hear him screaming. The boy was still unruly, and a strange alarm—a loud, repeating "quack-quack" sound–played throughout the building. "Quack-Quack-Quack-Quack! Help is needed in the Triage unit," it repeated calmly, over and over again. A small army of mental health workers arrived soon after to smash the boy to the ground. I overheard a nurse say, "Give him Ativan and Haldol," and then the boy screamed, "No! No Haldol! I'm allergic to Haldol! Call my mom! I get seizures!"

And this was the precise moment I realized that I was utterly fucked. I curled up into a ball on the floor of the room, my eyes streaming with tears. The nurses did not call the boy's mom, and instead several of them forced him to the ground and he was injected with something. I can't confirm whether or not they gave him Haldol. Halperidol is a serious antipsychotic drug, which can lower a person's threshold for seizures. A few minutes later, the phone rang in the triage and I heard a worker talk for a moment before she hung up. In a loud voice, she called to the other triage employees to say it was the boy's mother and that he does indeed have a seizure disorder and shouldn't have Haldol. By then, though, the injection was over, and the boy in a Jimi Hendrix T-shirt had returned to bang out a rhythm with his head against the wall that slowed and finally stopped. I didn't see him again until the next night at dinner. He recognized me and pointed to his forehead, all red and swollen, then asked proudly, "Did you hear all that?"

I said, "Of course."

He smiled broadly.

After an hour of lying on the floor, a psychiatrist stepped over me into the small, square room without comment. She was short and squat, with a slight grimace which never broke into a smile. We began yet another interview about my mental state and 15 minutes later, I had another handful of diagnoses: Major Depressive Disorder, Post-Traumatic Stress Disorder, Irritable Bowel Syndrome, Anxiety and Panic Disorder. The doctor didn't tell me what being "ED'd" meant, as the mental health workers called it; she didn't tell me how long I would be there, or when I could call my family. I followed a nurse to the locked ward where I would stay, from Sept. 29 to Oct. 4. I had to list everything I was wearing, down to the color of my underwear and bra. They took my hoodie away because it had a thin string in the hood, and tried to take my bra but I lied and said it didn't have underwire. Sure, I might've lost most of my dignity, but goddamn it, I was going to wear a bra.

My eyes slowly adjusted to the blur of bright overhead lights, the flurry of other patients flocking for a look at the new inmate, and the scuffed, hungry-white color of everything. As a psych tech showed me my bed and the one communal bathroom, an anorexic blond girl stepped on my flip-flops in her attempt to follow me.

"Dana, give her some space! You're stepping on her!" the tech shouted at the patient.

The girl stared blankly at both of us, and came to a stop in the hallway. For the next hour, Dana stood in that same spot without moving. She was a kind of ghost who stood in corners, who hovered near the nurse's station, who refused to sit down. She was one of the more peaceful patients, a harmless wraith of a girl with dark blue eyes.

Later that evening, after I'd begged through the plastic hole in the nurse's station for special permission to call my family long distance, I talked to my mom on a black payphone over the din of all the other chatter in our communal "living room." A lanky patient in her mid-20s paced the main room with a jerky stride, and talked to herself loudly as she picked at her spout of tangled hair with a hospital-issue brush.

"Ma, all I wanted was some peace and quiet," I cried into the phone. Tears seeped out of my eyes; I was exhausted beyond all measure. I begged my mom to find a private hospital, that I'd pay whatever the cost as long as I could get the hell out of OCCIC. She promised to look into it, then we hung up and I turned back to the white-washed room lined with gray plastic waiting room chairs. In the corner of the room was the scariest door of all—a genuine old-fashioned isolation room with two heavy slide-locks on the outside and one small window. The light was on, and the door was cracked open. A woman was lying on a bare plastic mattress in the middle of the floor, reading a book and twirling a strand of her long black hair around her finger. She looked up at me with angry blue-black eyes. *What kind of dangerous insanity is this?* I wondered, and reminded myself to laugh loudest at her jokes. Later, Chandra told me a little about her life, her frequent trips in and out of jail and mental hospitals for her aggressive behavior, up to and including threatening a local Braum's with a terrorist attack. Chandra was stuck in the isolation room for allegedly attacking another woman.

My room, shared with two other roommates, was farthest away from the nurse's station, which meant I was one of the least threatening people there. The rooms closest to the station and the living room were filled with more severe cases—women who murmured all night in the dark, whose relationship with reality was shaky at best, who coughed and hacked until dawn after years of meth or crack smoking.

One of my roommates was a lady in her sixties, maybe a hundred pounds, with wrinkles outlining her tiny face and mischievous smile. Kate committed herself voluntarily to detox from alcohol; she wanted to get clean and head back to Ponca City, where she liked to sit on her back porch and watch her grandchildren play. She told me she was up to a pint of vodka a day and beer on top of that. "Better than I used to be," she said with a smirk.

One night, when we were stuck in our room during a "quack-quack" alarm event, Kate told me about the last time she'd been locked up there against her will.

"I didn't remember anything for seven days. I had the DTs real bad," she said, still surprised after seven years at the force of her own withdrawal sickness. DTs, short for delirium tremens, is a withdrawal syndrome caused by cessation of alcohol but typically only occurring in the most severe cases of alcoholism.

Kate looked around our room, at the high, painted windows set into deep sills. "I was in this room last time I was here!" she remembered.

"I tried to kick the windows out but I ended up falling on my ass instead," she laughed. I cracked my first smile at this because I understood the feeling. Being in lockdown 24/7, stripped of everything but a rectangular plastic bucket filled with a client handbook, a hair pick, a tiny brush, and travel-sized toothbrush, toothpaste, and deodorant, will cause just about anyone to consider kicking a window out. Some days, I paced my room alone, only to stop occasionally and reach out toward those thick, opaque windows. The sills were so deep and the windows were so high and covered with so much paint that I couldn't touch them or see out of them. On the window closest to my bed, someone had etched the words, "Watch out! The ghosts come out at nite!!!"

With a turquoise crayon I took from the living room, I wrote in my room:

*I wait and I watch. Each evening, anxiety begins to pump through my veins. I feel like I can't breathe and my face is flush. I have an unexplainable, heavy, hot weight on my chest as it gets later and later into the night. I'm worried. Worried that tomorrow will never come, that I'll never sleep, that no one will ever get me out of here. Seems silly when I write it out like this, but I can't deny those itchy-vein, near-giddy feelings that creep up as the sun goes down.*

On the second night, I realized I was truly trapped until someone else decided I was "sane" enough to go home. This someone else was my psychiatrist, who saw me only three times during my entire stay: once when I was admitted, then for five minutes the next day, and for the last time when she printed my discharge papers. The psychiatrists and social workers were rarely seen on the ward at all. I was spit-fire angry at being detained against my will, so I did what any sane person would do: I wrote strongly-worded letters with my trusty turquoise crayon on the only paper I could find, my patients' rights handbook. Day one, I'd spent in a haze of denial and weariness, but days two and three were engulfed in rage, wherein I hissed impotent threats in the payphone receiver.

I took hot showers in the dead of night when most of the other mental patients had passed out on their plastic mattresses, when their smokers' coughs had deepened to a bass relief playing against the key of a never-ending fluorescent hum. With my thin towel in hand, I walked silently past open rooms where patients snored, curled under bleached-white sheets and blankets. Keeping clean was a queasy task, but each night I stepped past a moldy curtain into one of two shower stalls. I avoided looking at the clots of hair covering the tiled floor and clogging the drain. The water poured in a thin, hot stream straight down the wall, so that I had to stand flat against the slimy tiles to get wet. To wash, I either had to beg at the nurse's station for a paper cup of shampoo or use the bright-yellow antibacterial goop already in the bathroom. The shower stalls were often littered with wet paper cups, yellow and blue slime leaking out onto the tile. I learned to step over the paper cups, to ignore the hair and roaches, and to tamp down my gag reflex.

We had three toilets with no locks on the doors, so we frequently walked in on each other. I learned to knock on the heavy, faux-wood doors, and to identify myself when someone else walked in. The "mirror" in the bathroom was nothing more than a polished piece of metal nailed over each sink. When I dared to peer into it, I saw a dull, fish-belly gray stranger looking back at me with eyes that were dark and sad and lost.

On Friday, I cracked. I mean, outwardly. On the inside I was all raw egg, but on the outside I rarely betrayed emotion. When my social worker sat me down that Friday afternoon and told me I was going to spend the weekend in the hospital with a "chance" of being sent back to a Tulsa facility on Monday, I fell apart. I'd spent the whole morning and afternoon pacing the locked quarters, my ribcage stuffed with hope, waiting to see the psychiatrist. But I didn't get to see her that day, only my social worker, who slowly explained as though to a small child, the seriousness of my suicidal ideations and previous suicide attempt. I cried and pleaded. I said I hadn't been serious, that I didn't even know how to use a gun, that I didn't see the point in being locked up all weekend. I was at the bargaining stage of the grief process. But it was no use—Roxanne, my tall, imperious social worker didn't budge.

"It's already been decided for you," she said.

At this, I launched into a tidy little rant about how her facility didn't provide any therapeutic or creative groups, cognitive behavioral therapy or meditation classes, or exercise of any kind. The majority of my days are given over to re-runs, eating a little and pacing a lot, I cried. The state mental hospital experience is like living in a DMV waiting room for a few days. We were all waiting: some for homeless or battered women's shelters to open up a spot, others waited to detox or to be heard in mental health court, and still others, myself included, waited until we could behave ourselves before the doors would open again.

After all this, Roxanne softened a bit, and said, "Well, one of the reasons you're here is because you don't have insurance. When you don't have insurance, this is the type of place you end up."

I stared at her; I had no retort for that. She was right—these places don't have much funding, and what funding they do get is slashed year over year. On the surface, I understood that I'd been sent to this stripped-bare state-funded hospital because I had no insurance. I go to school full-time and take care of my young sons—two occupations that don't provide a great benefits package. But does that mean I, along with all the other suffering patients I hung out with, don't deserve good, quality mental health care? Is this what Roxanne was intimating?

I must've stared at her strangely for a long time because she gave me an "assignment" to work on over the weekend. Roxanne granted me permission to use a pen and legal pad to write with, and she wrote down several questions I needed to ask myself: What does your ultimate life look like? What are you doing now to get this quality life? Is it working for you? And if not, what are you willing to change?

And with that, Roxanne was gone. I was back on the ward with the weekend stretching out before me. These were hard questions to ask of anyone, sane or not, but I was glad to challenge myself with something beside sitting cross-legged in chairs while staring at old episodes of *House*.

When we weren't catching cat naps on our uncomfortable beds, the female patients sat around in the uncomfortable chairs. We did what I think most women would do: we talked. We changed channels but didn't really watch the TV. We discussed our problems. We complained about the food and the psych techs who worked what seemed like endless shifts, who tiredly dismissed us as irritants when we weren't lined up for food or meds.

"We had better food in county jail," my new friend, Jane, said one lunchtime as we picked over a greenish-tinged meatloaf, cold asparagus spears and a couple of canned, slimy peach wedges. I laughed at this idea. Jane is a perfect size 4 with a hypnotizing face and her hair chopped in odd angles, which set off her dark blue eyes and smooth features. She told me that her boyfriend had cut her hair off in a rage as he screamed, "No one will ever want you now!"

But Jane was the kind of girl who could tell you a story like that without a crease in her forehead. She had a rough life and bad things happened. Normal, acceptable, passé. So here she was sitting next to me and my near-lethal case of depression, after the same boyfriend had poisoned her. When it didn't kill her, he called the police at 5 a.m. to tell them she'd tried to commit suicide. Allegedly. I never questioned her sanity though I could never reconcile how someone could be poisoned with as much Xanax as she'd had. With its chalky, bitter-sour taste that quickly coats the tongue, Xanax just isn't the type of substance that can be easily mixed into food or drink, especially in massive doses. But I let the inconsistencies float away; I didn't care what she was lying about. We sat together on the locked ward day after day, and shared her emergency room blanket, stained here and there with charcoal vomit.

She didn't know where her boyfriend had gone with their 15-month-old daughter. Over our cold food and the din of *Law & Order*, Jane and I told our stories and cried over our babies. My toddler and tween were in good care, oblivious to my hospitalization. But all Jane had at that moment were the memories of her little girl, a downy-headed pixie she named Peace.

"When she plays in the backyard, she likes to pick those white weed flowers," she told me. "She smells them so deeply that she sticks 'em up her nose, and then puts 'em in her mouth!"

We both laughed so long, even as a sharp shot of pain through my body. I missed my boys; I missed the pecan tree and white shepherd's purse sprouting in my own yard.

I wrote by the sliver of fluorescent light from the hallway that night.

*By emergency order of detention, I'm still alive. Despite everything, the will to survive is within me. That's why I called Blake, to admit I had his gun, to admit I wanted to die. I screwed up my plans for a second time. As Neil Gaiman wrote, Sometimes you wake up. Sometimes the fall kills you. And sometimes, when you fall, you fly.*

*The first time, I woke up. This time, I hope to fly. Despite every hardship, every bad word, every fuck-up, every failure and prayer, every desperate act and missed call, every disappointment and violence, every act of God and man, my most primal self will not surrender. Even when we fight with ourselves, we often lose.*

When Monday finally emerged, I was up at 6 a.m. By breakfast at 7:30 a.m., I was already asking when the psychiatrists would see patients. "Oh, they get here around 8, but they've got a lot of patients to see. They don't make appointments," one annoyed psych tech told me.

I paced in a nervous cold sweat, and pressed down on the hope that again collected in my chest like cloud-white stuffing. I spotted Roxanne around 10 a.m., and pounced. "When will I see the doctor?"

"Just wait your turn. She's got a lot of patients today."

I paced some more; I stuffed down my hope of going home. Blake called, and he was confident I'd be released that day. He had already planned to take a half-day at work to come get me.

I sat on the edge of a gray waiting-room chair, and nervously chatted with Jane and everyone else. After our weekend on the ward, I could almost feel the fort of camaraderie we'd formed out of the only things we had—our voices and blankets and crackers. And I felt safe in it.

Another hour passed. Then another. Finally, Roxanne came back for me. I was allowed into the plastic-sealed nurse's station and said to the handful of nurses and psych techs, "Wow, it's strange to be on the other side of the wall." They chuckled as I followed Roxanne into another locked hallway, which she accessed by keycard, and into the psychiatrist's cluttered office. In an excited rush, I told her how much better I was feeling, and how much Roxanne's questions helped me clarify my life and my place in it.

The doctor gave me the poker-faced grimace, said she was glad I was feeling better, printed my discharge papers and signed them. Roxanne didn't smile. I didn't care about their lack of enthusiasm anymore. With papers in hand, I burst back onto the ward with a burning, dizzying ecstasy in the pit of my stomach that stretched into my cold fingers and toes. In a few hours, I would finally, finally walk out the doors, not handcuffed and wildly depressed but with eyes wide enough to take in the world! And the white, tender shepherd's purse! This time, I wouldn't walk past them in my yard; I might even pick a few, smell them deeply and try to eat 'em. Just to see. I was delirious with the idea of seeing the sun.

As I busied myself around the ward, stripping the thin white sheets and blanket from the mattress and heavy plastic pillow, giving back my rectangular bucket, a new patient was admitted. She was the size of a small hill, draped in a blue, shimmery muumuu. As she plopped down onto a double-wide gray seat, she shouted, "When I get outta here, I'm gonna smoke a Big! Fat! Joint!"

Blake arrived around 3:15 p.m., and a psych tech told me to get my things together. I hugged some of the other patients and wished them well, but Jane had vanished. I hoped she would be ok, and that she would find her little girl. I walked eagerly through short hallways, like a ship passing through locks in a seaway until I finally pushed open the double doors to the waiting room. Blake leaned back into a chair and I waved and smiled.

I kept walking until I was outside, and took a deep breath of pavement and hot sun and the fresh shock of being free. I faced down the building that held me captive. Blake handed me my purse in silence as I sat shakily on a curb and slid a menthol out of the pack.

"That was my room," I said, and pointed my cigarette toward a pair of painted-over windows, which looked small from the parking lot in slanted afternoon sun. I exhaled smoke curls into the October sky, and felt so light I could almost float away. ◤

# THE BOTTOMLESS ACHE OF THE REVOLUTION:

## A PREMIER CUBAN PAINTER ESCAPES TO OKLAHOMA

*by Michael Mason*

When I first saw him, José Antonio Pantoja Hernández was standing behind a display of several of his paintings. Just like several of the other artists lining the promenade in Havana, he had set up a makeshift booth for his work, leaning large canvases against a small folding table. At the time, he looked like a Cuban trying his best to look European: faded German clothes, a fanny pack, casual black lace-ups, and a ballcap. The clothes were from elsewhere, but his emaciated arms and bony cheeks were completely Cuban. In that sense, he looked like the rest of the artists lining the Paseo del Prado, each of whom the government had given special permission to sell their work on the street. Pantoja's artwork, however, was nothing like the standard rainbow of tourist-friendly artwork lining the sidewalk. His paintings shocked the gait out of most passersby.

I had heard Pantoja's name before, a week earlier during a carnival in Cienfuegos. I'd asked several graduate students from a nearby university who they thought was Cuba's most important living artist, and they all immediately answered "Pantoja." They explained that he was a street artist whose paintings were highly critical of the government. They guessed he would be dead or "carried off" soon. Then they told me how to find him.

At the time, August of 2008, I was in Cuba doing research for a book I planned to write. I had already broken free from the standard Cuban tourist track by booking rooms at various *casa particulars*, and was trying my best to blend into the culture by wearing old clothes and flip-flops. The ruse didn't work. Pantoja called me out right away.

"You from America?" he asked me in English, as I eyed his paintings. I smiled flatly.

"*Claro, chico*," I admitted. "*Pero que estas haciendo aqui con estes cuadros?*" I didn't ask him "what's up." I asked him what he was doing with his paintings. But my tone was concerned, as in, "What the hell do you think you're doing with these paintings?" He laughed a little and glanced at a nearby corner, where a policeman stood watching us chat.

"*Sientate*," he said, offering me a seat beside him on the bench. "I will tell you."

The policeman scratched a note on his pad.

•••

From 2003 to 2005, the Cuban government allowed the Proyecto Cultural de Comunitario to thrive along Prado. The country's most revered visual artists—those with the coveted Licensia de las Artes Plasticas—were allowed to sell their artwork along El Prado on Saturday mornings. At the time, it was the only real opportunity Cuban artists had to sell paintings directly to tourists without having to take a large cut at the few local (and heavily censored) galleries. Pantoja thrived in those early days—selling nearly a painting a week for up to $500. For a brief period of time, he rented a place in one of Havana's better boroughs, Vedado.

Unlike the sidewalk art displays in most cities, the artwork on Prado had a much higher quality of craftsmanship; there were a number of gallery-quality works on the street, many of them either surreal or abstract. Of course, there were several tourist-oriented displays full of brightly colored images of landmarks, giving you the impression that Cuba looks like Santa Fe or San Antonio. It's the Cuba that Cuba wants you to see.

By the time I met Pantoja, however, I had traded much of my tourist currency for *moneda nacional*, the currency of Cuban citizens. I had been spending about 70 cents a day on pulled pork sandwiches and orange soda, and zipping across Havana for quarters, using the unofficial taxi system. Although I had managed to dip my toe into the real Cuba, I hadn't been able to fully cross the divide. Save for the frequent propositions of *jineteras*, most Cubans in Havana wouldn't talk to me; the Cuban government discourages them from approaching tourists.

"I only paint my life," Pantoja told me, waving his hands at the paintings. His largest work, painted on burlap, depicted three brown and honey-hued skeletons surrounding a dimly lit table. At the center of the table lay three items instantly recognizable to Cubans: an empty bowl, a libretto (their ration book), and an egg. It was a nightmarish scene of starvation, the visual equivalence of a painful howl. Another painting showed a near-skeleton in repose, its fingers sprouting parched limbs.

Pantoja explained that he had lived through Cuba's "special period," a particularly brutal time during the early 90's when the entire island dealt with severe shortages. For about six months, Pantoja had subsisted on just one egg a day, every day. He told me that for most Cubans, hunger has become a way of life—so common that they refer to their refrigerators as "cocos," short for coconuts, because when you crack them open, there's nothing but water inside.

"You want to see the real Cuba?" Pantoja asked me. "I show you Cuba. Tonight, you come to stay with me."

As a small storm formed overhead, Pantoja rolled up his paintings. We waited under a nearby awning for his girlfriend Daileni to show up. Together, we hailed a series of cabs and buses until we reached the village of Bejucal, which is known for its community of carpenters (Pantoja is also a skilled woodworker). As we walked toward Pantoja's apartment, we saw a man on the street brushing his dog with a shiny black liquid. Pantoja explained that the man was coating his dog in motor oil to kills its fleas. When we arrived at the apartment, a withered, older woman—a girlfriend of Pantoja's father—was sitting alone at the small dinette table in the kitchen, staring into space.

"Don't give her money," Pantoja told me. "She only wants rum."

Pantoja gave me a brief tour. Even though the place was clean, it looked as though it had a permanent coat of gray grime. There was a small electric stove, and a fridge. The bathroom, Pantoja explained, was the open drain in the floor, where a toilet used to be. Small, busy bugs crawled in and around the hole.  If I wanted to shower, the single spigot sprayed only cold water. Daileni offered to make us coffee. When she opened the fridge, I saw a two-liter bottle of water and half-soured jug of milk and nothing else.

As Daileni prepared the coffee, Pantoja showed me his bedroom, which functioned as a studio. It might've been a hundred square feet, but felt much larger owing to the dozen or so oil paintings on the gray-blue walls. It was a gallery of the macabre: a skeletal pig rowing a pan in one picture, a farmer's head propped up by sticks in another. I stared at one particularly elaborate painting: a tortoise with a human head, made even more nightmarish by the sunken cheeks and eyes, and vines sprouting where hair should grow. The face looked vaguely familiar.

"This is Fidel Castro," Pantoja said. "The Cuban people, they see it immediately. When I put this painting in the park, it made many police to surround me."

Many of the portraits on the wall featured his father, the village alcoholic. In another painting, I noticed the woman from the kitchen, frozen at the empty table. He only paints his life. When I glanced at his bookshelf, Pantoja pointed out his four teachers, a set of art books featuring reproductions of Rembrandt, Goya, Dali and Repin. I asked him if he'd ever heard of or seen Jasper Johns, Cy Twombly, or Jean Michel Basquiat, and he just looked at me puzzled. Earlier, I learned that he'd never heard of Elvis Presley, either. I stopped asking such questions.

Pantoja's four teachers are evident in his work. He borrows the light from Rembrandt, and turns Dali's dreamscape images into starvation nightmares. His texture and color come from Repin, and the rage is all Goya. Looking at his paintings, you get the distinct impression that you're peering into a bottomless ache, one in which the past indicts the present. Pantoja made his own brushes and formulated his own paint. The coats are sparing and thin by necessity, and the colors are sad and anemic.

"You see that I am in a prison," he told me. "This island is killing me."

"Do you want me to get you out?" I asked.

•••

The Proyecto Cultural came to a screeching halt in 2005, when its director, Cecilio Aviles, shut the program down because it was becoming too "capitalistic" for artists. Pantoja—its most successful artist—was selling nearly a painting a week for around $500, the equivalent of an annual salary for successful Cubans. When police asked Pantoja about the increasingly strong images in his painting, he simply told them that they were reproductions of the Dutch renaissance painter Hieronymus Bosch.

"The police in Cuba are idiots," Pantoja said. "Thank god for that."

For nearly two years, the artists of Prado gathered each weekend to silently protest the shut-down. Each weekend, policemen dispersed the crowd. Seeing an abrupt end to his income, Pantoja scrambled to find a market for his work. He eventually met a friend who sold black-market goods to the wealthy Cubans of Miramar (most of whom are upper-level bureaucrats). "Mr. Hyde," as he was known, began hawking Pantoja's paintings to the Cuban elite.

"Many of the rich people of Cuba have my paintings," said Pantoja, "But they are not stupid. They hide the paintings."

Finally, at the end of 2007, Aviles agreed to resume the Proyecto Cultural. But this time, he explained, there would be many new regulations. All works would be subject to approval by Aviles, and each artist must have a personal evaluation of his work reviewed prior to displaying it on Prado. Pantoja was determined to return to the Proyecto, so when he arrived for his meeting with Aviles, he brought several still-life paintings of fruit, and a portrait of a famous homeless man in Cuba named the *Caballero de Paris*. Pleased that Pantoja's work had finally been subjugated, Aviles cleared the way for Pantoja to return to Prado.

After a few months of playing it safe, and enduring a downturn in sales, Pantoja began to reintroduce his more subversive works, this time painting them with even greater ferocity. Some paintings openly depicted the government playing marionettes with its citizens; others catalogued the terrifying hunger that continued to plague Cuba. He sold one painting—a hydrocephalic, monstrous portrait of the *Caballero*—to a Russian official for $1,500, his largest purchase off the street. It was during this period—during Pantoja's re-emergence on Prado—that I met him, and traveled to his home in Bejucal. By then, he had already sold about two hundred paintings over a five-year period, and was using the money to support himself, his parents, his girlfriend, and her family. Almost all of it went to food, he said.

•••

After returning from three weeks in Cuba, you get shocked by the cold air that comes rushing out of American doors. The brightly-lit grocery story aisles make you squint. Then the shocks fade, and you began to embrace the quick comfort and overstimulation the U.S. always offers. I waited a couple of months before trying to call Pantoja, and when I did, he was overjoyed to hear my voice.

"Everyone tells me they will call, but nobody calls," he told me. "This is a surprise."

I explained that I had been studying the various ways in which a Cuban artist might be able to get out of the country safely, and was meeting with a lot of challenges. Although I could get him an invitation to exhibit his work in the U.S., I was worried that it might undermine his ability to actually get a visa cleared by Cuba. If Cuban officials knew he was bound for the states, they would suspect a defection in the works.

While I was hunting for the right strategy and calling the occasional immigration attorney, Pantoja began reporting back on the pressures he was facing on the Paseo del Prado, saying that he was worried about Aviles. During one phone call, he explained that he had befriended a German engineer who was staying in Cuba, and the man commissioned several works from him, including a portrait in which Pantoja substituted the man's head for that of a bulldog. The patron, he said, was crazy about it.

A year passed by quickly, with Pantoja suggesting a number of desperate alternatives to the visa route. I could bring him a bogus Mexican passport. I could rent a boat in the Bahamas and he could stowaway. I called him each month, frustrated that I couldn't seem to find a good, safe escape for him. During the winter of 2009, Pantoja reported that he had finally been kicked out of the Proyecto.

"I told Aviles he could shove the *licensia* up his ass," Pantoja said. "Then I told him I was going to start my own project, and that I would sell my paintings wherever I wanted."

He guessed it would be a matter of time before they put him in jail. That winter, 26 Cubans died from hypothermia during one particularly cold bout of weather.

•••

After a few frustrating attempts at negotiating various art exhibits for Pantoja in other countries, I gave up on him. I couldn't seem to find a way around the obstacles that Cuba created. Even when the famed Cuban blogger Yoani Sanchez won an invitation to speak abroad, the Cuban government denied her visa. They weren't going to let a known dissident painter out of their grasp, I thought. Still, I called Pantoja and listened to him. He endured episodes of starvation and sickness and deep despair. But each time we talked, he thanked me and told me that our talks gave him hope.

The miracle, when it finally happened, came fast. I had befriended a Mexican fiction writer named Liliana Blum, who asked me how I knew Spanish. I explained my Cuban roots, and soon enough, we were discussing Pantoja.

"We will get your friend free," she told me. "I will help."

Liliana contacted a friend of hers who operated a small gallery in Queretaro, Mexico, and sent him photos of Pantoja's work. He recognized the brilliance immediately, and extended him an invitation to show his paintings. The invitation was sent by email, and I called Pantoja to tell him to check his account. He was giddy on the line, but my voice remained flat. I thought his odds were still around zero.

Aviles and the Proyecto had no bearing, nor any communication with the office that handled Pantoja's visa application. Cuba's National Council for Visual Arts accepted the paperwork—but it was Pantoja who greased the process along with heavy bribes to office workers.

"Everyone expects *un regalito*," he told me. *A little gift*, they call it.

Word spread among the art patrons of Cuba that Pantoja had received an exhibition to show his work abroad. One wealthy government insider, a man I'll call Pablo Perez, insisted that Pantoja sell him his most prized painting: a large portrait of the *Caballero de Paris* that had been five years in the making. He paid Pantoja ten thousand dollars in cash for the piece, and Pantoja gave him three other paintings in gratitude. When I spoke to Perez on the phone, he was understandably evasive about what those paintings depicted.

"They were somehow related to my own life," Perez told me.

"They each had very strong messages."

During this time, I called Pantoja and he told me there was one final step he must take before he could get his visa approved. He had to take his paintings before José Antonio Menéndez Viera, director of the National Registry of Cultural Property. Every Cuban artist who aspires to exhibit abroad must receive Viera's approval, and Viera's job is to make sure that every cultural property complies with the interest of the state.

•••

On Monday, May 30, of 2011, Pantoja walked into the Officina Patrimonio for his appointment with Viera. He brought a tube containing each painting he planned to exhibit in Mexico, eight oil-on-canvas works, the remainder of what he called his "Vegetation" series. A group of administrators asked him to lay the paintings out on a large drafting table for the inspection. Pantoja opened up the tube and unrolled the canvases.

"This guy has lost his mind," one woman said, "Take a look at what he's brought."

Another woman peered at the paintings.

"You can't do this," the woman exclaimed. "You can't paint the libretta, you can't put the head of Fidel on a tortoise—you must be a lunatic to draw these kinds of things!"

"They were trying their best to shame me," Pantoja said.

The women told Pantoja to take a seat. They rolled his paintings up and hauled them upstairs to the director's office. And they left Pantoja alone. With each passing minute, Pantoja became more and more convinced that his hopes of leaving Cuba were dashed. He wasn't bound for freedom, he thought, but either a Cuban prison or a sanatorium. The administrators didn't return for an hour. By that point, Pantoja had already accepted his fate. He had written down an attorney's number that he planned to call when the police arrived. Eventually, one of the administrators returned.

"The director wants to see you upstairs," one woman said.

When Pantoja arrived in Viera's office, the paintings were laid out across a conference table.

"Compadre," Viera said. "We have a very grave situation here. Do you understand what you have done?"

You can't take anything from a man who has nothing to lose, Pantoja reckoned. He decided that for the first time in his life, he would speak his mind instead of letting his paintings speak for him.

"Yes, I know what I'm doing," he said. "And I will not allow you or anyone else to criticize my work. This is all my thinking, my inspiration and my life and I will do it the same way every time and everywhere. These paintings will open the doors of Cuba. Raúl Castro said that the people must criticize the government to rectify any mistakes, and my paintings are proof of the Revolution's mistakes."

The room went silent. Viera demanded to know how Pantoja received the invitation from Mexico.

"From the Internet," he replied.

"And how did you get Internet access?" Viera asked.

"At the National Council for Visual Arts."

"And how did these people find you?"

"On the Facebook, of course," replied Pantoja. "I have many friends on Facebook who are all over the world, and many of them are journalists. They are very interested in what you will tell me today."

At the mention of journalists, Viera's countenance changed. He smiled and told Pantoja to relax, that he wasn't being interrogated.

"Don't worry, don't worry," Viera said. He signed off on Pantoja's paintings and handed them back to him. He was free to go to the airport.

•••

The paranoia that plagued Pantoja for his whole life followed him all the way to Mexico. He found his first plane ride terrifying and exhilarating, but still felt uneasy when he landed in Mexico City. He had a princely amount of cash on him, which he declared at customs, and they waved him through the gate. His eyes scanned the airport to see if any Cuban agents had followed him.

Pantoja grabbed the first available bus to Queretaro, where he planned to meet the gallery owner to arrange the exhibit. He stayed in the quaint town square for two nights, and called me on the second day, letting me know he was safe.

"This is unbelievable," he said. "This is the most beautiful city I have ever seen." In his forty years, he had only seen Havana and its suburbs; until recently, most Cubans were not permitted to travel, even within their own country.

The gallery owner never showed up, and Pantoja felt restless. All along he had planned to defect to the states, so he abandoned the idea of his exhibition and took a northbound bus to the border town of Laredo. When he arrived at the bus station, he paid a taxi driver to take him straight to the border crossing. At the border, he declared political asylum and asked for the protection of the United States.

He was detained for nearly two days in a small room with ten other Cubans who were defecting, two of whom were young teenage girls who had been seated behind him on the plane ride from Havana. After an early-morning asylum interview, the border patrol released Pantoja into the United States, and one of the guards directed him to a nearby hotel.

"I was finally out of the shit," Pantoja recalled. "In this moment, the fear finally left me. I started to feel human."

•••

Within forty-eight hours, I was housing a Cuban refugee in a spare room at my office. I introduced him to all my friends, who were taken by Pantoja's charm and unbridled enthusiasm for life. My family watched as he tasted his first blueberries and strawberries ("These are world-famous," he said). In the two weeks he stayed with us, Pantoja visited the Golden Pawnshop twice each day, explaining that it made him cry for joy to see so many things he had wanted his whole life. He told us that Mazzio's was the greatest restaurant in the world, and he asked us to buy him a bottle of ranch dressing because he wanted to put it on everything. He did put it on everything, including his rice. One day, he spent twenty minutes watching his clothes spin in our washing machine. I don't recall having a conversation with him that didn't include the words "unbelievable" and "crazy."

He complained that Oklahoma was too hot for him, but he seemed to adjust well. Pantoja insisted on painting a portrait of me in exchange for helping him; he turned my hands into talons because I "fight the bad," he said. Even though he was glowing with excitement over all the new friends and experiences he made in Oklahoma, he began to pine for the family and friends he had left behind. In the first few days, he spent $50 calling his girlfriend and family in Cuba, and quickly understood why so few people can afford to maintain contact with relatives in Cuba.

"We always say that the people who leave Cuba drink the Coca-Cola of Forgetting," he said. "But now I know this is not true—I can never forget my country."

After two weeks in Tulsa, Pantoja decided he should go to Miami, where an elderly uncle had a room waiting for him. I helped him book an airline ticket and also shipped a chainsaw and a guitar from the pawnshop to his new address. Before he left, my wife and I took him to an Irish bar downtown.

"I can't believe I am in a bar in America," he said, grinning and holding a pint. "This is unbelievable. It's crazy that this freedom is happening to me." ◥

# IMAGINARY OKLAHOMA

# ALWAYS AND FOREVER

*by Ben Greenman*

You try having a father who isn't equal to you in size. It's not easy. His boots are always bigger. His hands are always bigger. He can reach things I can't. At fifteen I find my voice is deeper than his and at first that's a victory that can't be measured, a world larger than any I can imagine.

I walk around Broken Arrow telling people things they already know, just so I can be heard wielding this new instrument. But then it sinks in that it's just a voice, and that it's just a little deeper than his, and that the things it's saying are not nearly as deep. Over time the novelty drains and with it the power of the voice and I am left with the fact that when we are photographed together I look, always and forever, as if I require his protection. So you try having a father like that. And while you're at it, try having a mother who notices the difference in size, and comments on it, and even narrows her eyes when she's commenting on it as if to suggest that things could be different if only I truly wanted them different, deep down in my heart.

There's an old woman in town who responds to every week of dusty summer by sitting down on the sidewalk, right there on South Main, and then looking up and announcing that she's praying for water to fall from the sky. She says she's Creek but she doesn't look it at all. Everyone accounts her a crank in more than one direction, and in the Ledger they have even given her a nickname: "Rain Dance." But how is what my mother wants from me any better?

I can look to the sky all I want and ask to be bigger but facts are facts and my father is bigger. Once I put on his shoes by accident and I was swimming in the things. Live with that at twenty, at twenty-five, at thirty. That's why I first entered a bar and why it took me years to come back out. Then one day, on the orders of the doctor, in an attempt to keep the woman I love, I came out. The sun was an affront.

I visited home and my father was busy in the back but my mother fixed me a sandwich and even offered me a drink. It took all I had to refuse. Do you know what it's like to deny yourself the only thing that ever comforted you? Glass half empty? Half full? It didn't matter as long as it was beer. That was my little joke back when I made those kinds of jokes. Here's my joke now: I put on my pants one leg at a time just like any other great man. I'm so scared. ◥◣

# OF ALL PLACES

*by Lori Ostlund*

His mother said it was Oklahoma that was making him nuts, blaming the whole state when the only place he ever went was to work, which was 4.3 miles away, meaning that he actually inhabited a very small part of Oklahoma, certainly not enough of the state for it, collectively, to be blamed for making him nuts. Still, it was true that he had gone through his life, thirty-four years, not being nuts and then he had moved to Oklahoma and suddenly he was. He told his mother that maybe what had made him nuts was not Oklahoma but everything leading up to Oklahoma, his wife telling him that she might be in love with one of her students, though his wife taught eleventh graders, and his mother calling every two seconds to see whether he'd left her yet. "Maybe it's you making me nuts," he told his mother, and she said, "Don't be silly."

"Of all places," his mother had said when he told her he was moving to Oklahoma, and he thought that the same could be said of the state she lived in, which was New Jersey. When he moved to New Mexico, where he met the wife who was now in love with a sixteen-year-old, everyone said, "Lucky you," people who had never even been to New Mexico, and when he'd moved to Minnesota, everyone said, "It's cold," as though he had no idea, but when he announced that he was moving to Oklahoma, people either said "Oklahoma?," like a question, or they began belting out the song from the musical, though most of them knew only the first word, which was "Oklahoma," singing it like it was a sentence on a rollercoaster, or a canoe gliding quietly down a river and then dropping straight over the edge of a waterfall. ◥

# SONGS

*by Aimee Bender*

Oklahoma, shaped with a pan handle and a deep pan, the piece of the U.S. puzzle that I always liked to pick up early and tuck right into Texas. Oklahoma, below the Kansas of Dorothy lore and the one they wrote a song for: I bet half the residents love that musical and feel acknowledged by it and the other half resent it because the song is so damn catchy and they do not like it in their head while the wind does its actual sweeping down the plain. That same wind is a pain in the ass for crops and animals alike. That same wind drives dust into the corners of eyes and down throats. At the corner store, Sadie works at a scuffed counter selling water and snacks and beer and gas to drivers who do not want to stop there. She is not in the friendly or homey area of Oklahoma. She is in smalltown transitional highway Oklahoma. She resembles the landscape with a windblown look to her skin and the pale blue eyes of certain skies in springtime. Enough already, she thinks. It is time for a new musical. It is called Tulsa. It does not rhyme with much of anything, but it's a mantra in her head: Tulsa, Tulsa. Full in the back of the throat, and unsentimental. ◥

# SEVERE STORM WATCH

*by Rivka Galchen*

We all thought the weather was god, didn't we? Whether it was the golf-ball hailstorm that ruined the business plan of the magnificent mile of cars or the crepuscular rays of a rainstorm at the horizon. A striking tornado was something we really wanted, wasn't it? A gale of importance, beating pompous and ludicrous as a cape lined in purple satin, sending us to the basements of nearby churches or schools, not that we ever actually went there, to the shelters, but we thought about it, and in the thinking we imaged a mottled kind of festive underground, a noble sharing of crackers and peanut butter with the extended Mormon family from across the street, an oddly jovial game of cards—like a commercial for life insurance—might break out amongst diffident adults. Yes the "severe storm" would sweep down and make our lives suddenly as important as a Greek tragedy, or at least an early Hollywood film now in Technicolor. Really. In reality, I remember, the few times when the emergency siren went off, no one in my family much cared. My dad would go and stand outside. It was nice, to be able to see in him an indifferent kind of bravery, or foolishness. It was almost a heroic stance, and one didn't get the chance to see him that way—he didn't get the chance to appear that way—in the negotiations of the McDonald's drive-thru or picking up a kid from swim practice. But with the sirens it was suddenly the lost world of warrior kings. Turn on the wind machine. It was the nobly unwinnable battle. The white buffalo one might even say. Man V. Nature! I'd brave outside too, cinematically. Those wall clouds looked like an advancing army of spirits from 1000 lost civilizations. Our land was one to be conquered; our destiny was hard, and welcome. Soon, if the scenes in one's mind gathered from movies and Channel Nine News were correct, roofs would lie on the ground, idle as an unreplaced flour jar lid. A flour jar lid? Or: roofs were blown off as easily as the seeds of a granny dandelion? The cars and trailers would lie scattered like children's toys out of a trunk, one stuffed bunny missing its button eye, the understated note of tragedy. Or... was it that the sky darkened like drippy acrylic paint from fourth period weeping across the newsprint paper? There had been a poem. The beautifully inscrutable radar images of crayola green and purple molds advanced across the state in the Petri dish round of radar signal data. Meanwhile, the rain finally broke. It built and then didn't. That was the storm, now headed South to Ada. Another storm soon enough. Yes: the storms were wild molds or melodramas or armies or gods or ghosts or historic wraths or good times as had only on screens. The storms were all sorts of things. But the one thing those storms were not—unlike the 11 items or less express checkout lane, or the pollen count, or the snapped shoelace, or the current price of oil, or the rate of bank foreclosures, or the Girl Scout Cookie time of year, or the way the dryer never quite fully dried denim—yes, in distinction to all that, the one thing those storms weren't—not the really strong ones, not the scary ones, the beautiful ones, the majestic ones—was real. Or, at least, that wasn't the part most worth noticing. ◀

# JEFF KEITH,
# LEAD SINGER OF TESLA,
# CONSIDERS YOUTH

*by Steve Almond*

There was that night in El Paso where the singer for Cinderella started bleeding from his vocal chords. Every time the dude opened his mouth, he made this, like, yakking noise. And there were all these red stains on the tile. It was some serious shit. It made you think about life, your body, how quick things could break down on the road. I was lucky. We were all so fucking lucky. We knew that. It wasn't like some riddle. Would you rather drive a septic truck around, or rock ten thousand paying customers? Shit.

But still, there were some nights when I thought about Oklahoma, being back in Idabel, even that one fucked up year in Broken Bow, and it wasn't any one thing, because those were some sorry ass towns, flat and mean and hot as all hell in summer. You could walk along for miles and all you'd see is strip malls and the road throwing up heat, the graveyard with the names of all the young dudes who went to war and got killed. Those summers were like one long dead end.

So I don't understand, I can't tell you, why I still think about them, sweating through my raggedy-assed jeans, walking around looking for that one Indian kid Kevin to sell us his shitty weed, listening to The Doors and CCR and Steve fucking Miller, and wanting, for whole hours at a time, to be dead, or not seeing the difference anyway – until that one note finally arrived on the down-stroke and the singer's voice reached up to nail it, and we did, too, all of us, singing, staring at each other, our dirty fucking hair and our pimples, and an actual breeze came rolling in for the first time in a month, and with it the smell of rain, and I was like, Holy shit, dudes, this is cool. We're alive. ◥◼

# POETRY

# DRIVEWAY

*by Ron Padgett*

Again I slid up over the horizon
and the lights of Tulsa spread flat out before me.
"Ah, there you are," I said,
"like a porch light left on
for almost thirty years."
                              "Don't get carried away,
Ron. Yes, the lights are on for you and anyone
else who wants to rush toward me in a stream of light,"
the awakened city said, "but I knew
it was you. Who else would talk to me like this?"
I said, "There always was this special thing between us,
no?"
        "Between you and me,
not between me and you. You're like all the rest,
you think you're the only one to come along, that
I was made for you."
                        "I know, Tulsa, but
remember, I was an only child."
                              "I know, Ron, but
you're not a child now, so why act like one?
Why don't you settle back and take a deep, long look
at things the way they are? Why not just let go
of your love-hate thing with me? Do you really need
this longing and regret and so much useless anger?"
"But what'll I have of the me who was a little boy?"
"Whatever you already have, no more, no less,"
the voice said evenly.

Suddenly I cried
into the dark, "Where's your mouth?"
"You don't know? It's all around you--"
I was pulling
into the driveway where I used to live
"--it's your skin"
and opened my eyes and was
here, in New York, typing these lines.

# CRITICAL MASS

*by John Brehm*

Lifted their bikes up-
side down above
their thousand
heads and
cheered
locked the grid
blocked the inter-
section shut
the whole East
Village down
cars jammed
against that
stopped moment
that break in
time's flow
nothing moving
nowhere
to go unless
inward until
the helicopter's
searchlight shook
the air and cops
billyclubbed
a couple kids
to set example
hauled off
a truckload of
others forced

apart the forces
that swirled
together there—
but what I still see
are the wheels
held upward
spoked with light
freed from
the pavement
spinning into sky.

# JAZZ ON A DIAMOND-NEEDLE HI-FI

*by Deborah J. Hunter*

Mama dropped the needle and my heart jumped.
It was fascinating, titillating,
be-boppin', foot stompin', traffic stoppin', biscuit soppin',
donut dippin', daytrippin', corn sippin',
make me wanna shout,
cuss somebody out;
it was without a doubt,
the most sinfully rappin', toe-tappin',
thigh slappin', happenin' event.

It was the sun risin', moon smilin',
bees hummin', lovers comin',
mamas cryin', souls dyin',
life goin' on
goin' on
goin' on.

It was
Coltrane shatterin' shackles,
Bird making the night air moan,
Dizzy gettin' busy with the brass,
Brubeck redefining time,
Miles moving mountains meter by meter,
Ella bouncing lightning bolts off the sky.

It was jazz.
Ooh, jazz.
Yeah, jazz.
It was ss-ss-ss-ss-ss-ss

*jazz.*

# HANDWRITTEN LETTER 1934 (A FOUND POEM)

*by Scott Gregory*

Tulsa Okla.
10th April

Mr. Henry Ford
Detroit, Mich.
Dear Sir. ---

While I still have got breath in my lungs
I will tell you what a dandy car you make.
I have drove Fords
Exclusively
When I could get away
With one.
For sustained speed
And freedom
From trouble
The Ford has got every other car skinned
And even if my business
Hasn't been strictly legal
It don't hurt anything
To tell you what a fine car you got in the V8 ---

Yours truly
Clyde Champion
Barrow

# THAT'S NOT FUNNY; YOU CLOWNS DON'T MAKE ME LAUGH

*by Lynn Melnick*

The woman in the grocery store on Sunset
stopped me in the produce,

her claws about my shoulders,
to bless me on behalf of her God,

on behalf of her hair, bleached
past the point hair can withstand,

so each strand became a defiance of her very God,
and her outsize lips, still blessing, could only up and down,

until what we think of as prophecy
was merely opening wide to say ah.

I took my remains and broke free,
my skin loose as I ran.  Meanwhile,

the butcher I'm dancing with refuses to change my face.
And the dye that spilled on the floor?

The kind of red your mother warned you about.
But no one warned me, I drank it straight.

Or hadn't you heard. Lately, it seems,
plastic surgeons are murdered far more frequently

than your more interior doctors.
How have I missed that crazy little thing

called conversion, when I could have called it that?
The plastic surgeons scalpel their tombstones;

it's not that they wanted to die,
they only wished to right the wrong bodies.

Was the cause perfection?  Whose isn't.  But everyone's face
is falling, and I don't want the circus come to town,

whether I'm the circus or the town.

# MINDING THE CENTER

# SOUTH BY MIDWEST:

## OR, WHERE IS OKLAHOMA?

*by Russell Cobb*

I'm not much of a Facebook person. Most of the time, I passively scroll through status updates while avoiding doing something else. Recently, however, I set off a Facebook conversation that lasted for days, with far-flung acquaintances and distant relatives chiming in on what I thought was a perfectly reasonable assertion.

Before I come to that assertion, let me ask you, dear reader, who I trust has at least a passing interest in the nation's 46th state: Where is Oklahoma? Were someone on the street to ask you this question, you might turn to a political map of the United States and point to the meat cleaver above Texas. There it is, you would say, in the mid-south-central portion of the continental United States. But where is it culturally? Is it part of The South? The U.S. Census Bureau says so. Generations of venerable southern historians, such as C. Vann Woodward, have said so.

And this was the assertion I casually made on Facebook. Actually, what I said was that, as a Southerner, the word "heritage" (as in "Southern heritage") struck me as slightly sinister, but I wasn't quite sure why.

I was quickly shot down by the sister of a very good friend, who happens to live in Birmingham. "Oklahoma is not the South, Russ," she said. "It's the Midwest." Another friend in Georgia sprung to my defense. "I've lived in the Deep South and Chicago. Oklahoma is definitely more Southern than Midwestern. Still, it's not quite the South either."

A Canadian friend was confused. "Where does the South end?" he wanted to know. "Is the South synonymous with the Bible Belt?" In a famous article, one historian asserted that the best way to define the contemporary South was to examine the audience for religious television. The bigger the market share for televangelists, the more southern the place. By this calculation, Tulsa was either the buckle on the Bible Belt, or, at the very least, one of its belt holes.

A good friend who considers a trip to Dallas to be a visit to a foreign country tried to argue that Oklahoma was its own region, that it shouldn't be lumped together with any other state, especially not Texas. But this seemed strange, too, because there are some affinities between Texas and Oklahoma. Still, Okies have none of the bluster of Texans, and it's hard to imagine a tourism campaign with the slogan: "Oklahoma, it's like a whole other country." We don't do arrogance. When I was growing up, the slogan on license plates was "Oklahoma is OK." Not great, not terrible, just OK.

The conversation went on for days. I could sense I was losing the argument. All the Oklahomans who posted seemed to think their native state was in the Midwest. This disturbed me, but why? There was something hopelessly dull and uninteresting about being from the Midwest. Someone else, a friend in New York, agreed. "It's in the Midwest, but I would rather it be in the South," she said. Why was the South an improvement on the Midwest? Being from the South had its own set of problems. And what about the Southwest? Maybe we were Southwesterners.

•••

Trace the old Route 66 via Interstate 44, and you will eventually come to a town where, depending on which gas station you visit, you will hear a nasally Midwestern accent or a Southern accent. The town is just across the Missouri-Oklahoma line, in Carthage, Missouri. On the southern end of town, near the highway, locals will say "highway forty-four," but will often turn the number four into two separate syllables: fo-or. Linguists will tell you that this is the hallmark the "Southern drawl": drawing one vowel out to make it sound like two.

On the other end of town, on the road to Kansas City, I-44 becomes pronounced as "farty-far." I can make this assertion with some authority, having traveled north and south across Missouri many times on my way to college in Iowa, which, unlike Oklahoma, suffers from no regional identity complex. Rolling hills of grain silos, perfectly red barns and miles of corn fields signify, in no uncertain terms, the Midwest.

Iowa, along with Nebraska and South Dakota, has produced a disproportionate share of broadcasters, in part because the accent in these states is considered the most neutral. This is the heartland of a type of English known as General American (SAE, or Standard American English, in another term of art for this accent), a place the linguist William Labov found to be the area most devoid of regional variations and irregular speech patterns. According to Labov's Atlas of North American English, General American encompasses an oval-shaped blob from eastern Nebraska and South Dakota to central Illinois, taking in much of Iowa and northern Missouri. Walter Cronkite, Ronald Reagan and Tom Brokaw all spent their formative years in General America. General America is where corporations go to test new products to see if they will succeed in the rest of the country. If all the children in Lake Wobegon are above average, all the children in General America are average.

When I first drove across General America in the early 1990s, I was shocked to learn how different it was from Oklahoma, which I always assumed was the most generic, milquetoast place in the world. The towns of General America, however, were tidier and straighter than anything I had seen in Oklahoma. The churches were whiter. The town squares looked like settings for Norman Rockwell paintings. So many small towns in Oklahoma looked like they'd just been hit by F-5 tornadoes or served as a setting for a movie about rural meth labs.

I also assumed that anyone not from a city spoke with an Oklahoma accent, which traces its genealogy back to Appalachia—a variation on the Southern accent. When I met my first roommate, Jake, from Hawarden, Iowa (population 2,478) at the University of Iowa, I was surprised he spoke General American. He looked like a hick in his tight Wranglers, mullet and Metallica t-shirt, and yet he spoke without a trace of an accent. I expected his accent to be something like that of Boomhauer's from King of the Hill: a twangy, monotone slur. (The creator of the show, Mike Judge, has stated that the inspiration for Boomhauer's accent came from an unintelligible phone conversation he once had with a man from Oklahoma City.) My roommate also had three more Advanced Placement credits than I did, completing the ruin of my sense of intellectual and cultural superiority.

Even more shocking than all this was learning that I had an accent. I shared a phone with Jake and two guys from Chicago next door. The Chicagoans drank Old Style beer at 8 a.m. and skipped class to watch hockey. One day, I discovered that I was missing a pair of socks and asked them about it.

"You're missing what?" one of them said.

"Socks," I said. "I can't find my socks."

The one I had been talking to went to find his roommate. He brought him into the common area, where we shared a refrigerator and a telephone.

"I can't understand this guy," one Chicagoan said to the other. "What are you missing?"

"My socks!" I said. "You put them on your feet."

"Sacks," said the other one. "He's saying 'sacks.' " They laughed and then mocked me. "Saw-ahks," they said. "I cain't find my saw-ahks. Shi-it!" To their ears, I sounded like an Alabama redneck.

So I set about detecting regionalisms in my speech and purging them one by one with the help of a fellow English major from Chicago. Greasy was not pronounced with a "z" sound but with an "s" sound. Words ending in "-ow" were pronounced with an "oh" sound, not with an "-uh" sound. "Pen" and "pin" were pronounced differently. "Milk" was one syllable, not "mi-yulk."

Going back to Tulsa, I noticed that somewhere south of Kansas City, Standard American gave way to Southern twang, leading me to eventually pinpoint Carthage as the transition zone. A 2004 study of national speech patterns boiled American dialects down to six major groupings. Northeastern Oklahoma and southern Missouri are the northwestern limits of the southern accent, while the "midland," that area from northern Missouri to Iowa, Nebraska and Illinois, was found to be the region with the fewest deviations from Standard American.

•••

Even if we Okies have a sort of Southern accent, though, that doesn't make us Southerners. The Census Bureau may designate Oklahoma as the South, but what explains the visceral reaction of Georgians and Alabamans when an Okie claims to be from Dixie? A friend of a friend from Tulsa replicated my Facebook experiment and was shot down by from someone from Arkansas. "It's the Southwest," he wrote. "The South starts with Arkansas." The next person to post was confused. "Upper central mid south west?" she wrote. "Please let me know what the answer is."

A friend of a friend who works for *Southern Living* magazine was sort of annoyed that Oklahoma was included in her lifestyle magazine. "It was a marketing decision," she said. "Everyone knows Oklahoma isn't in the real South." But where is the real South?

There was a time in the not-too-distant past when Oklahoma politicians made a deliberate effort to make the state part of the "Solid South," a peculiar institution that guaranteed the one-party rule of the Democratic Party. The heyday of the "Solid South" lasted from the end of Reconstruction until the end of World War II. The strategy was all about, of course, disenfranchising black voters and wielding monolithic political control over state politics. Danney Goble, the recently deceased Oklahoma historian, explains it this way in the *Encyclopedia of Oklahoma History and Culture*:

The fact that much of the future state was settled by immigrating southerners had great influence on Oklahoma's later politics. Its unwieldy constitution, its distrust of concentrated corporate and political power, its steady run-ins with federal authority, even its susceptibility to political corruption—all of these were qualities that the Sooner State shared with states of the Old Confederacy... Early Oklahoma Democrats campaigned and governed just like their fellow Democrats across the South: they openly and bluntly proclaimed their racism to win power, and they used power to affirm and institutionalize their racism. It was they who mandated separate schools under the constitution; they who segregated public transportation in Oklahoma's first statute; they who countenanced "white only" public accommodations, neighborhoods, even entire towns; they who systematically disenfranchised blacks with racist election laws.

The geographer Wilbur Zelinsky—one of the inventors of modern cultural geography—attempted to understand regional identity in the "vernacular." Zelinsky wanted to understand how everyday folks defined themselves in terms of regional identity. This was in the pre-Internet age of the 1970s and 1980s, and Zelinsky focused on the Yellow Pages. The telephone book, unlike, say, the Census Bureau, would give you a good idea of the regional place names that people used to identify themselves and their businesses.

Sorting through thousands of place names in hundreds of cities, he compiled a series of maps that showed how people identified their regions. Some of the regions were predictable: Boston businesses used a lot of terms like New England and Northeastern in their names or descriptions. "Southern" was a dominant term in phone books in Mississippi, Louisiana, Georgia, etc. But, looking at Zelinksy's maps today, it is Oklahoma that shows the biggest regional confusion. Strangely, Zelinsky never commented on this fact. He noted that some places, like western Pennsylvania, were kind of stuck between Northeastern and Midwestern, but it was Oklahoma that had the greatest amount of regional identities. Five of the twelve vernacular identities that Zelinsky came up with converged on Oklahoma. For phone books in the very southeastern part of the state, Oklahoma was southern. In the panhandle, it was the "West." Along the Kansas border, it was the Midwest. From Oklahoma City to the west, it was the "southwest."

Part of the problem with Zelinsky's research, though, is that it is static. It doesn't take into account the way regional identities change. Minnesota was once considered the Northwest; it is now firmly ensconced in the Midwest. Maryland was once considered the South, but few people would today characterize it as anything other than the Mid-Atlantic.

The Midwest, in general, seems to be gaining ground, expanding its reach beyond its western and southern boundaries. In 2006, NPR, while reporting on an outbreak of tornadoes in Tennessee, referred to the state as the Midwest. If the Midwest is the region of Standard American, this seems to make sense, at least on the surface. The common wisdom is that the proliferation of mainstream popular culture through TV, the Internet and social media is destroying regional identities, making us all one undifferentiated mass of Starbucks coffee shops and crappy reality television. Socio-linguists, however, have found that the opposite is true—at least in terms of regional vocabularies and dialects. New dialects are being born: California used to speak Standard American but now has its own accent, and regional variations are becoming more—not less—pronounced.

•••

There is always the case for the Southwest. But Oklahoma doesn't quite fit there either because the proper Southwest is a legacy of what was once Mexico, and, before that, the Spanish Empire. West Texas, New Mexico, Arizona, some of Colorado: all these places have Hispanic place names and visible relics of Spain and Mexico. Apart from El Reno—and one has to doubt that there were ever any reindeer (Reno is Spanish for reindeer) in central Oklahoma—there are no Spanish place names in Oklahoma. Coronado, apparently, wandered through the Wichita Mountains and lost a few pounds of gold along the way, but there are no missions, no pueblos. Our only decent Mexican food comes from recent migration patterns; in short, we have nothing that Americans recognize as archetypes of Southwestern culture.

Finally, in moments of brutal honesty, Okies will admit that their state is a variation of Texas. This is a painful admission, to be sure. "The whole state is like a suburb of Dallas," a fellow Tulsan told a Canadian friend. "It's Texas-light," someone wrote during my interminable Facebook conversation. Politically, culturally and religiously speaking, there's a good case to be made for this assertion. Texans and Oklahomans share the same affinity for hard-right, red-meat conservative politics, and they have large populations of Southern Baptists. Western Swing is a purely Texas-Oklahoma creation of Bob Wills, who belongs to both states. The accent is pretty much the same, although a bit stronger in Texas. There's the big role oil companies play in the states' economies. And, of course, there's football. Both states are football crazed, but therein lies a complication: there is no greater sports hatred than that between the Sooners and the Longhorns.

I've tried to deconstruct the annual hatefest that is the OU-Texas game for my wife, a native Californian, who, before meeting me, had never watched a college football game. Part of what makes the game exciting, I told her, is that it's played on a neutral site. So it's not in Texas or Oklahoma, she wondered? Well, it's in Dallas, I said. The idea that Dallas was somehow neutral seemed ludicrous, and, indeed, the more I thought about it, the more it seemed like Oklahomans had been bamboozled.

So, where is Oklahoma? It is in America's Heart, someone said. Well, not quite, I rebutted. If you compare the map of the continental U.S. to the human body, you would have to conclude that Oklahoma is America's pancreas. It's in the mid-south-central of the body, and, although it doesn't have the poetic resonance of the heart, it serves an important function. It breaks down proteins, carbs and fats. The pancreas is often overlooked until something terrible happens there, like a cancer—or the bombing of a federal building. But there it is, right there in the middle of everything, trying to make sense of all the substances coming through the system. Not all the substances that come through are healthy, but the pancreas soldiers on, keeping the body running. ◥◣

# LETTER FROM LONDON

*by Sarah Brown*

I've always been very susceptible to other people's slang. If I make a new friend, a month later, I'll have picked up at least one of their turns of phrase. This is more about my sponge-like love for language than any sort of Single White Female behavior, but I still try to keep it in check so as not to creep anyone out. This is why I was a bit nervous before moving to London. I can't even watch *Gosford Park* without thinking in a British accent for a few hours afterwards; how was I going to keep myself from mimicking and offending everyone I met while immersed in it?

I had a friend in New York who lived in London for a few years during grad school. When I visited her in London, I noticed a definite change in the way she spoke. She wasn't affecting any Madonna-like accent, but her cadence was different. Her sentences went up at the end; she'd finished questions with "yeah?" instead of "okay?" I knew she wasn't doing it on purpose because when we overheard some fellow Americans in a restaurant, she rolled her eyes and said, "It's so funny when people move here and suddenly sound like Gwyneth."

My fiancé is English, and after living with him in New York for just a few months, I'd already picked up some of his slang. Not his accent; just certain words or phrases. If he'd been American, no one would have noticed, but since he was English, friends would tease me for saying "fuck all" instead of "nothing" or "I'm not too fussed about it" instead of "I don't really care." So when we moved to London last fall, I was hyper-vigilant about not sliding down that slope any further. To be fair, I can do a much better British accent than my fiancé can do an American one. I actually sound like the recorded female voice on the Underground, while he sounds a lot like Dustin Hoffman in *Tootsie*.

When I first moved from Oklahoma to New York seven years ago, people would ask me, "Where are you from again?" and when I'd answer, they'd say, "Oh yeah, I can tell by your Oklahoma accent." This was always funny to me, because I don't have an Oklahoma accent at all. My father was born in California, and my mother was born in Texas but raised in Canada. Neither my brother nor I have an accent, although we do both drop our Gs in -ing words. No one in my immediate family says *y'all*. Although once, when I was preparing to be on *ABC Nightline*, my mother warned me, "I don't want to hear that Okie *yeaaah* come out of your mouth on national television!"

My first job in New York was a temp job at a construction company. My first week there, I was waiting at the copier with a man with fancy cufflinks and a crewcut.

"Where do you live?" he asked in a thick Jersey accent.

"Brooklyn," I said.

"Nah ah ah," he shook his head and wagged his finger. "Where are you *from*?"

I answered, "Oklahoma," and he said, "Yeah, I thought you sounded like a hillbilly. No offense intended." And I honestly don't think he meant it rudely; I quickly learned that people who've always lived in New York can only differentiate between From Here and Not From Here. Now that I'm in England, no one could pick out my hometown in 100 guesses if I gave them a running headstart, and sometimes I wish I had a *Sopranos* extra to baffle again.

I've been in London for seven months now, and I'm proud to say I've held fast to my American English, much to my fiancé's frustration. We have a lot of disagreements about spelling and pronunciation. His argument is always, "But my way is correct."

And often it is, but the rest of the time I have to explain to him that only moody, flowery poetry-writing American teenagers spell it *colour* or *favourite*. At the same time, I don't want to go out of my way to be difficult while in a foreign country. If I'm ordering in a restaurant in England, I'll ask the waitress for chips, but I'll eat fries. If I'm helping our friends' toddler get dressed, I'll call her underwear *pants* and her pants *trousers*, but my sweater is never a jumper.

I've noticed recently that now when I'm asked where I'm from, I answer "New York." Maybe this is because I know that if New Yorkers can't find Oklahoma on a map, there's no use trying with Londoners. Maybe it's because I know I'll get immediate cool points with whoever's asking. Or maybe it's because I'm missing my home of the past seven years, the place where I carved out my adult life all by myself. I think of New York as home now, but Oklahoma will always be where I was born and raised, and supported and encouraged enough to set out on my own. It's a good place to come from. ◀

# ESPECIALLY THE ZEBRAS

*by Amy Leach*

Two giant Aldabra tortoises with wide dark eyes are on the move around their scrubby domain. The front one stops. Not willing to participate in gridlock, not wishing to change lanes, the rear tortoise climbs over the front one, like a Fiat driving over a stopped Fiat. The one underneath objects wrathfully and shakes the surmounter off. Another giant tortoise hauls himself over on thick pigeon-toed legs and the three of them face each other like the complacent lobes of a shamrock. A fourth tortoise in the shed has lost all his go.

Two female giraffes arrived in Tulsa ahead of the heat wave, one from Missouri and one from Kansas. For now, a fence separates them from the male giraffe, but the fence is low enough so they can "interact with his head." They sniff his head, nuzzle his head, take cues from his head: at first the two of them were startled by all the roaring (the Tulsa Zoo is next to the airport), but then they looked at Samburu's head, which was cool as a cucumber. He was born here in 1992, and knows that jet planes are as natural as wagons full of grape-eating children and the intermittent ditty of the carousel. A tall platform is being constructed where the carrot-bearing public will be able to climb up and "interact with the giraffes' heads." It must be a thankless job to be the body of a zoo giraffe, always transporting the far more popular head around. But recently Lexi and Pili were let into the main yard, to join Samburu in the circulating shadow of his canvas umbrella, a three-giraffe sundial.

It is so hot the leaves flash like mirrors. The cicadas get riled up and cottonwood fluffs around. Two little gray Sicilian donkeys marked like hot-cross buns are in a stupor. A spindly little girl in the Frogger Jumping Harness dangles in the air like a pixie, too light to actually touch down on the green bouncy mattress. Gravity can be a good friend, but I have noticed that he plays favorites. Three chunky zebras are safely grazing; the cheetah lives behind an unleapable fence. Oklahoma looks like Botswana, especially the clouds and the zebras, but you can tell you're in Oklahoma because the cheetah is visible.

In the Children's Zoo, a red wattle hog mixes himself some mud with his snout—start with some dirt, add some sump water, a little more dirt, mix mix mix—and plunks himself down in the oozy sludge, his big notched ears flapping forward over his eyes. His explanatory plaque says that red wattle hog numbers dwindled when people found fattier hogs for making soap. It also says that red wattle hogs have some wild relatives in Texas—the Texas relatives must have quit the soap-making business to pursue mud-making full-time. In the Contact Yard, I try to make contact with an extra wide goat, stroking her rusty-wire hair. She does not appear to notice. One little crackpot goat is running around butting other goats in the rear, and they definitely notice. Here is someone who knows how to make contact that sinks in.

A grizzly bear has her nose pressed against the window, watching the children watching her. Apparently she was found at the same dumpster or campground three times, and the rule is three strikes and you're out, and they know who you are because they tattoo your lips. Grizzly bears have such a powerful sense of smell that even if tranquilized, crated, trucked 300 miles away, lectured to stay put and eat the local ladybugs and huckleberries and wild potatoes, they still might show back up behind Buckshot Bessie's Bar and Grill, ransacking that peerless dumpster, that consummate dumpster, that dumpster surpassing all dumpsters. The polar bear died so the Tulsa Zoo had room for a recidivist.

## THE EMBASSY OF DEAD BRANCHES

A Scottish Highland cow with shaggy red bangs and tufty eyelashes is breathing so heavily that her long curved horns rock back and forth. The word *animal* comes from the Latin word for "having breath." Every time I walk by the alligator snapping turtle's aquarium he is slanted up his slope of rocks. I don't understand why he's always in the same position until I see him stretch his head up to the surface to breathe. His stony-plated armor looks fortified for fending off Gog and Magog, but here, submerged in his tank in Tulsa, all he needs to fend off is a small fish friend and death, so he positions himself for convenient access to air.

Close to a mini-bayou graced with two alligators and a cabana, there is a triptych of small embassies: swamp, bog, marsh. The barking tree frogs representing marsh are stuck to the wall. The tiny bog ambassador is lying exposed in a dish of mud; the description of bog turtles says "they are very secretive." She is not alone among secrets, having been transferred from a ferny bog into the public eye. Appearing for swamp is a spotted turtle that could fit in the palm of my hand, swimming hard into the window, making the water churn around his fake mangrove roots. As I walk back and forth he follows me, climbs onto his minute bank, falls pinwheeling into the water, paddles back to the glass, cranes his neck towards me. If he were an ambassador from outer space instead of just a swamp, I guess we'd all be amazed; or if he were a mar.made turtle programmed to mechanically paddle after a person. I wish I were Ariadne, I wish I had a ball of thread.

In the back of a heptagonal snow-and-sky diorama, furnished with dead-leafy branches, a snowy owl sits swiveling his head to the left, around to the right, around to the left. Two different people who pass by inform their companions that owls can turn their heads all the way around but they wonder why he doesn't do it. A hefty girl pounds on the glass and shouts, "That is a sexy owl!" Two teenagers in cut-offs conduct an antiphonal conversation involving someone else on the other end of a cell phone: "Have you been in the truck?" "I've never been in the truck." "He says he's never been in the truck." A caravansary of preschoolers is ushered through. At first, they are excited that the owl has his very own bath, but then the excitement turns Aristotelian as they debate whether it's a bath or a shower. Pre-school does not mean pre-intellectual. The sign says "the snowy owl's range includes the entire Arctic Circle."

A few pre-intellectuals are strollered past the dwarf antelope huddling in the shadow of her twelve-foot wooden fence; they seem to be the only people not asking "What's that?" "What the fuck?" "What the hell is that?"—the only ones whose interest in the animal is not deflected by the answer "a dik-dik." One little boy waves at the antelope silently; two dark-haired babies in yellow dresses stare, open-mouthed; a small girl in gold-heart sunglasses cries out "Goodbye" as she is wheeled away. This all helps me understand why only two-year-olds are allowed to go on a Camel Tour:

1. Riders must be 2 years old and able to hold on securely

2. No kicking, biting, spitting, or other offensive acts toward the camels

3. The load limit will not exceed 300 pounds

Two camels lie under a tent, patiently wearing blue seats. Who is worthy to be carried by such faithful creatures, except nonviolent two-year-olds under 300 pounds? Babies should qualify too, because of the hallelujah quality of their minds, but they might fall off.

## THE WISDOM OF GUNDA

Outside the chimpanzee house there's a red metal outline of a chimpanzee bolted to the concrete. It looks like a chimpanzee cookie-cutter; a woman has her daughter get inside it, to compare physiques: "Scooch forward, stick your butt out—" A chimpanzee has very long arms and very short legs, so to fit in the outline a person has to contort herself. But none of the actual chimpanzees I see would fit in the cookie-cutter either, not Bernsen, the little pirouetting one, or the huge one, Morris, who catches flying bananas and lemons with one hand.

Somehow I sense I am living in the age of anatomical expertise. Signs at the zoo say things like "Langurs have tails up to 43 inches long," "A chimp's muscle tissue is denser than ours," and "Elephant tusks are incisor teeth." At the Elephant Demonstration, visitors ask, "How many bones do they have?" "How many toes do they have?" "How many teeth do they have?" An elephant has four molars like a dead elephant, but a dead elephant can't hold a candle to Gunda here, enjoying her broccoli and her hose bath, her particular freckles emerging from the mud.

The elephant keeper, the giant tortoise keeper, the grizzly bear keeper, the chimpanzee keeper and the sloth keeper all tell me how different their animals are from each other, in their fearlessness, pushiness, irascibility, taste for togetherness, mothering styles, interest in people or antipathy to them. Three Fiats with homogeneous bodies will yet behave in heterogeneous ways, one creeping hesitantly to the pharmacy, another zooming to a toga party, and one, having forgotten to fill up, slowing down and stopping. You might think a sloth would have little behavior to differentiate it from its fellows, but Ty for one likes to sleep in a bucket, and after months of sweet-potato blandishments, does not mind the keeper lifting his long, curved nails up out of his bucket into the air. The only animals interchangeable like dollars are the ones not indigenous to this planet—the GloFish®. So that you must purchase the fluorescent fish from a retailer, the manufacturer makes them sterile. Perhaps something in this process has bent them out of true: all of the GloFish® at the Tulsa Zoo have the same personality: deceased.

Once the elephant keeper worked at a zoo where they'd take the elephants for a walkabout in forests and meadows, and he said if you didn't keep an eye on them, you'd lose track of them, their footfalls are so silent. It's true—I watch the male elephant trudging around his dusty yard, twirling the end of his trunk, swinging his tail back and forth, fanning his triangular ears, but I cannot hear him, gravity's darling, any more than I can hear the dark purple butterfly fluttering back and forth in front of me. One got all the mass, the other got all the autonomy, but they are equally inaccessible to the ear. There is more than one way to escape scrutiny.

As I am leaving the zoo I pass a sign that asks, "What animals do you want to attract?" I consider and decide that, of all the animals I have seen here, I would most like to attract the red wattle hog and the reticent goat and the lithe green lizard I saw resting his chin on a log, and I enter the Habitat Garden to learn how. However, I find the Habitat Garden to be strongly skewed toward the attracting of toads. "Overturn a clay pot in a damp area for toads." "Large rocks and rock piles make good shady places for toads." "Attract toads with a slow-dripping faucet." Although I am glad to learn how to sweeten the life of a toad, I leave the zoo not knowing how to be someone the hog, the goat, the lizard, the dik-dik, the gibbon, or the saki monkey, or the snowy owl want to be close to. In the parking lot, two little birds who were sheltering from the sun under my car fly away. ◥

# THE HAND OF MAN

*by Ginger Strand*

On a recent Tuesday morning, around 36 8-year-olds and I were watching a bright yellow longhorn cowfish bob around its tank at the Oklahoma Aquarium when the *manus deus* descended from above. Actually, it looked less like the hand of God than the hand of man: it had neatly trimmed nails and came down from the heavens of the tank clutching a long glass tube. The cowfish fluttered its fins, snail-horns alert, its mouth an O of surprise. The hand directed the glass tube into the tank's pebbly substrate, rooting around until it raptured up some long stringy things. Fish poop. The cowfish turned modestly away. It didn't look at all like a cow. But we humans are incorrigible when it comes to naming sea critters after things we know on land.

This was one of those moments, not uncommon in aquariums, where the immense effort involved in faking nature is revealed. Somebody has to deal with the fish poop, the mechanics of colossal tanks of water, the optics of super-thick glass, the chemistry of piped-in water. Not to mention the economics of paying for it. Like many of the newer public aquariums, the Oklahoma Aquarium has made much of this process transparent. Exhibits explain the technology behind them, wall copy frequently notes how fish were acquired, and placards on the tanks denote financial sponsors. The aquarium's director of science and mechanics Kenny Alexopoulos has even given *The Journal Record* his recipe for imitation coral (press rock salt into wet concrete spread over plastic mesh; rinse away when concrete dries for realistic pock marks). In fact, strolling the nearly ten-year-old facility, you might find yourself thinking the complexities of manmade systems are just as cool as the ecosystems the aquarium honors. And that would be appropriate. Because it's not really nature that's being celebrated here—it's something trickier and more complicated: the evolving connection nature and man have been working out, nowhere more than right here in eastern Oklahoma.

Take, for instance, the exhibits marked "Aquatic Oklahoma!" They include some of the region's most characteristic megafauna: alligator gars, blue catfish, and, of course, paddlefish, who have been freaking out area anglers since before Thomas Nuttall, a Harvard botanist, arrived in 1818 and heard tell of "a singular fish . . . destitute of scales, and with the upper jaw extended in front a foot in length, in the form of a peel or spatula." That spatula-shaped rostrum gives the paddlefish its Jurassic appeal, but it also holds electroreceptors for finding plankton in murky plains rivers. Though if you walk out onto the aquarium's patio and look at the early summer Arkansas River—a generous name for what looks like a gravelly collection of mud puddles—murk doesn't seem to be the main problem: lack of water does. It's hard to imagine any of the aquarium's megafauna could survive in large segments of the river; they must be living in the reservoirs made by dams. They may be native Oklahomans, but their aquatic habitat is manmade.

Then things in Aquatic Oklahoma get weirder: tanks hold largemouth bass and sauger, which are not native to Oklahoma, saugeye, which is not native to anywhere since it's a biologist-produced hybrid, and striped bass, which is not even naturally a freshwater fish, but an Atlantic Ocean anadromous fish—a saltie who migrates up rivers to spawn in freshwater. The story goes that a group of stripers got trapped behind a South Carolina dam, and when they thrived there, Fish and Game departments nationwide thought "Hey, let's stock those bad boys here!" Stripers are a popular sportfish, bringing added revenue to the state.

Like most of the fish in the Oklahoma section, the striper exhibit includes a sign touting the state angling record for the species. In fact, fishing is so much the point of the Oklahoma section, I began to wonder what I was really looking at in Aquatic Oklahoma: a celebration of ecosystems or a celebration of state agency omnipotence. In addition to the stocked sportfish, there's a whole wall in the Ozark Stream section touting the stream "restoration" at Evening Hole, a spot on the Lower Mountain Fork River near Broken Bow. There, the wall tells us, a boring, sluggish stream was whipped into trout-friendly shape using "big imagination, heavy equipment, and the latest in the science of streams." While they were at it, state wildlife officials excavated an old dry ditch and made a new stream called Lost Creek. A better name might have been "Found Creek." Clearly, the hand of man has been hard at work—and not just inside the aquarium.

Then again, what's wrong with that? After all, Tulsa's predominant water feature is a human-nature hybrid itself. The Arkansas River has been undergoing improvements since the nation's first River Act funded the clearing of debris from its mouth to its confluence with the Neosho River. In the 1880s, Colorado started diverting water from the Arkansas for irrigation, and ten years later, Kansas got in on the act. That changed river dynamics again: by the early 1900s, so much water was being diverted, the river went dry by July.

But it was fear of floods that led Congress in 1946 to authorize the Army Corps of Engineers to begin re-engineering the river for real. Today the Arkansas is impounded by two power-generating flood-control dams upstream of Tulsa, creating Kaw and Keystone Lakes. And from Muskogee down to the Mississippi, it's not really a river at all, but a series of stepped reservoirs linked by eighteen dams and locks known as the McClellan-Kerr Arkansas River Navigation System. The first cargo arrived in Catoosa, 448 miles inland from the Mississippi, in January, 1971: 650 tons of newsprint for the *Tulsa World*.

Faced with this level of transformation, it's hard not to wonder: what does Aquatic Oklahoma even mean? Which fish can we really consider Oklahomans? Which can we even consider wild? Fortunately, the Department of Wildlife Conservation is housed right next door in the aquarium complex.

"When you take a river and put a series of dams on it and create lakes out of it, you are going to change the species dynamic," Mike McAllister told me. Mike is an information and education specialist at the DWC. In Mike's eyes, the changes to the species dynamic were all good. In fact, Oklahoma's Arkansas River was improved when the Corps of Engineers took it in hand. "A plains river in its natural state really ain't anything pretty to look at," Mike told me. "It's just there." Mike is not alone in this opinion. A mile wide and an inch deep; too thick to drink, too thin to plow: there's no shortage of insults designed for rivers like the Arkansas. Plains rivers tend to be shallow, slow, brackish and turbid—downright boring in fact. That is, until April, when they bloat with spring rains and snowmelt and start swallowing houses and cattle. The Arkansas did plenty of that before being transformed by one of the most expensive projects in the history of the Corps. Many of the huge federal water projects in the West and Midwest we now know were pricey and often pointless boondoggles—irrigation projects that benefit a handful of corporate agribusinesses, dams that can never recover their operating expenses, aqueducts that burn coal to pump water uphill. But the Arkansas River projects are widely viewed as successful. They were, as *U.S. News and World Report* declared in 1979, pork that paid off: "Dams and levees have turned the formerly turgid river into an azure ribbon offering fishing, water skiing and boating," the magazine enthused.

Of course, there are effects beyond better recreation. Dams disrupt the river's natural sequence of bubbling riffles and deeper, slower pools. The flowing parts of the river become faster and colder. Cottonwoods downstream of dams die off, leaving fewer shady spots for fish to hide in. In the reservoirs, sediment builds up instead of flowing downstream, and the colder, clearer deep water creates a new kind of habitat, less friendly to bottom-feeders and electro-sensory fish like the paddlefish and more friendly to sight-feeders like striped bass. Chubs and prairie minnows, long adapted to grope around for prey in slow, muddy water are replaced by largemouth bass and carp.

The hand of man has thus transformed the region's rivers into a kind of hybrid, neither river nor lake but both. Tulsa visitors can be flummoxed by the way locals call bodies of water by both names. Grand River is the same as Grand Lake. Part of the Arkansas River in Tulsa is called Zink Lake. The Corps of Engineers has it both ways: they refer to Kaw Lake, for instance, as "a lake on the Arkansas River." But this elides their part in the story. They're not calling it "a lake we made out of part of the Arkansas River."

It all reflects the interesting place we have come to in humanity's relationship to the planet. Control of nature—the mastery celebrated in structures like the Hoover Dam—is no longer uncritically admired. That's partly because we've lost confidence in it. Hurricanes, twisters, droughts—nature keeps offering up proof that we'll never really get the upper hand. And then there's blowback: the mounting evidence of the damage our own hands have wrought. Search a scholarly database for "Arkansas River" for instance, and you reap a harvest of scary sounding research papers: "Flow Regulation and Fragmentation Imperil Pelagic-Spawning Riverine Fishes," "Delayed Effects of Flood Control on a Flood-Dependent Riparian Forest," and my favorite, a paper on the speckled chub from the *American Society of Ichthyologists and Herpetologists:* "Declining Status of Two Species of the Macrhybopsis Aestivalis Complex in the Arkansas River Basin and Related Effects of Reservoirs as Barriers to Dispersal." Translation: You don't get a flood-control omelet without breaking some (fish) eggs.

Faced with this dual problem—we are too powerful; we are not powerful enough—we have dropped the language of mastery in favor of the language of management. But management-speak can downplay the amount of meddling we do. We aren't really managing nature; we're altering it to suit our needs. Why shouldn't we be as up-front about our recipe for reservoir as the aquarium is about its fake coral? Mike McAllister seemed downright reluctant to talk about the state's stocking programs. But an *Outdoor Oklahoma* magazine I picked up in his office provided the stats: last year, Oklahoma wildlife officials stocked around 16 and half million fish in the state's waters: 895,017 largemouth bass, 996,002 hybrid striped bass, 19,039 paddlefish, well over 12 million walleye.

"We don't stock the Arkansas River," Mike told me. But then he did note that the DWC had stocked stripers in Keystone Lake. If I really wanted to know more about it, he concluded, I should drive up to Miami and talk to agency biologists. They were all at something called the paddlefish event. He gave me a map.

"One of the unfortunate things we have to live with is that we've taken species we like to catch and put them places they don't belong," Brent Gordon told me. Brent is Northeast Regional Fisheries Supervisor for the Oklahoma Department of Wildlife Conservation. It was a slow day at the paddlefish event, which is a research and processing station the DWC sets up near Spring River during paddlefish season. Anglers get their paddlefish cleaned and processed for free. In return, the DWC collects research data from the fish, as well as any eggs. The eggs are sold for caviar, which funds the program.

Brent readily admitted that many of the most popular game fish are not native to the region. As we stood at the cleaning table, he laid out how state biologists work to balance the desires of sports anglers with an eye to preserving existing ecosystems. They pay attention to balance: striped bass, Brent pointed out, were first brought here to control crappies. Hybrid fish were created to lower reproductive rates, making populations easier to control. Still, sometimes introducing non-native fish creates problems. Asian carp, a notoriously invasive species, were introduced to manage aquatic vegetation. They ate the plants and then they started eating everything else. Now there are electric barriers in Illinois to try to keep them from wreaking havoc in the Great Lakes.

"A pond or a lake is going to hold so much biomass," Brent says. "You can tie it up with a whole bunch of little fish or a few big fish."

Listening to Brent talk gave me a sense of how much research and science and good old trial and error is involved in managing aquatic Oklahoma. He made it clear that there were pros and cons: things are lost, others are gained.

"The Arkansas River was a perfect example of a big prairie river," he said. "It had minnows and darters and things that aren't on everybody's radar, but you hate to see them disappear." Then again, everybody loves stripers. The sport fishery contributes a lot to the state economy, and fishing is a way of passing conservation from one generation to the next.

"We have a trophy striped bass fishery right in the middle of Tulsa!" he said. In fact, the DWC collects its brood stock right below Zink Lake's low-head dam. But today, he noted, the fish weren't running, because two of the Corps' upstream generators were down.

"If the Corps is generating, they'll run," he said. "If not, they won't." I blinked, thinking for a moment I had misunderstood him. I hadn't. The Corps of Engineers dammed the river so it wouldn't flood, installing turbines to fund the project. That made good striper habitat so the DWC stocked them. Now the Corps must run the turbines so the dammed river will flow so the DWC can harvest spawning striped bass so the hatcheries can raise new fish so biologists can restock the state's reservoirs so anglers can go out and bask in the wonder of nature.

"Anglers are part of the process now," Brent summarized, which seemed almost like an understatement. It might be more appropriate to say that the Oklahoma Aquarium ends at the state line. Or, looked at another way, that insects and fish and anglers and power generators and biologists and water-skiing boaters—whose fees help pay for the stocking programs—are all wound up in one chain of interconnectedness that looks a lot—if you think about it—like an ecosystem.

After talking to Brent, I drove back down to the Oklahoma Aquarium, which is open late on Tuesdays. There was a mellow vibe there as evening fell on the strip malls outside. Inside, a mother moved from tank to tank with her shark-mad son. The Ozark Stream beavers canoodled in their den, visible on beaver-cam. A big-lipped blue catfish hunkered down at the bottom of its tank. The paddlefish cruised back and forth, shoving their spatula-noses into the pancake-flat water. The striped bass floated serenely beside a backlit sign: "Catch a lifetime of memories: go fishing!" They looked like immigrants, hybrids, wild things partly domesticated by the constant human need to remake the world. In short, they looked a lot like us. ◥◣

# OF VICE AND MEN:

## A KILLING

*by Gordon Grice*

A paved road in rural Oklahoma; on either side, miles of rolling grassland, the grass tall and pale with autumn. My friends, a married couple, coming along the road in their pickup truck, ought to have been insulated from the natural world. A motion in the ditch caught their eyes. It was enough to make the man, who had the wheel, slow down; he didn't want to hit a deer. It was, in fact, a deer, but something was wrong with it. They could tell from that one flicker of motion, before they were even certain what sort of animal they were seeing. It had that peculiar spastic quality that suggests incipient seizure, a wounded spine or brain.

They stopped, got out of the truck. The deer saw them, staggered almost to its feet, folded back down. A muscular wave went through it, as if it meant to flee but couldn't get its legs under it. The man eased closer to see. The deer had been gut-shot.

He was a hunter; his wife had always been around men who hunted. He had been hunting this very week, in fact, and both had eaten the venison. They were not the sort to think they could put the thing in the truck and take it to the vet.

The way he saw it, someone had done something wrong. Someone had shot the deer and failed to follow it up, or had not followed it assiduously enough. This unknown hunter had failed to follow the code. A man may kill an animal, but he must minimize its pain. The anonymous hunter was cruel to let the deer go gut-shot. Its death would be painful; maybe dogs or coyotes would eventually run it down, or maybe it would simply die a lingering death. But it would be wrong to say that cruelty was the whole of his complaint. He mainly objected to the broken code.

He is not particular about rules in general. I know him as a hard drinker, a breaker of traffic laws and rules of etiquette; but he doesn't break laws just for fun. Like most of us, he weighs the material advantages and risks, multiplies by the coefficient of his own conscience, and makes a decision. But the rules of killing are something different. In his mind they are not subject to expedience or interpretation. Whoever had done this thing had proven himself less than a man. It is too little to say he had failed at a sort of civic responsibility; he had failed at humanity, or at least at masculinity.

Since he was not carrying a gun, he had to use the hunting knife he carried in the truck. He was not used to slaughtering animals by hand. He had to psych himself up for it. He paced before the truck, working himself up until he was snorting like a bull; he might have been a power lifter preparing for a personal best. The deer might still be a danger to him, but he was past caring about that. His wife was back in the truck, out of harm's way. When he was at full pitch, he strode to the deer to seize its neck in the crook of his left arm and plunge the knife into its heart.

Here's what she saw: Her husband taking on an excitement familiar and, in this context, disturbing. She looked on the man she loved, ready to plunge his knife into the heart of the wounded deer, and felt disgust.

At his touch, the deer seemed to take an electric charge. It stretched its neck and bounded, a hint of healthy motion, enough to carry it beyond his reach. The man ran after it, and though its gait showed he'd been right that it would never recover, it out-distanced him. He ran into the grass, his arms pumping at full run, the knife ready. He ran until the deer was lost in the fluid grass, gone to ground somewhere in that wide and treeless horizon. After that the man wandered, looking for it. The rush gone, he was weak, and even his eyesight seemed less acute than it had been a few moments before. He looked until he heard the blast from his truck's horn, calling him back. ◣

# KAFKA'S NATURE THEATRE OF OKLAHOMA:

## THE CLANDESTINO'S DREAM

*by James Hawes*

Kafka called his unfinished novel *The Man Who Disappeared*. But the fact that nobody outside academia does so is perfectly justifiable, and not just on the obvious grounds that if everyone had respected Kafka's recorded utterances about his works as gospel, his major works would not exist. For all his flaws, Max Brod knew damn well what Kafka really wanted, and his title is bang on the money, for *Amerika* has a good claim to be the first attempt at the Great American Novel of the 20th century (and not just because it contains what is almost certainly the first description of Coca-Cola in "serious literature").

Since Kafka never even saw America himself, this may sound like a strange claim, but his failed novel wonderfully encapsulates the myth of America, as seen from the outside, in the last decade when the gravitational centre of "Western Culture" (even to most Americans) was still Europe.

The story of Karl Rossmann—who travels Kafka's imagined America as wide-eyed as Harry Potter in his first days at Hogwarts (and initially with a similar sense of almost magical privilege-by-birthright)—is that of a youth ejected from a traditional class-based structure (his sexual initiation back home having broken the bonds of social propriety) and sent to a place which is not only the land of freedom and opportunity, but also a convenient place to send people forever.

Not for nothing did Irish communities, right up to the dawn of cheap flights in the 1980s, hold "American wakes" for emigrants: the journey to the land of the free was generally assumed to be a one-way trip to a half-discovered country from where only postcards and money-orders ever returned. This myth of America as the land of (social) death and (personal) re-birth is as potent now as ever.

But the magic which insulates Rossmann at first soon fails, leaving him adrift in a world filled with hierarchies of dominance and subordination that differ from those in *The Trial* or *The Castle* only in that they are naked expressions of the power to hire 'em/ fire 'em, untroubled by any of the ramshackle pretensions to metaphysical underpinning that are so striking in Kafka's Old World power-structures. As Rossmann's dreams fade, his infinite "flexibility" in the labour market is as ironic a commentary on a certain definition of "freedom" as you could wish.

And then comes salvation, in the form of the Nature Theatre of Oklahama (the manuscript misspells the name, having famously been taken by Kafka straight from the caption of a photograph depicting a white-on-black lynching). Here, *everyone* is going to be hired.

Nothing in the rest of the book has prepared us for the Nature Theatre, and the reason is simple: it scarcely belongs with the rest at all. Its genesis is separated by a gap that is not only chronologically substantial, but represents a great chasm in Kafka's creative biography. The body of *Amerika* belongs with the other 1912-13 works which, in the years of Europe's last hurrah, won this well-connected, up-and-coming young millionaire's son glowing reviews and the Fontane Prize (the status of which has been extraordinarily downplayed by Kafka's hagiographers, as has the distinct whiff of insider dealing about how exactly Kafka came to get it). The Nature Theatre, though, is part of the same blaze of wartime creation that is witness to Kafka's new concern with the public, organizational functionings of power, and which also yielded *In the Penal Colony* (which got by far the worst reviews of anything Kafka ever showed the public).

In the Nature Theatre, as in the Cathedral scene of *The Trial* (of which it is a clear relative), Kafka uses references to chiliastic Biblical imagery in expressing the hold that the vision has over the protagonist. In both, we find Kafka's great insight, his creative USP, the breakthrough vision he had in *The Judgment*: the way in which we are ourselves suicidally complicit in constructing heavens we can never reach.

How can we simultaneously believe that a Doorman can be bribed—and that he holds the key to The Law? How can we believe that an organization really can hire absolutely anyone who turns up— and yet not be completely disillusioned when the bureaucrats of that organization demand to see our banal, everyday papers?

Finding himself (fatally?) id-less at the moment of apparent salvation, Karl Rossmann, palpably sliding down the scale of hope, ends up calling himself *Negro*. He might just as well be called *Clandestino*, for his dilemma—and his all-too-human mental fudge—is exactly the same as that of the hero of French-Spanish pop singer Manu Chao's irresistible hit:

Perdido en el corazon
De la grande Babylon
Me dicen el clandestino
Por no llevar papel[1]

The use of religious imagery in describing a search for employment is the creatively vital mismatch, then as now. Like a modern Green Card-less migrant, Rossmann comes to the Nature Theatre somehow believing that it has the impossible capacity to absorb everyone's demands for work *and* deliver everyone's quasi-religious dreams— only to find that the Promised Land is barred, not by an angel with a flaming sword, but by a functionary insisting on a very earthly *papel*.

The Nature Theatre thus illustrates Kafka's most central point: We modern, post-death-of-God people have fatally blurred our desire to be "taken up" by a Higher Power with our quotidian struggles in the grubby reality of a world. All of Kafka's great protagonists—Rossmann, Samsa, Bendeman and the two K.'s—define themselves above all in terms of their work and yet feel the need for quasi-theological answers. But the physical and metaphysical worlds are (as in Kafka's wonderful parable of the crows) by definition insulated one from the other.

No power on earth can provide us both with the paycheck we need and the belonging we yearn for, not even that fantasy world of so many dreams, whether in 1911 or 2011 America. ◼

## ENDNOTES:

1. Translation via lyricstranslate.com: "Lost in the heart / Of the great Babylon / They call me the Clandestine / 'cause I don't carry any identity papers"

# PROFILES FROM THE MIDDLE

# LOST IN TRANSLATION

*by Laura Raphael*

When I was 14, I began a passionate love affair with William Faulkner.

As you might expect in such an unusual pairing (he being dead and Southern, me being lip-glossed and wanting my MTV), we had a few problems to overcome, chief among them the fact that I couldn't understand nearly half of what he was telling me.

He used words I'd never heard—exegesis, perfunctory, ameliorate—and so was like a young suitor who spoke in half-English and half-Italian, or Chinese, or Klingon.

No matter. In the first heady days and months of my ardor, I reveled in the dizzying complexity of his beautiful sentences, the layered depth of the world he shared with me, the sad and searching characters caught in a history not of their own making. That was enough to capture my heart and keep me returning. Or turning, as it were.

But then, impatient with the gulf of words widening between us, I decided to learn my love's full language. I began my vocabulary quest with a paperback copy of *The Sound and the Fury*, a slip of construction paper purloined from art class that doubled as a bookmark, and a pen. Every time I encountered a word I didn't know—doggerel, miscegenation, tautology—I'd write it down, along with the page number, and then I'd keep reading. After every session, I'd consult the dictionary (the bound one that ruled the day before dictionary.com or the "define" feature in Google), turn back to the paperback, and reread the sentence or passage with my knowledge of the word.

Indeed, it worked so well that I can still recall many of them—peripatetic, chimera, unctuous—wonderful words, magical words, words that began to erase our language barrier so that our passion would flourish and I'd finally—one day, maybe— be able to not just read but pierce the deeper meanings of my holy grail: *Absalom! Absalom!*

The discoveries were fun, even if they made me obnoxious. "Hey, did you know that what we're doing right now is *palaver*?" I regaled my friends at lunchtime. "Isn't that cool?" I wrote bad poetry (and made my parents read it) that somehow rhymed *fecundity* with *profundity*. And I'm sure my sister was thrilled to be told to hurry up in the morning because she was "as slow as a *terrapin*." I couldn't help it—using this new language was my way of saying, "Meet my new boyfriend! Isn't he dreamy?"

Something similar happened to the genius filmmaker Guillermo Del Toro when he was a young lad in Mexico. In his case, it was a full-on language barrier: he discovered a monster movie magazine, in English, but such was his love of monsters (and movies) and desire to know more about them, he learned English so he could understand it.

Both cases—my adolescent Faulkner passion, Del Toro's childhood monster movie obsession—point to something fascinating about how we learn the words we learn. Well, not *how*, but *why*.

When I taught English to 7th graders, I tried 1,001 different ways to get my students to acquire new vocabulary. We made word maps, wrote songs, created 3-D play-doh models. Some of these methods even worked. But that's just it—they were *methods*, they focused entirely on the *how* of it all, when I should have been paying more attention to the *why*.

People most often learn new words because they have a compelling *why*. Sometimes it is to please a teacher, or to pass the SAT so you can get into a good college, but more often, the words that stick will probably be the ones you learn when falling in love with a computer geek or trying to understand an episode of *Buffy the Vampire Slayer*. Ultimately, these whys come from wanting to connect with something outside of yourself—whether it's a dead Southern writer and his Yoknapatawpha County, tentacled monsters and their makers, or that cute nerd in your physics class. We need to know that we are not alone, and learning new vocabularies and sometimes even complete languages allows us to leap over natural (and manmade) barriers between people.

One of the stated goals of a public library is to be a resource of knowledge—to act as a kind of "people's university" where all can ignite and explore what interests, excites, and fascinates them. I love being the catalyst for these initial explorations—"Hey, if you're interested in X, you might like Y." But I must admit that my favorite part is when people come in who are already clearly in the thrall of a topic or author, and they just want me to locate the materials that fulfill their unique passions. Antique firearms. Contemporary Irish literature. Raising chickens. Listening to them makes me want to rediscover my own passions—and maybe revisit *The Sound and the Fury* and all of those wonderful words I learned way too many years ago.

I did eventually get around to the intellectual workout of *Absalom! Absalom!*, but I always return to the first novel of his I read, because that is where we fell in love... and where I learned to speak fluent Faulkner. ◥

# BUSTER KEATON WAS NOT AN OKIE

## (HE JUST SAID HE WAS)

*by Jeff Martin*

Several months ago, I was in New York City for a few days, traveling alone and on a tight schedule. But there was one thing I promised myself not to miss. The Jewish Museum, located on Manhattan's Upper East Side, was hosting an exhibition focusing on the work and life of escape artist Harry Houdini. As I toured the galleries, just inches away from his handcuffs, straightjackets, and other props, I wondered, "Did Houdini ever pass through Oklahoma?"

In that spark of a moment, I promised to look into it when I got back to Tulsa. Houdini, as you'll soon learn, actually did have a connection to our fair state. But what I assumed would be a lead role was quickly relegated to that of a supporting character, lending light to a much more compelling and surprising, well, half truth.

I catch myself thinking differently about everything these days. Each experience, every new finding, gets filtered through some sort of Oklahoma-shaped lens.

Perry, Oklahoma doesn't get much in the way of press. The last real nationally newsworthy event involving Perry occurred April 19, 1995. A man driving a yellow 1977 Mercury Marquis was pulled over for speeding on Interstate 35. Hours earlier he had executed the largest act of domestic terrorism in U.S. history. But Timothy McVeigh is nobody's poster child of civic pride. Still, in the 16 years since, nothing else has quite been able to surpass that dubious distinction. But part of Perry's true legacy, its real claim to fame, has been all but lost on the people of Oklahoma.

On October 4, 1895, a century before the Oklahoma City bombing, Joseph Frank "Buster" Keaton was born in Piqua, Kansas. His parents, Joe and Myra, had no real connection to the town of Piqua. But in the days before Dr. Spock and induced labor, babies were often born on the spot, be it in the back of a horse-drawn carriage or the home of a hospitable stranger. It was just two years prior, in 1893, that Joe met Myra while her family's medicine show was traveling through the territory that would later become Oklahoma. But what is a medicine show, anyway?

Though they continued up to World War II, medicine shows reached the height of their popularity in the 19th century. The shows were usually made up of traveling horse and wagon teams selling "miracle cure" medications and other products. These "cures" came to be known as "snake oil," a term now used to insinuate that a product's claims are false. The charismatic leaders of these outfits would suggest to unwitting crowds that these elixirs had the ability to cure any disease, smooth wrinkles, remove stains, prolong life, or cure any number of common ailments. Between the business and hard selling, entertainment was provided to distract the rubes foolish enough to believe these ludicrous assertions. This often included a freak show, a flea circus, musical acts, magic tricks, jokes, or storytelling.

Though the medicine show in this incarnation is a thing of the past, think about those late night infomercials. Same thing, new look.

Myra Edith Cutler (she never took the name Keaton) came from a long line of hucksters, showmen and irascible characters. Her father, Frank Cutler, co-owned the popular Cutler-Price Medicine Show. Though he was suspicious of this young drifter named Joe Keaton from (no kidding) Dog Walk, Indiana, Cutler hired him both to help behind the scenes, and to perform small parts from time to time. In a 1958 interview conducted by Columbia University, Buster recalls his father's early days:

"He first heard about the gold rush in California, so he rode freight cars and bummed his way out to get into that. Not much luck. He got back home. About that time, Oklahoma opened up the Cherokee Strip, so he went into that, and he got himself 160 acres near Perry, Oklahoma. He became great friends with the man going alongside of him at the same time; that man was Will Rogers."

When Keaton talks about the Cherokee Strip being "opened up," he's referring to a second Land Run, which occurred four years after the legendary run of 1889, on September 16, 1893. The "Cherokee Strip" in this case is actually the "Cherokee Outlet," a 60-mile wide strip of land south of the Oklahoma-Kansas border. The real "Cherokee Strip" was a two-mile stretch that ran along the Outlet's northern border, and came as a result of a surveying error.

According to the Cherokee Strip Museum in Perry, "By horse, train, wagon and on foot more than 100,000 land hungry pioneers raced for 40,000 homesteads and the valuable town lots available in the Cherokee Outlet Land Opening." Eventually Joe Keaton acquired two city lots in Perry. But it appears at first glance that Buster, having either heard conflicting or perhaps even exaggerated versions of actual events, didn't have the facts and chronology in order. He speaks of his father returning "a couple of years later" for another land run, what he refers to as "the day of the 'Sooners.'" This reference indicates that Buster is talking about the land run of 1889 as if it happened *after* the Cherokee Strip Land Run. But what he is actually speaking of is the much lesser known land run of 1895. This was the final, and by all accounts the smallest land run in Oklahoma.

So it seems that Buster's recollection is at least based in truth. However, what about that claim of his father's friendship with Will Rogers during his initial land run experience? In the fall of 1893, Joe Keaton was 26 years old. Will Rogers, on the other hand, was about to turn four. It seems highly unlikely that this young child could have been Joe's "best friend" and "the man alongside him," as Buster recalled. In his wonderful 1993 biography on Rogers, Ben Yagoda writes, "Will saved as mementos a business card upon which Joe Keaton, father of Buster and proprietor of a celebrated knockabout act, had scrawled, 'Dear Carl, Give This Boy the Room you have—he's my friend." Maybe Buster never did the math. Perhaps he didn't care about the "truth." Coming from a long line of hucksters and Vaudevillians, what was truth anyway but a malleable tool?

## NOW YOU SEE HIM, NOW YOU DON'T

After leaving the Cutler outfit and striking out on their own, Joe and Myra began working with a burgeoning magician-illusionist named Harry Houdini. A partnership was formed and the "Harry Houdini and Keaton Medicine Show Company" (also called "The Mohawk Indian Medicine Company") was born. At the time of Buster's birth, this was the family business. It was Houdini in fact who gave young Joseph the name "Buster."

"I was 6 months old," recalled Keaton, "in a little hotel we were living at in some town. I crawled out of the room, crawled to the head of the stairs, and fell down the whole flight of stairs. When I alit at the bottom and they saw that I was all right, I wasn't hurt badly, they said, 'It sure was a buster,' and the old man said, 'That's a good name for him.' I never lost the name." The Keaton-Houdini partnership fizzled quickly. Within a year of Buster's birth, the Keatons had ventured out into a new world, Vaudeville.

## 'HOW CAN YOU DO THIS TO THIS POOR BOY?'

When Buster was between roughly 7 and 14 years old, "The Three Keatons," as they would come to be known, were the roughest "knockabout" act around. Joe would do humorous monologues,

Myra would provide the music via saxophone, and Buster would be thrown around in all sorts of ill-advised, yet no doubt hilarious, acrobatic routines. In today's world, parents often feel reluctant to slap a child's bottom in public. A 1905 ad for The Three Keatons read: "Maybe you think you were handled roughly as a kid—watch the way they handle Buster!"

Life became even more nomadic, and young Buster had no real place to call home. He would visit his grandparents back in Perry during the summers, enjoying the peace and childhood adventures that life in the country could offer. After escaping the family act and Vaudeville circuit alive, Keaton headed to New York and met one Roscoe "Fatty" Arbuckle. Fatty gave Buster his entrée into films with 1917's *The Butcher Boy*, in which Buster is smacked in the face with a sack of flour. He was hooked.

What followed is legendary. He wrote, directed and starred in more than two-dozen films including *The General* (1926), referred to by Orson Wells as the "greatest comedy ever made." His amazing physical feats and deadpan delivery made him an icon fit to rival Chaplin. His "golden era" took place mostly in the silent era of the 1920s, but he continued acting and making films well into the '50s and '60s, appearing in such films as *Around the World in 80 Days* and *A Funny Thing Happened on the Way to the Forum*.

## IT GETS IN YOUR BLOOD

Although Buster was a Hollywood man and a longtime California resident, Perry never strayed too far from his mind. In 1957, Sidney Sheldon (later known as an acclaimed novelist), wrote and directed the feature biopic, *The Buster Keaton Story*, starring the nimble Donald O'Connor (*Singin' in the Rain*) as Buster. As part of the promotion for the film's release, the actual Buster embarked on a nationwide tour.

As part of this campaign to promote his own life story, Buster made a point to stop in Perry for a special "premiere."

The film was poorly received and lambasted for its inaccuracies. In her book *Buster Keaton: Cut to the Chase*, biographer Marion Meade writes, "In point of fact, *The Buster Keaton Story* embarrassed him. Reviewers roasted the picture." "Apparently pure fiction," decided the *New York Herald Tribune*. In the film, many details of Keaton's life were altered or completely fabricated. For example, his family was never part of the circus and his father did not die performing in it.

In many ways this biographical embellishment made perfect sense. Buster Keaton was never a real person. He was a character, a performer. Buster Keaton wasn't born, but created. Even his death in 1966 at age 70 seems quite inconsequential, because Buster Keaton lives on. Knowing this, it's completely understandable why those quiet, simple memories in Perry meant so much to the man. As Meade points out, "All his life Keaton had dreamed of owning a home in the country. His most vivid memory was of visiting his grandparents in Oklahoma. He could remember little about the old people or the town of Perry, only the pleasurable feeling of the land and how he hated to leave."

He died in Los Angeles. ◥

# THE MAKING OF MISS HORNET

*by John Waldron*

I've been teaching high school social studies for 18 years, so it's hard for me to be shocked by the behavior of students. But every once in a while, someone manages to surprise me. One day last year I looked up at the auditorium stage to hear one of my students deliver a speech that changed my idea of what it means to be an American.

As you enter Tulsa's Booker T. Washington High School, the eyes of history are upon you. The portraits of women stretching back in a line to the 1930s form a gauntlet, the faces staring slightly down at passersby. Each one was named "Miss Hornet" for her class, as the embodiment of virtue and school spirit. The tradition is nearly as old as the school, founded in 1913.

As you walk the main hallway, a culture of inclusion unfolds. Hair styles change to reflect the ideal of glamour for a young black woman of a bygone era. In the 1970s, the afro suddenly asserts itself, loud and proud. In 1979, the first Asian face appears: a young émigré of Vietnam. That's a good story. A few steps beyond and a white face appears among more black ones. In the last decade, the pattern portrays an explosion of diversity: South Asian, African-American, Caucasian, Hispanic. A reflection of the new America? Perhaps.

Then the last face: a smiling young woman, her hair covered in a resplendent white hijab.

Welcome to Booker T.

The same year the voters of Oklahoma approved a measure banning the practice of Sharia law in the state—a practice I am sure few of us understood and even fewer of us actually witnessed here—the voters of Booker T. Washington high school chose as their Miss Hornet a woman who wore head scarfs and practiced a different religion. If you believe in the power of education to promote appreciation for cultural diversity, individual expression, and freedom of choice, then the appearance of Fareedah Shayeb on the Miss Hornet wall is an American success story. But, as is usually the case, a story offers as many angles as a portrait.

To run for Miss Hornet, you have to fulfill certain basic qualifications: GPA, attendance record, other measures of participation. You also have to pass peer review—selection by a number of homeroom classes. The real showdown takes place at an all-school assembly. The young women and men (there is also a Mr. Hornet) appear onstage and each takes a few minutes to leave lasting impressions on the student body.

Maxine Horner, a member of the class of 1951 and one of the first black women to enter the Oklahoma legislature, once said about BTW: "That school put a shine on you. You walked out of there and you didn't know there was even such a thing as segregation. They put a shine on you and you felt like you could do anything." Looking at the faces on that wall, you see pride, confidence, poise, and power. In those Baby Boom days, the ceremony was arranged by a teacher everybody called "Mama" Bratton. You did not cross Mama Bratton. The ceremony had all the trappings of a royal coronation.

In 1979, Thu-Hong Tran appeared onstage with a bundle of balloons of different colors. Losing one, she said, "This is what happens when you let one person rise." Opening her hand, she released the rest of the bouquet. "And this is what happens when you let everyone rise together." The student body, which had been integrated in 1973, got the message. She still relates with pride her time at Booker T., though she now lives in Boston, where she teaches science.

"Booker T. has a special place in my life," she told me in a 2009 letter about how she tries to emphasize the value of education and discovery to her own children.

Today, the winner of the Miss Hornet contest is one who can turn unknowns into friends. The candidates usually sweep their peer groups, the people who know them best. The freshmen are the largest bloc of students with no real knowledge of any of the seniors, so they form a key swing constituency. To win their vote, candidates usually dance, sing, or perform something silly and outrageous. Raps and funky moves are common. It can be a fun show, and the September 2010 competition was no exception.

Until Fareedah approached the podium.

She'd been a student in one of my social studies classes every year for four years. You couldn't miss her: She always sat in front, always asked questions and follow-ups, was happy to give you plenty of sass. And, of course, there was the hijab. Rather, many hijabs—she was no stranger to fashion, and could go a whole month without repeating her choice of scarf. "You will never see my hair," she told me once, though on occasion I had noticed her scarf slipping a bit.

She was Booker T. through and through. Her mother, an alumnus of the school, teaches in the English department. Fareedah, who is African-American on her mother's side and Palestinian on her father's, was active in student organizations and took the most rigorous classes. She loved the pep rallies and the games, and she was always beaming. Her smile lit up any room. She had experienced some challenges as a Muslim girl in a Midwestern state—stares, awkward questions—but in general she had found a happy home for herself in our diverse student body.

But, could she be elected Miss Hornet by a body of 1,250 students?

I think she remembered the story of Thu-Hong Tran when she prepared her speech. When she reached the podium, she smiled broadly and said:

"Hi, my name is Fareedah Shayeb, also known as the girl in the scarf or as Ms. Asad-Pratt's daughter, and I just want to start out by saying thank you *so* much for nominating me for Miss Hornet! I am going to start by explaining what I think Miss Hornet represents, then the good stuff will come later...

"So, basically, Miss Hornet is the girl in the senior class that embodies everything that is Booker T. So I am here to tell you why I think I could be that girl:

"Number 1, I love Booker T. so much. I know everyone on this stage does, too, and I am honored to be up here with all of them. I also think I represent how diverse BTDub really is. My name is Arabic and it just so happens to mean 'unique.'

"So how many Muslim Miss Hornets have you heard about? Well, I am about 100 percent sure that I would be the first. And, honestly, how many Muslims do you know to begin with? All right, well, how many black, Arab, Native-American Muslims do you know? I know some of you wanted me to rap but I'm not sure that would have worked out very well so I am going to do something else. Because we all have to work with what we are given in life.

"You know some people wonder whether or not I could even fit a crown on my scarf and let me assure you that I can. And I am sure that every single person in here has, at least at one point or another thought: What does her hair look like?"

And then, before a hushed student body, she began unfastening the scarf. Hair tumbled out. She did not sing, or dance, or perform a rap. But she held that audience in her hand.

I was as transfixed as anyone else. It was a beautiful moment. The students voted over lunch and she won, of course. But then something else developed. Fareedah had been wearing a wig! She hadn't actually revealed her natural hair.

The rumor mill had already been turning, of course. Some students had wondered whether her unveiling had meant she was no longer a Muslim. A few were upset, feeling that they had voted under misleading conditions. It's hard for a teacher to sample student opinion on a point like this, so I'm sure I don't understand the public mood completely. But I do know that Fareedah bore the questions with her usual character and courage. She wore the scarf again every day and went about her business.

Talking to Fareedah, I knew that she had given the matter a great deal of thought. Growing up in Tulsa, she had endured the looks and questions for a long time. Her scarf was an endless source of speculation. Coming of age after 9/11 didn't help, of course. And while she is classified as black or African-American, she didn't always fit in with black culture here in Tulsa. She had grown up living in multiple worlds. Maybe this is what had prepared her for the event. When you consider the row of Miss Hornets from the last decade, it becomes clear that the winners are the ones who can cross cultural lines. I think Fareedah was having a bit of fun at the expense of anyone who had ever questioned her: If you think there is something magical about my scarf, or that it defines me as a person, then you deserve to be fooled.

It was as though Andy Kaufman had been elected prom queen.

That was in September. The year wore on and Fareedah was crowned in a beautiful ceremony and her picture was added to the wall. She busied herself with her studies and high-school life. She wrote papers, took exams, applied to schools and hung out with her friends. She was very much the ordinary, if over-programmed, modern American teenager. Life continued, and it turned out that most people didn't really care about the scarf. It's a diverse school after all: We select students on a geographic basis and there is no racial majority on the campus. Since there is no one dominant group, students have traditionally felt freer to express themselves as individuals. They learn to make choices about themselves. In general, the students accept and move on. In many ways, I think they are better than adults at accepting change.

Finals came with a rush, and the year raced to an end. Then, in May, during the Senior Farewell Assembly, Fareedah closed the story. Amid the testimonials and the farewell performances, Miss Hornet 2010 appeared on the stage to say goodbye—in curls. No scarf this time, no wig, and no gimmick, just a bright teenager with a gleaming smile. As she said later, "Why should something as insignificant as a scarf matter? The Qur'an doesn't say that women must cover their heads. It just says to be modest.

"Plus, it's not that great for my hair."

In her own terms, Fareedah revealed herself to a school she had grown to love over four years. She had grown from a precocious freshman into a more mature young woman, capable of making her own decisions about her identity. She was happy and ready to take on the world. Last month, Fareedah wrote to me reflecting on the event.

"People fear what they don't understand and I live amongst people that are chronically misinformed. And that not only does that make my life more difficult because of cultural misperceptions, but it adds another strike against me in a male dominated society."

Ironically, I barely noticed the event. Like most teachers, I was standing in the back of the auditorium talking about schedules or some other minutiae when she appeared on stage. It took me a minute to realize what was going on. Maybe that was because of the student reaction. Some of them already knew what was going on, and some of them didn't particularly care. In the end, the story was not that a Muslim girl was elected Miss Hornet, or that this proved that the school was culturally tolerant. Students don't think like educators, and teenagers don't think like their parents. For them, the scarf was ultimately no big deal.

That's the lesson. ◥

# VINTAGE SMITH:

## THE SAMMY HAGAR OF SYRAH
## PAINTS THE TOWN RED

*by Mark Brown*

WALLA WALLA—The Lost Weekenders were seated on the lawn, awaiting instruction, when their leader emerged from the house holding aloft a portrait of Bob Wills.

"He comes stumbling out with the Sara Bowersock painting," said Scott Large. "For the rest of the two days, Bob went with us everywhere. He was the official mascot—on the bus, in the vineyard, the bar, wherever we went that night.

"The spirit of Bob."

To appreciate how winemaker Charles Smith, his Oklahoma rep Scott Large, Tulsa artist Sara Bowersock, and Texas Playboy Bob Wills go together, you have to understand a little bit about blending. And Lost Weekends.

Smith, Washington winemaker du jour—one of the hottest things in wine since the 1976 Judgment of Paris, when the French got their asses handed to them by the Californians—is the force behind K Vintners, whose "Kung Fu Girl" has been making wine drinkers out of beer drinkers and Riesling fans out of most. To reward the biggest promoters of "Kung Fu Girl," Smith threw a three-day hoedown of food, wine, and controlled mayhem: the Lost Weekend. Oklahoma drank enough of it to earn both Large and Alex Kroblin, his Thirst Merchants partner, spots on the list.

"He started out at 2,000 cases and now he's at 75,000 cases a year, all of it from the same vineyard, all hand-picked," said Large, whose Thirst Merchants owes 10 percent of its portfolio to Smith. "And he makes 'Kung Fu Girl' the same way he makes his 'Royal City' Syrah. You just don't find that."

More miraculous, perhaps, is that Smith found us. Tulsa was not on Smith's radar when Large called and said K wines needed to be in Oklahoma, nor was it when he came to town in the autumn of '09 for a Thirst portfolio tasting and wine dinner hosted by Lucky's on Cherry Street. But Smith has a way of taking over a city's airspace. So after a quick "breakfast, lunch, and dinner" that featured farm eggs, pancakes, lamb sausage—with the 2007 K Viognier, served in a coffee cup—chicken-fried bacon BLT, tuna casserole, cold pizza (in individual "used" pizza boxes) and cold fried quail with sage gravy, Smith and Company went out.

"At some point in the night," Large recalled, "when we were all at the wine bar (Vintage 1740), Charles decided he wanted to pretend he got hit by a car. We'd been going back and forth across the street from 1740 to the Mercury Lounge, getting pretty crazy. So he said, 'I'm going to lay in the street and you guys pull your car up like you just hit me and let's do a photo shoot.' So now there are all these 'dead' photos of Charles at 18th and Boston."

Before he left town, Smith loaded up on T-shirts at Dwelling Spaces; ate back to back to back at Coney Island, Weber's, and Nelson's Ranch House; proposed to the love of his life, a drop-dead Roman named Ginevra Casa, at the Full Moon Café where he, in his words, "proceeded to drink my face off"; and spent some $10,000 at Parkhill on South Lewis. Restocking his cellar from the Lost Weekend.

The idea was to reward 34 wine reps across the country who'd kicked butt in a 2010 "Kung Fu Girl" sales contest. A tireless promoter, Smith uses such opportunities to show appreciation and just plain show off. For their efforts—and their pains—Smith awarded the lucky 34 with a trip to Walla Walla, a multi-course Italian feast on his front lawn, and bag of ibuprofen, water, and phone numbers to the local police and emergency medical units.

"He hit this one guy so hard in the face with his fist," said Large. "Kind of slapped him a little bit. It was wild."

A wine drinker of utmost sincerity, Smith keeps about 2,000 bottles on hand, for personal use. In a game called "Raid the Cellar," a runner from each of five tables ran to the cellar to pick any bottle in Smith's collection. Two rules: One, there had to be at least one other bottle of whatever you grabbed still on the shelf. Two, no sharing with other tables, not even a smell. Breaking either rule would result in immediate elimination and no more wine.

Which, to Smith, must border on hell's own kitchen. Large and the other Lost Weekenders drank, between them, 32 bottles, everything from 30-year-old Dom Perignon to great Burgundies and Bordeaux. Generosity is part of Smith's charm, but the message being served in every glass was one of respect and acknowledgment, of being on the same page.

"The idea is that we didn't serve *my* wine with lunch. It wouldn't be pearls before swine. That's no fun, right? The trip was very little about my wine. It was more like this is what I do, and this is how I throw a party."

So right. Nor would it be a Charles Smith show without a road trip. The Lost Weekend began with a party at Smith's Anchor Bar in nearby Waitsburg, with DJ Howie Piro Intoxica! (the bass player in Danzig, for a stint) spinning records and The Big John Bates Grindshow providing rockabilly and burlesque. Not all of Waitsburg's 1250 citizens appreciated the invitation, though all were invited.

"I was born and raised in Holland, so nothing shocks me," said Imbert Mathee, the owner the *Waitsburg Times,* who covered the event. "They were more dressed than me when I go to the beach."

"I sold 200 tickets to the public," Smith said, in effort to make everybody feel welcome. "So, basically, I created a party around them. It was simply, 'You guys won, you're supposed to be having fun.' Not like some insurance seminar. They got the anti-pitch."

Best part about the Lost Weekend is how close *we* were to hosting it. Explaining his concept, aware of how nutty it sounded, Smith cracked a smile.

"Initially, we were thinking about bringing everybody to Tulsa. We really considered taking it on the road somewhere."

You can see the elements coming together ... concert at the Cain's, coneys and corndogs to soak up the wine, a truck from Parkhill or Ranch Acres, or both, pulled up to the ballroom alongside an EMSA truck, red lights spinning, and a tour bus ready to haul everybody back to the hotel so that the rep from Hawaii who threw up on the guy from Washington wouldn't end up on, say, Boston Avenue with his pleats around his knees and Tulsa's finest ready to add cuffs.

Is this any way to run a winery? It is if you're Charles Smith, *Food & Wine* Winemaker of the Year, the antichrist of the wine trade, its John the Baptist, at least, waist-deep in a steady stream, drinking mead and tearing the wings off locusts, finding converts around every bend.

"Two different Winemaker of the Year awards, 300 points in a row from Robert Parker for 'Royal City.' It's not in terms of volume," said Large, "it's the wake he leaves. The wave he's causing."

"He's very different from traditional winemakers. Not his wines, but the way he markets them," said Philippe Garmy, organizer of the OSU Wine Forum. "It's like heavy-metal counterculture. Each of his syrahs is one of Ozzy Osbourne's children."

"The guy's been a big success, and everybody's realized that, even though he doesn't do it the traditional way," said Duane Wollmuth of the very much a mouthful Walla Walla Wine Valley Association. "He's gained a lot of respect because he has been out there doing it his own way. Charles is definitely making some quality wines. It's certainly not a 'Two-Buck Chuck' type of thing."

Out there meaning the Smith place in Mill Creek Road, the antebellum home of K Vintners, where the ankle-deep Titus Creek cuts a clear if tiny swath between an award-winning vineyard of stone and bone and the bluegrass lawn that laps at the wraparound porch. Out there, meaning, out there.

Why Walla Walla? Why not!

"I didn't move to Walla Walla because this is where the action was," Smith said. "It still isn't here! It was not my intention to get great reviews. I didn't run to get the wreath. I ran to run. The wine business is a gauntlet. If you stop, you die."

Smith isn't even the largest winemaker in Walla Walla, let alone Washington. Walla Walla's Precept Wines owns several brands, among them the Magnificent Wine Co., Smith's first winery, the one where he launched his now-legendary House label (House Wine, Steak House, Fish House). But with his Modernist Project—a series that includes the can't-miss labels "Velvet Devil" Merlot, "Boom Boom!" Syrah and, his calling card, "Kung Fu Girl" Riesling, Smith is making new history.

Smith read the study that said 95 percent of all wine is drunk the day it's bought. The Modernist wines are meant to be drunk now and are priced for a market that doesn't cellar wine anyway. They all retail between $12 and $15 and all come with screwcaps instead of corks, which isn't unusual anymore but still sends a message.

"I'm not trying to trick them," Smith said of his fans and potential market. "I want them to be able to find the good bottle among the 30 for sale with the labels that say something fake, like something 'River' or something 'Lake' or 'Sky.' Mine bucks the trend by not trying to sell it as something you shouldn't have access to, like you're not a member of that club. I want to communicate the language of wine to everybody because not everybody speaks wine. If you use the language that people already have, they'll have easier access to your wine. You're doing them a favor and yourself a favor.

"Wine is for everybody. It's been for everybody forever. It's like bread. It's like tortillas or pasta."

It's partly this realization—that America is about to embrace what Europe has known for centuries—and partly Smith's ability as a winemaker that makes Garmy, among others, fans of the project.

"He embraces a spirit—a paradigm of the pioneer in winemaking. He's very democratic. He has a wine for everybody."

Even the entry-level wines defy industry standard. Other Thirst Merchant lines, like Owen Roe ("Sinister Hand") and Orrin Swift ("The Prisoner"), have caught on with consumers in the market for cool. But their entry level is a bit steeper than Smith's, and they lack his range. "You can either guzzle them, or read them," said Parkhill's Milton Leiter. "You can gloss over, or spend an entire evening. His go either way." Parkhill carries the Modernist line, but not the high-end Smith syrahs—big-sticker bottles better suited to a restaurant menu than a shop rack. "Syrah's a sticky wicket," Leiter said. "Especially $100 syrah. People know cabernet. They know what they're supposed to do with cab."

Leiter fields more requests for the easy-drinking Middle Sister "Forever Cool" Merlot or "Surfer Chick" Sauvignon Blanc than any of his beloved Costieres des Nimes. It's still retail, and that's consumer behavior. And if a wine shop is like a library—lots of titles gathering dust because nobody cracks them—then "some wines are Janet Evanovich and some are Ian McEwan." Meaning some wines are page-turners, while others give pause. What consumer picks which—the sexy thriller or the think piece—depends on that most elusive of labels: taste.

Smith's runs the gamut, and his policy of inclusion allows for monster bottles like the rich, red beast he calls "The Hustler," a syrah so transformed that its aroma of roast pork and flavor of black licorice (Smith doesn't do red) makes it an enticement, if not a steal, at $140. *The Wine Advocate* speculates the 2003 "Hustler" will peak in 2035. By then, the Middle Sister should be well into menopause.

"I like him, he knows what's he's doing," Leiter said. "And if there's growth to be had in the market, it should be there, in that $10-$15 range."

In America, wine tends to flow east, over the divide and into the middle trough. The bulk of it comes from Napa and Sonoma, but also Oregon's Willamette Valley and Washington's Columbia River Valley. It's there, or in the runoff of there, that Smith set up shop.

Walla Walla used to be known for its sweet strawberries and sweeter onions, Walla Walla Sweets, a bulb so fine they named a minor league ball club after it. Since the arrival of Smith—you might say his rise has coincided with that of the region—wine's taken over. Washington wine was on the rise, but Walla Walla remained an unknown quantity. Sweetness aside, you can't build a tourist trade on the strength of an onion. Then Smith bought an antebellum farmhouse on Mill Creek Road and there went the neighborhood. That he slept on the floor his first year and subsisted on Top Ramen and taco wagon is less sexy than his antics, or even his hair.

"I can't say I've always done the right thing. Maybe I drink too much and say the wrong words in front of the wrong people sometimes, but the idea is at least I'm authentic. People look at me like I must be cheating. A lot of people love my wine, and that's awesome. But, as with any business, if you stick your neck out, you're going to get a few lumps and bruises. But, if you stay in your shell, you'll get nothing."

•••

Walla Walla is that weirdest of places, so familiar, so not. You've heard of it, imagine you can … imagine it, only to find that it's hiding in a middle of nowhere more stuck than your own. And if you're coming from Seattle, it's even stucker.

Washington has two uneven sides, green and blonde, the Seattle side and the Other side. The coasts get the traffic and the press, but it's the rest with its Columbia River Valley and wheat fields that run to Canada that's throwing up dust in the world of wine. To get there from Seattle, you cross the Yakima River Valley, where the Rattlesnake Hills rise and the Cascades fade into a lush memory. Further on, toward the confluence of the Columbia and Snake rivers, the land flattens and the hills become round, routine, and endless. There is a suggestion of Big Sky country as the Blue Mountains lay a backdrop over the Tri-Cities area, where the roads and rivers bend.

Walla Walla is a Nez Perce term meaning "place of many waters." And some of the waters turn to wine.

Thirteen miles west of Walla Walla sits little Lowden, home to L'Ecole No. 41 and Woodward Canyon, two respected wineries in the region. Ten years ago, the local wine industry consisted of 30 wineries and 800 acres of vineyards, according to an association timeline. Now it's more than 100 wineries and nearly 2000 acres.

On a billboard there, the new poster child of Washington wine lurks behind a pair of shades and more hair than all of Winger combined. Welcome, says Charles Smith, a California escapee who rides the golden hills around Walla Walla on his 1947 Harley-Davidson Knucklehead, hair pulled back in a five-pound knot (unleashed, it swells and falls like the Gardens of Babylon), the summer sun raspberrying his Ray-Banned face—the pariah and pretty boy who puts his money where his oversized mouth is.

"You gotta spend some to get some," Smith says of his $8400 roadside attraction. "Eventually they'll come here. Maybe."

Here is a place far removed, especially for a guy like Smith, who left his west Seattle wine shop to come make wine, and before that left Copenhagen, where he'd followed his Danish girlfriend, where he hung out in night clubs managing rock bands, where everybody had really long hair, wore rock 'n' roll clothes and was good-looking, Smith claims, "because they're Danish."

"I moved here to do what I do, and I didn't know it would turn out like it did. Come on ... Copenhagen, Denmark, to Walla Walla, Washington? I moved here because this is not for the faint of heart."

Smith set up shop in Walla Walla ten years ago, but his evolution in wine goes back to his youth, when he slaved in restaurant kitchens as a 19-year-old. As a busboy at the Palm Springs Hilton, he dumped a tray of orange juice into the lap of

Roger Smith, then-chairman of General Motors (and soon-to-be subject of filmmaker Michael Moore's *Roger & Me*.)

"The head chef chased me out of the kitchen with a large knife," said Smith, who turned 50 in August. "But he weighed 300 pounds and I was a skinny, poor 140, and I ran backward giving him the finger. Until I fell, then I got up and ran really fast."

When he stopped running, he came to his senses.

"You work in a kitchen you work the longest hours, doing the dirtiest work to get paid the least. That sucks. I realized that the guy who had the best job was the guy who bought the wine. He gets to come in later, leave earlier, and he gets to drink all night. I'm like, 'That's my kind of job!' I excelled at that."

A Sacramento native whose dad sold used cars until he starting cutting hair under the sobriquet "Mr. Andre," Smith embraced his calling and honed his chops. He lined his mouth with the yeast and must of untold vintages, starting in his own backyard.

"I learned in Napa Valley," he said. "And I don't mean sitting in the tasting room listening to Windham Hill. I'd be in the cellar, the music's cranked, and you're drinking wine from a barrel. That's where it's going on."

Smith got his first glimpse of Washington not in a winery but from the front seat of a Chevy Astro van. He and one of his charges—Sune Rose Wagner, lead singer of The Raveonettes, a Danish indie rock duo—were on a three-month road trip doing what rockers do best.

"That's how I found it. I wasn't looking for it. I didn't even know I was going to make wine. I had $5000. I could hardly make anything."

•••

A high-plains drifter of sorts, Smith came to Walla Walla not to blend in but to stand out. Walla Walla is known for its cabernet and merlot, but Smith wanted to be known for something else. He made his name with K Syrah, a cheeky play on words but more a brand, like the kind you iron into a screaming calf. A head-high, white "K" greets you at the winery entrance on Mill Creek Road east of town.

"I was tired of the stupid Euro stories behind American wineries. Some faux chateau thing. I live in America and I wanted my winery to sound like it. You don't even have to be able to fuckin' say it and you'll be able to buy it in a wine shop. It's got a fuckin' K on it!"

When I met him, in his spanking-new tasting room that used to be a garage, the fire-red Bob Wills T-shirt wrapped around his trunk seemed to have shrunk a size. "I was home 23 days between January 12 and June 21," he said, "and weigh 23 pounds more."

Smith does nothing like you'd expect a winemaker to do it. He drives a car in the Walla Walla Fair demolition derby—a big, black sedan called the Battle Wagon, whose roof has a white skull with a black sword thrust through it. He calls it his day in the dunk tank. Hanging from the steel-and-wood rafters of his tasting room are four 90-pound woofers, for rocking the hard way when a dinner party or wine event calls for it. Cases of wine sit on pallets next to minimalist furniture. Light pours in like golden chardonnay. A menu of the available vintages is cut-and-pasted on a large wall in that graphically compelling, black-and-white K Vintners way. A six-glass "maximus" runs you $5.

"They'll get loud," Smith says not of the wines but the woofers, "but in a way that just sort of envelops you. It's a real, even sound."

To prove it, he cranks them and the air in the room begins to hum slightly. Your ears don't shrink but your chest swells. An older couple doing a tasting begins to swing dance. Napa seems a world away.

A few nights earlier, he'd thrown out the opening pitch for the Sweets, Walla Walla's representative in the West Coast League, where they play the likes of the Bend Elks, Bellingham Bells and Wenatchee Applesox. He'd been using his spacious tasting room as a bullpen.

"I actually have a great knuckleball," he said. "When I was 14, I was a pitcher. My knuckleball floats and then drops … kaboom! Then I get to the park and they hand me an onion." So he threw a fastball. "A strike."

Not all of Smith's pitches find the plate. A few years back, he bought the Pastime, an Italian mom-and-pop that had been serving Walla Walla for 100 years. The move did not sit well with some of the locals, who view every move Smith makes with suspicion.

"He told me he's known around town as the guy who killed a pastime," said record-store owner Jim McGuinn. "But the guy was going to sell it to somebody."

McGuinn runs Hot Poop, one of those now-lost record shops that reek of incense and independence, where fans roam the stacks in silence beneath Beatles and Clash posters, concert fliers and a garage-like assortment of rock 'n' roll bric-a-brac. McGuinn, whose long hair has grayed from the rock of ages, was the town mystery man, before Smith came to town.

"I compare him to Levi Strauss," he said, meaning Smith left the safety of the city for the gold in the hills. "There are rumors—he gets his money from dealing heroin, he's a rich boy whose parents set him up. None of which is the truth.

"I like him. He took the edge off me being an eccentric."

"I got here at the right time," said Smith. "The economy was bad. People weren't buying plane tickets but they were still buying wine. The ones who were buying $40 bottles started buy $20, and the ones buying $20 were buying $10."

"People do the same thing with speakers," said McGuinn, who sold Smith a piece-meal stereo system when he hit town. He credits Smith's success to the mystique he removes from the traditionally reverent wine trade. "The only brands I usually buy are Annie Green Springs and Red Mountain. But my wife and I were in Bayside, Maine, one Fourth of July and we pulled into a little roadside shop for provisions. They had fireworks, watermelons and both the 'House Red' and 'Kung Fu Girl' Riesling. I thought, 'Wow.' "

For all the notoriety, K Vintners comes not from a plan but an impulse. When he first got to Washington, Smith fell in with another transplant, Cayuse Vineyards' Christophe Baron, the first Frenchman to establish a wine estate in Washington. Baron begged him to come to Walla Walla, and sweetened the pot with enough fruit for 15 barrels of wine.

"He said I'll give you the grapes and you can pay me when you sell the wine," Smith said. "He was from France and he wanted somebody else who was no-bullshitting, tough, Euro-centric, knew about food and travel. He was my partner in crime."

"They each had capes made," said Large, "and they would walk around Walla Walla in these capes and I guess that's when people around there started to hate Charles. Nobody can keep up with him."

Or them. Baron and Smith were the "Toxic Twins," known for entering a restaurant with seven bottles of wine between them. "They'd say, how come you guys bring so much wine? We'd say, 'In case one of them's corked.' We'd drink six bottles of wine at dinner. We were the passionate ones."

Thus emboldened, Smith walked into a Seattle bank in June 2001 to ask for a line of credit. He'd been making wine for two years. He flipped through his business plan—an underwhelming three-pager with a spreadsheet and a couple of flowcharts—and explained away his odd job history. He spoke Washington wine with enough authority to get a sit down.

"They said we really like your idea and the people you're working with all look really good. I said, 'But I have no collateral.' They said, 'We'd like to taste your wine.'"

They all met, Smith and some bankers, at a wine bar the following day, he with a range of anonymous bottles—he had no bond and, hence, no winery name; he had no license and therefore no label.

"I filled their glasses, and they swirled it around, smelled it, tasted it, then the guy reaches out his hand and says, 'You got a deal. We're going to give you $250,000 and this wine is your collateral.' I'm like … 'Awesome.'"

With the line of credit, he was able to find a property, create a label, buy a house. The latter dates to 1860. Coyotes roam near enough to keep the Shih Tzus under wraps. Behind it is the building that houses K Vintners. There's a temperature-controlled warehouse lined with barrels, and a tasting room he used before opening the one downtown. On the back of the house, down a rickety flight of steps, is his personal stash. It holds a couple of thousand bottles. Smith grabbed a French one and led the way.

Upstairs in the living room, a stray cat padded across the floorboards. The master sat back against a sofa, sipping at his glass, oblivious to the toy dog licking on his bare feet. Feet that soon will crush 120 tons of grapes—7000 cases worth. He'll climb into the 5-foot deep crusher and pound 4 feet of fruit into submission. He's looking forward to the exercise. "I can't wear most of my shirts and pants," he said, resting the glass of Chateauneuf du Papes on his belly. "A Domaine du Caillou. Pretty good, huh?"

Of course. It was good enough for popes. But I wanted to sample some of the house wine. He went to the cellar and brought up a pair of bottles: a 2005 vintage of "The Deal," from a place called the Wahluke Slope, and a 2007 version of "The Hustler." After the Chateauneuf, they were a mouthful. Like a dose of Jack Kerouac after a diet of Victor Hugo.

Smith, I learned from several videos online, would rather drink than talk, masticate than pontificate. Wine notes are a slippery slope, and he can talk tannins and balance and structure with the best of them. But he's better at just talking.

Smith does a wine called "Old Bones," a syrah that *The Wine Advocate's* Robert Parker gave 99 points and deemed "hedonistic." Its label (black-and-white, always) depicts a sword fight to the death, pitting against each other two crowned skeletons who can't and won't be killed. The story behind it goes:

When the house on Mill Creek Road was homesteaded in the mid-19th century, there was a log cabin there. In it lived a Native American who led a band of Indians out of the Blue Mountains. His name was Old Bones, and he befriended the man who owned Smith's house. Together, they would make trips to trade with the Indians of the Columbia River.

A small vineyard now sits between the house and the big K that marks the entrance. Smith was going to name the vineyard "Old Bones" in honor of those who'd come before him. But in the year the first vintage was ready for release, his neighbor died. He was an Indian named Phil Lane. And now, he has a vineyard named after him, with a clear-running, half-foot deep stream that separates it from the bluegrass lawn that surrounds Chateau Smith.

•••

Tulsa and Walla Walla share two things, anyway—both sound more Indian than they now are, and both are seeking to be known for something by somebody from somewhere else. Smith found a sweet spot on the nowhere side of Washington to make his wine, an "oasis in a sea of wheat," a fellow transplant called it. But the middle of nowhere is a state of mind. Who knew that, when the wine revolution came, it would be led by a pig-tailed warrior girl pitching a sleepy German varietal? Who knew America, and Tulsa in it, was ready to take Riesling and like it?

"I was told it was going to be my kind of place," Smith said of our town. "I didn't go there because I was selling a huge amount of wine there. They liked what I was doing and embracing it and I wanted to come. Size-wise, for what I do, Oklahoma is an over-performer for its category.

"It's like me—I'm an over-performer for my category."

Smith could have stayed in Seattle, could have stayed away from Tulsa, could be 23 pounds lighter and however many pence none-the-richer. That's just not how he sets the scale.

"I had to give up a lot to come here, and I didn't give up that to get the jackpot. I got sleeping on the floor making 15 barrels of wine. What I have now is something different because of what I put into it, luck and timing and everything else.

"This is kind of the frontier, for people willing to risk it all."

We're in his Suburban, driving north, through so much waving wheat that I begin to get sea sick. The landscape has lost its scope. We could be anywhere, and nowhere.

"There's a camel," he says, interrupting a conversation on his cell.

Another time he points out a pioneer cemetery, its crosses glowing bone white in the western sun. "I tried to buy that," Smith said, pointing to a cinema. "I wanted to do Sunday matinees, you know, for kids? Because there's nothing to do here."

Here is nowhere fast. Waitsburg, a little 'burg on the eastern edge of Washington, so far below Spokane that even Idaho is closer. Here is where the Smith ethic of pick yourself up by your bootstraps takes on significant meaning.

"I got $460,000 in the town," he tallies. "It gives this place value—value to me. You have to contribute to the community, to invest in it somehow."

One way would be to buy the defunct American Legion Post No. 35 and paint a big, black-and-white Stars and Stripes across it. Which is what Smith did, calling it the Anchor Bar, inspired by American naval prowess and, well, a lot of grog in an airport bar. The locals crucified him for it, but Smith is on a crusade undeterred.

"My business is wine but I make my life rougher by doing some of this other shit. I mean, I make over 200,000 cases of wine a year. So, if I make over $10 a case … "

Which is his way of saying, put up or shut up.

"It keeps me busy. I'm not doing this other stuff for the money. I'm doing it because it's what I want to do. Turns out that it's work too. I want to contribute and do something. If it doesn't exist, stop complaining and do it yourself. I don't want to listen to anybody complain. So I said, screw it, I'll do it myself."

Smith's sounds like one of those stories that only happen in Danish fairytales. He got the girl, he got the millions, he's never lost the hair. When all's said and drunk, Smith will have had it his way—like Sinatra, emerging from the pack, but more like Sid Vicious, all bloody and shitty, in skinny jeans and rock 'n' roll tees and riding Harleys to nowhere and back. If only you could bottle it, whatever's fueling him.

"The only problem is if your success implodes you and you become a jerk. You have to be willing to do everything and risk everything to do it. To thine own self be true. That's my thing." ◀

# MOTHER ORPHA:

## THE BEER, BRAWLS AND BITCHES
## BEHIND TULSA'S TOUGHEST BAR

*by Natasha Ball*

The 1970 Cole's Cross Reference Directory—an avocado-green volume in the corner of the fourth floor of Central Library—lists 112 W. Fourth St. as the home of Orpha's Lounge. Upstairs, at 110 ½, was Orpha's Hotel. On the same page, there's a number for Oral Roberts University and its Dial-A-Prayer line, and a listing for the Orpheum Building. There's also a personal address tucked among the commerce listings: Orpha Satterfield. She's been dead more than 10 years, but she continues to receive mail at the address.

Orpha's Lounge, Inc. management says that the bar opened in the three-story Irving Building in 1958. In the years between, the street and phone directories show Satterfield operated a bar northeast of Orpha's on Second Street, a place listed as the Post Office Bar. A space in her name lingered in the direct vicinity until she bought the Irving Building with the help of a small loan from her son-in-law. She moved in above the lounge two years after it appeared in the listings on Fourth Street, between the Coney Island Hot Weiner Shop and the Downtowner Motor Inn.

Satterfield, who also owned and managed apartment buildings at 1901 Riverside Drive, ruled her properties from behind a desk on the second floor on Second. She'd sit there watching daytime TV in the breeze of a small desktop fan, her presence like gravity on tenants and what they owed for rent. Her neighborhood was flush with attorneys' offices, stenographers services, insurance and financial companies, hotels and barber shops. When her family came to town to visit, she pretended to live in an apartment at her 19th-and-Riverside property, the one with the wrought-iron fence and award-winning gardens.

Satterfield—who in her later years looked not unlike Momma in *Throw Momma From The Train*—had been in Tulsa since the mid-Fifties, when she worked at Bishop's Restaurant. The Norman-born Orpha Mae Gibbs, whose name means "neck" in Hebrew, served the governor, local celebrities and entertainers at the downtown lunch spot. It was a far cry from the clientele she served at her mother's restaurant and at the Burger King in Bristow, where she worked as a teenager. By the time she was 18, she'd married William Satterfield, an oil refinery worker. She was a housewife before she stuck herself out as a bar owner and landlord.

Orpha's Lounge, Inc. was in Orpha's name until 1996; she died at her Mansion House apartment in 1999 at the age of 85, on the first day of June. She was survived by at least 20 children, grandchildren, great-grandchildren and, yes, great-great-grandchildren, many of whom resided in Oklahoma at the time of Orpha's death.

"If someone showed up at her place hungry, Orpha made sure you were fed," her obituary read. "If you needed some cash, she could find an odd job for you to do. She would cook holiday meals and feed anyone who showed up." A former tenant of hers remembers how she'd offer beer coupons to anyone who paid their rent on time and in cash. She made mothering a lucrative business.

Since Orpha's time, the neighborhood along Fourth Street has changed a bit. The BOK Center opened in the fall of 2008, putting Orpha's Lounge on a thoroughfare between a couple of Tulsa's renovated hotels, a vast inventory of surface parking lots and the 19,000-seat arena. It brought nearly 200 events and more than 360,000 ticket holders to downtown in 2010. On nights when the BOK Center doors are open, the crowd at Orpha's turns into a mix of regulars and ticket holders, sharing cue sticks and turns at the jukebox.

•••

Orpha's Hotel is now a set of 18 efficiency apartments, lining the halls of the second and third floors with single occupants and communal bathrooms. Jerome Garvin, an Orpha's Lounge regular, manages the business. He can't say how many fights he's gotten into downstairs. It's not because he'd rather not say. It's because he's lost track.

"The BOK arena has had this drastic ripple effect on downtown, especially Orpha's," he said. "They get so much business from people going to and from the shows that they were forced to clean the place up. There aren't stabbings there anymore."

Jerome was living in one of the apartments when the owners of the building asked if he'd be interested in managing the property. He was the resident who'd been around the longest when the last manager quit, so they offered him the job.

The apartments rent for about $100 per week. It's a rate that Garvin said serves as a stepping stone for residents of the nearby homeless shelters, the people on a first-name basis with the women who tend the bar downstairs. He said the old hotel is just as storied as the lounge, allegedly serving over the years as a drug house, a whorehouse and a residence for oil field workers during Tulsa's boomtown days.

"Managing this place has been gratifying, but it can also be really disappointing," he said. "There's a reason that person is on the streets. Some people make it, others don't. When they don't, and it's at my expense, it bothers me bad. I don't like to kick people out when they don't pay their rent, but yeah, they gotta go. No pay, no stay."

•••

It was Thanksgiving Day the first time Lee Sales went to Orpha's. According to the tradition established by Orpha herself, the bar offers a full spread on major holidays. Sales ate supper and washed his hands of the place. He didn't return until years later. He took over as manager of the bar about three years ago.

"The people who ran this place after Orpha would let people get piss-on-themselves drunk, and then they'd just drag them out the front door and leave them," Sales said, shifting his large frame in his barstool. "When I first started to come down here, you'd have to step over people to get into the doorway."

His first order of business once he stepped in as the main man was to shoo troublemakers.

"There are a lot of places I can't go here in town now," he said, grinning. "Some of the people I had to kick out I liked, but they had to go. When I took over, EMSA was in here three and four days every week. Someone would go into a seizure, or someone would get into a fight. I mean, God, it was pretty bad."

The 61-year-old Sales—whose congeniality and smile belie his history as the manager of some of the roughest bars from New York City to his native California—drives to work at Orpha's nearly every day from Wagoner, a round trip of about 80 miles.

"Where else can you work and get paid for shooting pool?" he asked, his smile showing from under his white Fu Manchu. The back of his gray mullet had curled with sweat. "Audrey's the one who really runs things. She's the ramrod. Anytime someone's causing trouble, I tell them, you can deal with Audrey."

•••

Audrey had been behind the bar for three years when Sales took over at Orpha's Lounge. She's a westside girl, brought up in Garden City, the riverfront neighborhood known for its shotgun shacks, refineries and how it took the brunt of the flood back in '86. She's built like a linebacker, and she carries herself like she'd be the only grandma to play the strongman game at the fair and win the five-foot teddy bear. Though she wouldn't look me in the eye, she called me honey when she pointed me toward an open barstool at Orpha's.

The interior of the lounge is situated so that everyone, especially Audrey or whichever bartender is on duty, faces the entrance. Everyone sees anyone who walks through the door—what they're wearing, what they're carrying, the color of their skin. The barflies studied me with something between suspicion and something like incredulity. Maybe they thought I was there to pass out tickets to everyone who had double-parked their junked-out shopping carts.

There's a small door along the east wall of the bar. It's easy to miss because the wood of the door matches almost exactly the wood paneling on the walls. Sales told me that he'd heard Orpha rigged a dumb waiter/elevator behind that door, and that she used it to go between the bar and her room upstairs. Behind me the walls were covered in signed dollar bills and birth announcements, scrawled on printer paper with photos of babies Scotch-taped to the bottom. Below were Easter Sunday's pool tournament brackets, barely readable in the light of neon signs.

In June 2008, *Tulsa World* reported a stabbing at Orpha's. A young man picked a fight with a few patrons. Audrey, the bartender on duty that night, told him to go. Her back was turned when she felt the man's knife rip twice through the skin on her back.

"Who told you that?" she asked, looking up at me from underneath her long, dishwater-colored bangs as she dug for ice under the bar. She was wearing an extra-large Orpha's t-shirt, the kind that looked like she'd bought it at an airport. "Yeah. I let my guard down, but he got it, too."

She explained that a few regulars pinned the offending customer onto a table.

"I beat him senseless," she said, looking toward the door. "I just wanted to draw blood."

Two days later, Audrey was back behind the bar. For the time she was out, it was Misty, another long-time bartender at Orpha's, popping tops and pulling drafts. Not long after Sales took over, Misty added Orpha's to her family tree as well as her resume—she married Sales's son, and now they have a baby boy. Ashley is the newest member of the staff, and though she's too chatty to be tough as nails, Sales thinks she has potential.

•••

While Tulsa's Banana Republicans sipped martinis at the bar on the roof of the Mayo Hotel and lounged at the tables on the oasis-like patio at Arnie's, a trio of drunks wearing dirty jeans and truckers' hats sat slumped over the bar at Orpha's. One shouted repeatedly for Audrey as she uncapped bottles of three-two beers for a couple of pool players.

"Audrey's a pretty gal," Sales said. "She's got beautiful blue eyes. But I've watched her come out from behind that bar, and when she does, her shoulders drop and her blue eyes turn to little, tiny red spots. She gets on them ol' stocky legs and whenever she grabs you—she grabs you on about a half a run, low—and she'll carry you straight through that door. I've seen her do it more than once."

The eyes of everyone sitting at the bar were on Audrey and this man. She turned and put her hands on her hips, and her head nodded as she shouted in the man's face: "What do you want, you old bar drunk?"

He giggled, like a little boy who says dirty words solely to get his mother's attention. He only had a few crooked, yellow teeth. I could see that Audrey was laughing too. For awhile she propped herself on her elbow and joked with the man and his friends, until a regular shuffled to the bar and wanted to trade her a CD and an old desk calendar for a bottle of beer. ◣

# HIGHS AND LOWS IN
# BRADY HEIGHTS

*by Michael Berglund*

Miss Anne lifts a rainbow-colored scarf from the small cage sitting on the picnic table in her backyard. Angry black eyes on a white, ratty-furred face peek out through the metal mesh. "A possum," Miss Anne, my 80-year-old neighbor, tells me. "I caught it in the cage last night."

It is Saturday, and while she'd been trying to catch this possum for months, she didn't anticipate that the little guy would inconvenience her by sneaking into the trap on the weekend. She tried to call animal control: closed until Monday.

"You know someone who needs a possum?" she asks.

I don't. I don't even have the guts to trap a possum. We had a possum family that lived in our tree for a summer, and when my partner and I would come home late at night, they'd be resting on a low branch, their eyes glinting from the reflected porch light. Despite my partner's reassurances that they're harmless, I'm certain they're demon-possessed and out to get me.

Fortunately for her, Miss Anne doesn't share my paranoia. In fact, having lived next to her in the Brady Heights neighborhood for the last six years, I've learned one key trait about Miss Anne: she's resilient.

Miss Anne moved to Brady Heights in 1964. She's raised three children in the neighborhood. She's suffered the loss of her husband. She's watched the neighborhood transform from a safe, family-oriented neighborhood to a hotbed of racial strife; she's experienced the exodus of neighbors to south Tulsa, watched as empty houses became dilapidated, hoped as new neighbors moved in to revitalize the historic homes. Through it all, Miss Anne lived in the same house, sat on the same porch, watched the neighborhood bloom, wither and re-grow.

"We bought this house in 1964. We'd been living in an apartment across from where the Tisdale is now," she says. "We were wanting more room, and I used to walk down Latimer to catch the bus. I saw a 'For Sale' sign, and so we contacted the lady and bought the house, and we've lived there ever since."

Miss Anne leans down to inspect the possum closer. It inches towards the back of the cage, bares rows of sharp teeth, and hisses. "Oh, now, come off it," Miss Anne says gently, "you'll be fine." She sees me step back and reassures me. "He's just scared," she says. "Nobody likes to be caged, right? He'd never hurt you." I don't feel better.

"There were a lot of kids who lived here who went to Roosevelt and Central High School and Emerson. It was a real homey neighborhood and everybody knew everybody else and would sit on the front porch and wave when they saw people in the evenings. There were enough children of different ages so that there was a lot of companionship and fun things for them to do. It was the kind of neighborhood where everybody looked out for everybody else's kids, you know, just like a small town would. In fact, it was like a small town in the city."

The mid-60s, according to Miss Anne, changed the neighborhood. The Civil Rights movement was gaining steam in Middle America. In 1963, the NAACP Youth Council of Oklahoma City began sit-ins at lunch counters. In March of 1965 local and state police in Alabama used violence to stop marchers attempting to walk from Selma to Montgomery. The atmosphere in Brady Heights began to reflect the racial tensions occurring nationally. Miss Anne believed in the message of the Rev. Martin Luther King, Jr., and she worked to instill his message of peace and equality in her children. Friendly interaction between blacks and whites was commonplace in and around the neighborhood, but in the mid-60s, at times, groups of African-American teens from adjacent neighborhoods, feeling empowered by King's message, forgot the ideals of non-violence that sat at the core of King's dream for America.

"A group of kids knocked my son Tony down and beat him up," recalls Miss Anne. "It scarred him emotionally more than anything. And he came home and said, 'Mom I wanna know, you always say there's as many good blacks as there are bad ones. Where were those good ones when they were beating me up?' And I told him, 'You know, those good ones were just as scared as you were.'"

The neighborhood began to change, as did the perception of tranquility in Brady Heights.

"People started moving south," she says. "For a long time there weren't hardly any children at all up here."

The condition of the historic homes, once built and lived-in by historic Tulsa figures such as Tate Brady, G. Y. Vandever, I. S. Mincks and "Diamond Joe" Wilson, started to deteriorate as they were left abandoned and neglected. A once upper class, fashionable Tulsa neighborhood fell into relative obscurity.

Through the tumult that occurred over the next 15 years, Miss Anne remained devoted to those in the neighborhood. In one instance she befriended two elderly sisters whose house had become virtually unlivable.

"They had a hole in their roof. One slept on the floor and the other slept on a chair."

Miss Anne tried to convince them to move to healthier conditions in an assisted living facility downtown. After much cajoling, they finally did, but the house remained dilapidated.

Another shift began when the Brady Heights Neighborhood Association (BHNA) formed in 1980. Wes Young, a Tulsa Race Riot survivor, was elected the first president of BHNA, and he set to work to list Brady Heights as the first Tulsa neighborhood on the National Register of Historic Places. Miss Anne suggests that since then, families are moving back into the neighborhood. She hears the sounds of children in yards again, and she boldly walks through the neighborhood to check on those around her. When my partner and I leave town, we don't worry about our house. Miss Anne has our phone number.

"I don't know how it is down south, but I don't think they're as close-knit a neighborhood as it is up here, and I really wish that people would become that way. We really have lovely neighbors up here."

In addition to "lovely neighbors," the neighborhood boasts some of the most unique homes in Tulsa. From styles such as our Greek revival home, to a mansion in the style of Robert E. Lee's Arlington home, to prairie style, to the only Queen Anne style home in Tulsa, Brady Heights encapsulates a time in Tulsa's history when divisions such as class and race mattered less than expressions of individuality.

I take one last look at the possum as Miss Anne places the scarf back on the cage. When I realize he's just as scared of me as I am of him, he doesn't seem as frightening. I ask her what she's going to do with it.

"I don't know, but I sure can't keep it," she replies. As I walk back to my house, I see her gently pick up the cage and walk towards a stand of trees behind our houses. She sets the cage down under a weathered sycamore and opens the front door. ◥

# HEAVEN AND HEART:

## THE TENSE PAST OF MICHAEL BEEN

*by Thomas Conner*

**M**ethodist church basement, northwest Oklahoma City, 1987. Yes, there is wood paneling. Yes, the carpet is shag, a rich cobalt blue. Yes, a threadbare pool table, a stereo with illuminated VU meters, two speaker cabinets taller than I am at age 16. About half a dozen of us have shown up this evening. I attend church youth group for two reasons. One, that look on my parents' face when I say, "I'm going to church"—I can dash out with that line and come home late. Two, Sondra might be there. I've been enduring youth group since I got my learner's permit because sometimes I get to drive her home. Tonight she's here and wearing that shimmery, fuzzy, opal-colored sweater, and tonight the group is going to talk about God and pop music, the spirit and the flesh, love and lust—and I'm supposed to figure out which is which.

The discussion topic is titled "With or Without Who?" and centers on U2's new single ("With or Without You"). As in, who can't Bono live with or without? Is this a God thing or a woman thing? We talk about other songs, other bands, and inevitably we get to The Call. That band's singer, Michael Been, is from Oklahoma City, too, and I suspect he's seen his share of church basements and shimmery sweaters. We listen to "Everywhere I Go," from The Call's "Reconciled" LP the previous year, and it's a step beyond Bono's conflation of religious yearning and gut-wrenching desire. Everywhere Been goes, he thinks of _____, looks for _____, needs _____. Years after Sting stalked his human prey in "Every

Breath You Take," Been is either a monk considering his maker or, given the increasing urgency of his pleas ("I *neeeeed* you!"), utterly infatuated. He doesn't sing like a man who gets filed next to Bill Gaither and Michael W. Smith down at Sound Warehouse. He starts barking and yelping and moaning, and Sondra's doing that thing where she tucks her hands inside the sleeves of that sweater and then leans back and stretches. "*Smiles, eyes, powers to confound me,*" Been sings, low, patiently. Then his voice thins, gets tighter, on the verge of something: "*I lose my nerve / Your voice, it echoes all around me.*" God's voice, or her voice? I'm hedging, praying to both. I'm 16, and I just can't see the freakin' difference.

•••

Those were heady days for youth pastors across America. Pop music afforded them new ways to connect with the kids. A band of session geeks called Mr. Mister scored a No. 1 hit with a blatant hymn titled in biblical Greek, "Kyrie." Amy Grant made a pop record with synthesizers and wore leopard prints on the cover. By the time U2 released *The Joshua Tree*, bearing songs such as "Where the Streets Have No Name" and "In God's Country," our youth group topic was inevitable. God had once again taken an interest in the devil's music.

This was the environment in which The Call thrived. But The Call — even the band name could be a religious allusion, or not — was just the peak of a lengthy career for Been (pronounced like the legume, not the past participle), one in which a deeply personal tug-of-war between spirit and flesh had played out within a large, tuneful catalog of songs. Back and forth he went, from Christian bands with earthy sounds to roots-rock bands with spiritual songs — always swinging widely between heaven and heart. But on Aug. 19, 2010, the latter lost the battle. Been, 60, was backstage at the Pukkelpop music festival in Belgium — he wasn't on the bill, his son was — where he collapsed of an apparent heart attack.

•••

It's 1997, and, after being AWOL most of the decade, The Call has released a greatest-hits compilation ahead of a new album, "To Heaven and Back." For promotion, Been films a chat with a "star" interviewer, Kevin Max. The choice is meant to be ironic; Max is the lead voice in a trio called dc Talk, then at the vanguard of the mid-'90s resurgence of Christian pop music.

By way of asking a question, Max makes a statement about The Call: "That's what people want to hear from The Call. They want to hear the fight between the principalities of powers."

Been agrees. "I think we separate life too much from spiritual," he says. "I don't know what it is. I was talking with a friend of mine just last night. One of my favorite authors is a guy by the name of Frederick Buechner, and Buechner wrote about the trouble with, like, church. The trouble with church is we all go in and sit quietly — it's totally unlike the other seven days of the week and the rest of the pretty much other 23 hours of Sunday. It's this one hour when we have to be in and be so reserved, and it's tense and it's quiet and everyone gets real uptight if the kids are making noise. He was saying this kind of thing should be done in the midst of children running around playing and having fun. We separate this flesh and blood, nuts and bolts, children laughing, screaming, Grandpa over there snoring — all of that is supposed to be part and parcel of life."

He follows with a story about seeing Martin Scorsese's 1973 film "Mean Streets," which opens with Charlie (Harvey Keitel) in a Catholic church, holding his finger over one of the candle flames. He's practicing, building up a pain threshold. When Charlie was a boy, he watched a priest do this for a long, long time. Charlie's opening lines to the film, in voiceover: "The pain of hell has two kinds. The kind you can touch with your hand, and the kind you can feel in your heart, your soul. The spiritual kind. And you know, the worst of the two is the spiritual."

Immediately, The Ronettes' "Be My Baby" kicks in.

"I thought, God, it's spiritual, and then, 'Be My Baby,' " Been says. "Rock 'n' roll and the spiritual — all this stuff became one thing to me. Finally my life really turned into this kind of struggle between spiritual and the flesh, between 'Be My Baby' and that holy candle."

•••

Years earlier, 1988, Been was actually on one of Scorsese's sets. I didn't even recognize him as the Apostle John when I first saw Scorsese's adaptation of *The Last Temptation of Christ*, after elbowing my way through protesters outside a Memphis multiplex. Here's a different story of the life of Jesus, not as an incorruptible deity among men, but a divine being in a human body — and thus subject to the same doubts and desires inherent to the form. His temptations are real. He finds himself, like all of us, struggling to do God's will.

"When the old authors first wrote the Bible, they had this guy Jesus," Been told the *Los Angeles Times* that year. "He's a man, everybody knew he was a man, everybody knew where he was born, they knew he died, they knew he had followers, he had a reputation as being demonic and revolutionary and every other word at the time that they called heretic. And then these guys who wrote the New Testament had this massive job of proving to everybody that this man was God. So the emphasis of what they did was on [the man's] God qualities, divine qualities — which are all accurate, all true, to me. ... But 2000 years later, the job's reversed. You have to remember he was a man, because if he wasn't a man and didn't go through everything we went through, it wouldn't mean anything to me.

"I remember at one point in my particular life, somebody saying to me if I was in a lot of pain or struggling or doubting, questioning my life, in that kind of turmoil, and somebody would say, 'Well, Jesus knows what you're going through,' I would've said, 'No way does he know what I'm going through. Not if he's God. Not if at any time he can call upon his God side and rise above the problem. He wouldn't really know it. If he did know it, it would be patronizing, condescending."

•••

Been was raised in Oklahoma City but moved to Chicago when he was 12. He saw Muddy Waters and Jimmy Reed, and he toyed with comedy (even beating his pal John Belushi in a state comedy competition). His swings between heaven and heart began there: He formed a band called The Saints, then joined two bands already in progress: Aorta and Lovecraft.

Been first helped turn Aorta from a middling psychedelic band, to a country-rock band with Christian overtones on 1970's "Aorta 2." Been loved Dylan, Van Morrison, especially The Band (whose members Garth Hudson and Robbie Robertson eventually recorded with The Call). Whenever Been picked up an acoustic guitar, "Knockin' on Heaven's Door" wasn't far behind.

"We got in to see The Band [after a Chicago concert]," said Chicago-based jazz guitarist James Vincent in a recent conversation. Back then, he was named Jim Donlinger and was Been's songwriting partner in Aorta and Lovecraft. "For him it was like meeting The Beatles. That's where it was for him, that pop-oriented, maybe slightly country music with big ideas in it, sometimes spiritual, sometimes very earthbound. That's what changed Aorta and really made Lovecraft. You can hear the beginnings of Michael's thoughts there, anyway. There was always some religious component to his songs, but not in a way you could call gospel, you know? ... We weren't writing gooey love songs, either of us. We were trying to make a statement. Some of the things we wrote about were almost — we were kind of fascinated by death, I guess. Don't know what that was all about. One song we wrote together was about somebody who had a consciousness after death. It was that person's perspective of what the experience was like. I can't remember what it was called. It was serious, though. Michael was serious. He wanted to understand it. He wanted to understand it all."

•••

The rest of the '70s find Been sporting a sculpted mullet and bouncing around different bands, looking for the right middle ground between the spiritual and secular. At first, he fell in with full-fledged Christian bands, playing bass on an album called *Laughter in Your Soul* and with the family gospel band 2nd Chapter of Acts. His next two bands were named for more sensual pursuits: Fine Wine (to which Been contributed the songs "Heaven Knows" and "I Wonder If It's All Worth It?"), and The Original Haze, a name shared by a particularly potent strain of marijuana.

By the time Been and Musick formed The Call, New Wave was beginning to wash ashore a propulsive strain of rock 'n' roll that welcomed Been's instrument, the bass. The connective tissue between the black-and-white beat and the melody's Technicolor, the bass flourished in the romantic corners of New Wave music, driving both sides and sometimes blurring the distinctions entirely (New Order, Japan, the beginnings of Duran Duran, the end of Roxy Music). Been's bass, next to the drums of Scott Musick, a fellow Oklahoman who'd moved to San Francisco with Been and been behind the kit in Original Haze, drove much of The Call's music.

New Wave also was populated by many like-minded idealists—Bono in U2, Mike Peters in The Alarm, Mike Scott in The Waterboys, Jim Kerr in Simple Minds — inspired by the righteousness of punk but also the arms-wide scope of '70s arena rock. Here, Been's illusions of grandeur had plenty of room to roam, between heaven and earth, and a driving style to support and enhance the urgency of their messages.

The band had its moment in the sun. The Call made music that was shown on MTV and played in church basements. It wasn't wholly religious, and it wasn't completely secular. By the band's second album, *Modern Romans* in 1983, they opened with "The Walls Came Down," a superb rock hymn about Jericho that never mentions Jericho. Instead, it turns the city back into a fable, a story, a symbol, and like so many Call songs, it turns into an allegory of modern war. *"I don't think there are any Russians / and there ain't no Yanks,"* Been sings, drawing the song to a conclusion by pointing out and trying to knock down a contemporary wall, *"Just corporate criminals / playing with tanks."*

A ying-yang dichotomy pervades The Call's catalog, often in clever ways. Songs include "Day or Night," "Flesh and Steel," "Back From the Front," "With or Without Reason." He even seems to cop to it: *"I've been tortured by this riddle / and I don't know how to stop"* ("Too Many Tears"). In "The Morning," he sings exuberantly of the spiritual (right?) things he does want: *"I wanna live, I wanna breathe, I wanna love hard / wanna give my life to you."*

Also in that song, one of his best, he again admits: *"I'm divided / but I've decided / it's my nature."*

•••

In a 1997 interview, I asked Been whether The Call was a Christian band.

"Certainly not in the definition of it today, where there's an entire genre of Christian rock,'" he said. "We're not part of that. This just had much more to do with the way I was raised and the way I learned how to write and express myself. I was born and raised there in the Bible Belt — it's classic Southern guilt. Those religious ideas got a hold of me as a kid, and none of it struck me as spiritual. It was all rules and threat and punishment and fear. You hang onto those things later in life, and they come out. I'm no peddler of Christianity. It's just the language I use."

The issue was hotly debated in some Christian circles, especially as the religious pop music market became a bigger commercial concern. A September 1990 article in Christian Century magazine, "The Call's Cry in the Wilderness" by Brent Short, analyzed the band with scholarly detail.

"Unlike much of 'contemporary Christian music,' The Call uses no religious rhetoric and attempts no proselytizing," Short wrote. "Their style is at once driving, confrontational, rhythm-oriented, vulnerable and self-deprecating. ... Their records show not a trace of the self-righteous theologizing and Bible-quoting that ruins so much 'Christian music.'"

I wrote about pop music for the Tulsa newspaper throughout the '90s, as the ghetto of "Christian rock" was overcrowding. I interviewed a lot of Christian rock acts — dc Talk, Third Day, Audio Adrenaline, Jars of Clay. Every one of them told me how much they hated (er, struggled with) the "Christian" pigeonhole. These were Been's children, young songwriters living their Christian faith not in a bubble but in the world. They were writing songs that weren't merely modern-language transcriptions of psalms, and they couldn't understand why their occasionally religious lyrical content damned them to a distant corner of the record shop.

"The odd person will come out to one of our shows and realize that we're playing the devil's music because it's too loud. What I want to know is, exactly what decibel level does the devil come in at?" Peter Furler, singer for the Newsboys, told me in 1996. "We're not trying to play to please the mainstream or to try and please the Christian market because either way you lose. We try to stay focused and do what we do best, making sure we feel our own convictions that we're doing the right thing. ... But I don't want us to be just a Christian version of Pearl Jam."

"I think the best thing you can say about a song — whatever experience I had writing it — [is that] all the feelings are so universal," Been said. "Experiences everyone goes through, just different circumstances, different names, but it's all similar. If you can write a song [to which] someone can go, 'I relate that to this part of my life' — then you've really done it. That's the best you can do. The most you can expect is to spark somebody's life that they've got going."

As he sang in "With or Without Reason" (with or without who?):

*How you gonna tell your story*
*Are you gonna tell it true?*
*Either with or without reason*
*Love has paid the price for you.*

•••

Beer and barbecue joint, Tulsa's 18th and Boston district, 1997. Yes, there is Budweiser neon. Yes, there are two sauces on each table in pointy-tipped bottles. No, it's not the kind of venue The Call expected to be playing the year they released a greatest-hits collection. But the place is packed, shoulder to pork shoulder.

Been walks in, and suddenly I'm sorry I've come. I'm ashamed of my reasons. He's heavy and moving slowly. There's more of him for gravity to love. He sets up a stool behind his microphone — God, he's going to sing sitting down, a big broken body, like B.B. King. It's going to be the kind of night where he just sits still, the kind of night where he just won't move. He's squinty and blotchy and every square inch the aging, also-ran has-Been.

But spirit conquers all. The crowd claps and the band lumbers into its set, the usual mix of new songs and greatest hits, and Been's voice purrs and growls. He sits on the stool and creeps toward its edge. He slips into "Oklahoma," his most potent lyrical blend of God the father and Mother Nature, and his low voice rumbles like the approaching storm: *"We were shakin' in our beds that night…"* His legs twitch, his feet start scuffing the floor. *"There was movement in our hearts that day…"* He wants off that stool.

Steamrolling into the catalog, Been finds himself once again restating the determination of his belief. He begins: *"I've been in a cave for 40 days…"* He wants to give out, he wants to give in. He sings with closed eyes, he chews his lips between lines. Drink orders are being shouted at the bar. He still believes, through the lies, the storms, the cries, the wars, he still believes. Someone's brought their kids, and one of them, a little girl, twirls around in front of Been, at his feet. Tossed on the waves, through the darkness, despite the grave, he still believes. Through cold, heat, rain, tears, crowds and cheers — and someone actually cheers. Others follow, mid-song, whoops and hollers. The electricity is crackling now, the voltage ready to spark.

Been drives toward the end of another laundry list of things that will not deter him, and finally cries, "Oh, I still believe!' — and he's off the stool like a shot, like it exploded. Red-faced, sweating, he grabs the microphone and spits his sermon. *"I'll march this road / I'll climb this hill / upon my knees if I have to."* More cheers, noise, cacophony, everything church is not supposed to be. *"I'll take my place / up on this stage / I'll wait till the end of time / for you like everybody else."* ◥

# PLAIN HUMOR

# WESTWARD WHOA:

## GAY COWPOKES SADDLE UP TO TEACH AN OLD SPORT SOME NEW TRICKS

*by Sheila Bright*

I'm sitting in the stands at the Sooner State Stampede amidst the smell of grain-fed cow manure and the clink-clank melody of metal. The steers standing near me snort their way out of the chute before unwillingly participating in a wrangle and release program. The crowd whoops, hollers and moans as the cowboys and cowgirls hit the dirt, then dust off the backside of their tutus and saunter out of the arena.

This ain't my first gay rodeo. I have friends who are serious contenders and once traveled the gay rodeo circuit. They have the belt buckles, expensive horses and bragging rights to prove it. Still, it's been awhile so it takes me a few moments to get used to the blur of rhinestone belts, bad prom dresses and tangled Barbie hair mixing it up with rawhide rodeo reality.

Nothing shakes up the cowboy culture more than a cowboy in a dress. At the 2010 Sooner State Stampede and other gay rodeos across the country, the cowboys wouldn't be caught in the arena without one—at least not in the Wild Drag event.

An audience favorite, Wild Drag features three contestants: one male, one female, one drag partner likely sporting a Goodwill castoff and a bad wig. A steer is released from the chute, two cowboy/girls chase it down, catch it by the rope then push and prod it toward the drag queen/king who must ride it past the finish line until all four hooves cross it. The steers apparently don't like taffeta or men with bad lipstick applications for there is a lot of bucking going on.

Next up, Goat Dressing. Two contestants—one wearing Fruit of the Loom briefs on his arms—stand 50 feet away from a goat on a rope. A whistle blows, the men sprint toward the tethered goat, turn it upside down and slide the underwear over its rear hooves quicker than you can say "Yippe Ki-Yay."

Panties on a goat may look like comic relief, but it's serious business. You can win money for this.

## COWBOY/COWGIRL UP

You don't have to be gay to compete in the gay rodeo, but you usually are. For some participants, it's the chance to show off their rodeo skills. For others, it's a chance to simply show off and experience acceptance in another arena. There is more than an emotional investment required for the rodeo. It takes a lot of monetary investment to be a serious contender, especially in the roping events. A good roping horse can cost thousands of dollars. Rough stock events, which include bull and steer riding and bareback bronc riding, can be real bone-crushers. You can train for a year just for the chance to stay a few seconds on the back of a beast. You can easily crack a rib. Explain that injury back at the law office.

## THE DIRECTOR

Rodeo director Tim Dickmann worked hard to return the Sooner State Stampede back to Tulsa for the 2010 season. Volunteers landed a site—Bridle Creek Ranch in Sperry—and rustled up enough sponsorships to cover the costs of the October event. Some 71 contestants rolled in from as far away as Canada to compete in traditional rodeo competitions like bareback bronc riding and barrel racing, as well as the camp events like wild drag and goat dressing.

Back in 2002 when the Sooner State Rodeo Association was first formed, its goal was to give gay, lesbian, bisexual and transgender people in the Tulsa area a chance to participate in western-related events. They didn't ride into Rodeo Town with rainbows blazing that first year. Instead, the event logo featured a rainbow printed only in black-and-white for fear of anti-gay backlash. Today, the banners, posters and event programs send a clear message that this is a rodeo of a different color, many different colors, proud colors. Still, there is a major kink in taking the Sooner State Stampede to the next level. It centers around privacy.

"We do run into the problem that we need more people to attend the rodeo to make it raise more money. More money means more publicity. More publicity means more exposure," explains Dickmann. "And there lies the problem: Some of our contestants still aren't out of the closet so making the rodeo more known is going to take away some of the freedom that they experience here."

## BEHIND THE SCENES

As owner of Bar M Rodeo Company, which supplies stock for rodeo events, Mike Pershbaucher thought he understood the world of rodeo until he got a call in 1996 from someone needing steers and bulls for "a funny rodeo."

"We were operating out of Sulphur, Oklahoma, and, honestly, I was a little embarrassed to tell anyone about the job at first," says Pershbaucher. "But I loaded up the stock, drove to the arena and watched how these cowboys and cowgirls poured their hearts into everything they did. Now, we tell everybody because it is a great organization, and I laugh all the way to the bank."

Bar M Rodeo Company supplies the stock for more gay rodeos than anyone else in the United States. Pershbaucher and his straight cowboy crew travel the gay rodeo circuit from Ft. Lauderdale to Palm Springs. He's been hit on once at a rather rowdy campfire after party. His friends quickly put the cowboy with the malfunctioning gay-dar in his place. And there's been an unexpected bonus: "Gay guys have good-looking straight female friends. Who would think a straight guy could go to a gay rodeo and get hooked up?"

Because of the camaraderie, laughter and pride of seeing serious and not-so-serious gay cowboys learn the rodeo ropes, Pershbaucher enjoys the gay rodeos as much or more than the multitude of small rodeos he attends across this state. Still, after years of learning to understand the culture and proudly defending it, this straight cowboy faced another challenge about four years ago.

"That's when I became a Christian," he says. "Morally, I admit I did struggle with it for a while, but then I realized that there are a lot of things we do that we don't always agree with. I've made a lot of good friends that I might never have allowed myself to know if it weren't for the gay rodeo."

•••

At the 2010 Sooner State Stampede, only a few vendor booths lined the wall. Shullbitters boasts the slogan "Hang Around And We Guarantee You Will Get Some," and sells rhinestone belts and leather-scented lotions. A few steps away, a huddle of men best described as burly were bunched up around the Green Country Bears table. They are the kind of men you expect to see at a tractor pull or a feed store in western Oklahoma or a cattle ranch in Osage County. That's the point.

A sub-group of the gay community, Bears describe themselves as "friendly, fun, cuddly, frisky, teddy bear kinds of guys." They don't shave their bodies or say things like "You go, girl." Many are packing a few extra pounds and lots of facial hair. Their vanity isn't on display quite as much as the designer-clad "Twinkies," or so they say. Dressed in Wranglers and XL shirts, the Bears and their cubs (men who prefer Bears) struggle to find their place within the tight-ab-waxed-chest world prevalent in the gay community.

"We are just as gay as any other gay person," says Curtis, who still hasn't come out to his family and friends. "There is nothing more prejudiced in a gay community than prejudice within the gay community."

And so they hand out literature, wear buttons declaring "I just look straight," compete in the rodeo events and offer support to other gay men who don't fit the stereotypical gay man mold. They sport shirts featuring a bear paw and muted rainbow colors. Even in a predominantly gay crowd, they tend to form their own den of comfort. Many of the cowboys have spent years working cattle on Oklahoma ranches and learning the cowboy ways through 4-H or Future Farmers of America. For others, a lifelong search for acceptance has landed them in the foreign world of rodeo. They have bought horses and learned to ride not because of a love of the wild west, but because they have a love that needs room to roam. Wide open space where a man can be a man and love a man at the same time.

Coming out of the closet in Redneckville is frightening and dangerous, the men say. Staying in can be a perpetual nightmare.

"There comes a point when your fear of not being happy outweighs the fear of being found out," says a spokesman for Green Country Bears. "Everyone reaches that point eventually."

## RODEO QUEEN

Anita Richards, a drag queen often seen performing at Renegade bar in Tulsa, has spent years gluing on fake eyelashes, wriggling into tight shiny dresses and teasing her hair to staggering heights—all in the name of entertainment. So going all cowgirl glam for the 2010 Sooner Stampede was just another day in the office except for the manure-laden dirt floor that can ruin a good pair of heels if you don't watch your step.

One other difference: Anita usually only dresses in drag when there's a paycheck in sight. This gig—Miss Sooner State Rodeo Association 2011—is a freebie for a good cause.

Besides offering rodeo competition for the gay and lesbian community, most gay rodeos boast a fund-raising arm. Entry fees, sponsorships and event ticket sales provide funds for local charities each year.

"There is an overall general acceptance of the gay population in the Tulsa community, but we still have a way to go. I want to do my part whether it's by supporting the equality center or promoting the SSRA," says Anita.

## OVERHEARD AT THE GAY RODEO

Gay cowboys and cowgirls are funny. Not funny as in "Look there's a cowboy dressed in a mini skirt," although that's funny too, but funny as in nearly everything they say makes you laugh until you're snorting sawdust. It's like a celebrity roast with no celebrities and no FCC bleep control.

"My finger just went up that calf's ass." "I'm sure it wasn't the first time."

"On any good day in Tulsa, you can see a bad crossdresser. You just paid $4 to see me."

"I didn't eat enough Wheaties for that fucker."

A quote from a rather germaphobic steer wrangler: "Always wear a latex glove when you're sticking your hand up something."

Heckling is a sport all its own at the gay rodeo. As the contestants tighten their reins, strap up their chaps and readjust their blinged out belts, crowds of their friends shout out phrases like "Ride 'em bitch" and "It's on Daddy." Dudes, dudettes and everything in between may fall off the bull in a mili-second or not even make it out of the chute at all, but as long as they fire off a quick one-liner or provide a good laugh, all is well in the gay rodeo world.

"Do you ladies ever get hairspray on your phone screen?"

"Those steers are serious today."

"I'm going to take a nap during all this roping crap."

"Oh, he dropped something shiny. Leave it to the gay guy to spot the bling."

"Butch up!"

"Ride 'em like you did last night."

Sure, the International Finals Rodeo sports top bull riding champions, expensive horses and live television coverage, but the International Gay Rodeo Association ropes in a running commentary of sexual innuendo and belly-busting humor that you just can't find in the Wranglerized world of a ThunderBull event.

Midway through every gay rodeo, the light-hearted mood shifts as a riderless horse enters the arena for a memorial recognition of contestants who have lost their lives in the past year. Although not AIDS specific, the ceremony draws special attention to the fact that the disease still claims many friends.

It is in that special moment that you realize there is more to this rodeo than cheap costumes and high-dollar horses. You see friends sling their arms around the shoulders of friends. You see cowboys take off their hats in respect while others tip forward their hats to hide a few tears. You see a community coming together for the sake of memories: the good, the bad and the sometimes ugly. ◥

# RODEO DAZE

*by Barry Friedman*

It's the manure that gets to you.

Saturday, August 6. It's the final night of the 25th Annual Pawnee Bill Memorial Rodeo, and we're at the Lakeside Arena, two miles outside of town, and it smells like every animal here has suddenly and simultaneously defecated.

"You have to get used to it," says Melissa, my girlfriend, who grew up in southwest Kansas near meat processing plants, feed yards and flatulent livestock.

"And why are we here two hours early, anyway?" she asks, standing in the heat (101° according to the last bank) in the dirt parking lot.

"Why? I hear ten thousand people will be here, that's why. By the way, glad you wore shoes, considering what you're four inches away from stepping in right now?"

"And what do you know about it? You're from New York. You ever been to a rodeo?"

No.

We drive back to Harrison Street and decide to eat at Click's Steakhouse, rather than El Vaquero, which is open but has no cars in the parking lot. We see a sign for the rodeo.

*Advanced tickets: $6 per night. 3-Day Pass $20*

We can't be reading that right.

We are.

I'm thinking even without the rodeo in town, Click's is packed on Saturday nights. Kids with spurs, teen girls in boots and cutoffs, and XXL men in XL large shirts stand outside. A man inside, sitting with his wife, is trying to calm down his children. His youngest is screaming, his wife is bouncing the older one on her thigh" —a thigh, I imagine, that's significantly larger than the one he married. The man's head is in his hands.

He can't be older than 20.

There's a story, it's on the menu, that when Click owned the place, someone ordered fries at dinner, something Click did not serve. "Who ordered the @!#?@! fries? They can go across the street to the @!#?@! Tastee Freeze for that!"

You hope the story is true.

Click is long gone; I ordered the @!#?@! fries.

Traffic is now bumper to bumper on the way to the arena. Up ahead, we see a panting dog, standing on a toolbox in the back of a pickup, his head moving in and out of the open window of the cab.

"Write that down," I tell Melissa, *"Mangy dog in back of a pick-up."*

"The dog isn't mangy."

It's a little before seven. The rodeo starts at eight, but we want to see the Pawnee Bill Memorial Rodeo Pageant, whose application includes the warning: *NOTE: Should the Pawnee Bill Memorial Rodeo Queen or Teen Candidates become married or pregnant during her reign, she will automatically forfeit her crown, buckle, saddle, banner, and trailer to the first runner-up.* The application also alerts the girls that each night after the competition, *You will return to your lodging accommodations and will not leave for any reason.*

Animals aren't the only ones locked up after a rodeo.

Employees of Hampton Rodeo Company, the event's producer, collect admission by the sign in the parking lot that reads ...

*Contestants and Vendors Keep Right/ Everyone else go straight*

We go straight.

Gordon William Lillie [a.k.a Pawnee Bill] produced Wild West Shows in the early part of the twentieth century, including, "Pawnee Bill's Great Far East Show," where he hired Mexican cowboys, Pawnee Indians, Japanese performers, and Arab jugglers.

Rodeo is an American show.

"Rodeo is not my God anymore. You must be born again in the name of Jesus Christ."

The man speaking is in the booth on the north side of the arena, sharing his testimony, asking us to repent, reminding us that if we break one commandment, we break them all (I think about the crackers we stole from Click's), and promising to be around tonight for "fellowshipping."

The beauty pageant contestants-- Princess, Teen, and Queen categories--all in heavy makeup and sequin shirts but none from Pawnee ride in on horses. Before the winners are crowned, a girl is named Miss Congeniality, one wins for Horsemanship, others are runners-up. Every girl is something. They leave, one last ride, fast, around the dirt field, waving and smiling.

A man on a tractor--he's on his cell--the giant rototiller behind him unearthing the ground, begins circling the pit. He's the *Zamboni* machine operator between periods of a hockey game.

The announcer for the event, Danny Newlin, a bald man in a cowboy hat with an unruly mustache and a wireless mic, enters on horseback, circling the arena, extolling the wonders, beauty and metaphor of the sport.

"I am the luckiest man in the world," Newlin says, "because I get paid to do what I love. I could talk forever about the rodeo."

At times he does.

The IPRA (International Professional Rodeo Association) is in Pawnee this week as part of the second annual Oklahoma Twister Rodeo Series. Last week, Salisaw; next week, Hanna, Oklahoma. Summer for rodeo is like spring for the NBA. Someone wrote that schedules like these make professional sports more like vaudeville.

Newlin keeps making reference to tonight's *performance.*

Rodeo contestants are paid only if they win, place or show in an event (they're like horses in that respect). If they finish in the top eight at the end of the IPRA season, they will also be awarded a commemorative belt buckle. Most, though, are lucky to cover expenses. There's no guaranteed money, no salary. They will pay the $80 entry fee tonight, sleep in trailers and pickups on sun-baked fields, do their own laundry, crack ribs in the mud.

Chris LeDoux sings about it.

One cowboy, Newlin tells us, got married earlier today.

"Wonder how long his wife'll put up with it?" he asks.

I'm a comedian, I've traveled. I can tell him. Three years max.

It's 8 p.m. The stands are full. Ten thousand? Maybe not, but still more than attend a weekend of Tulsa Shock games. The performance starts after the national anthem, after Newlin proclaims that John Wayne is his hero, why vegetarians would benefit from eating burgers, and how God needs to protect us from terrorists. I look across the arena, up one section, down another, and other than the African American in the blue Hampton shirt who helped us find parking and who is now on horseback on the south side of the field, I see only white faces.

A rodeo clown on the infield wears a *Stillwater Steel and Welding Supply* sign that hangs to his ass. He and Newlin have a routine.

"Hey, Danny," the clown says, "heard someone say you were sexy and wanted to meet you."

"Really?" says Newlin, in mock excitement.

"Yes. The note was signed by Tom and Steve."

During tie-down roping, a particularly brutal event, a calf is released, chased, thrown to the ground (it's called flanking) and then tied up by at least three of its legs, upside down. One of the calves breaks free from the rope (the pigging string). It lingers for a moment, like a ballplayer admiring a home run, then proceeds to run around the arena, a victory lap, a triumphant *Fuck You* to both the rider on the ground who wanted to humiliate it and a crowd that came to see its subjugation. Melissa, who *did* go to rodeos and got drunk afterwards with guys who had initials for names, calls out, "Run, little calf, run!"

Soon, though, it is corralled, returned to the staging area—its moment of freedom, *schadenfreude*, vindication over.

The clown enters the arena driving a red jalopy with a man in a wig in the backseat and a "Just Married" sign on the bumper. The skit ends with the clown throwing large brassieres out of a suitcase, the "groom" chasing, a little kid in the driver's seat, and the car backfiring and doing wheelies.

I start thinking about that scene in *Diner* where Fenwick asks Boogie, "You get the feeling there's stuff going on we don't know about?"

I walk down to get a water, a lemon Popsicle, something to combat the stillness and stench of the night air. I find a port-o-potty. Waiting, I am fourth or fifth, I see an elderly man to my right who is clearly angling to cut in line. He is slightly bent, crazy thin, an OU hat on his head. My urge to go is not great and my prostate is just a guest here; I should let him in. He has an aging urinary track; this is a home game for him. But there's a principle at stake, a protocol.

*No.*

He looks at me; I look back. He inches forward; so do I. We're two lanes of traffic merging into one figurative and literal shithole.

"The line's back here," someone says, saving me from having to. I'm not sure I would have.

"An old guy tried cutting in line to use the bathroom," I tell Melissa when I return.

"You let him, I hope."

During the Wild Cow Milking competition, one of the cows collapses. According to IPRA rules, cows in this event can only be milked on all fours; so while the Roper and Milker stand over it, the cow struggles to get to its feet. Something is wrong. It stands for a moment, then falls again. It gets up, wobbles, falls for the third time. Breathing, but erratically, it lies motionless. Rodeo personnel ride around it, watch it, but don't attend to it. Newlin rattles on about upcoming events and thanks more sponsors, a diversion often used by rodeo announcers when an animal is in trouble. Eventually, the cow stands, steadies itself, and limps to the pen. The crowd cheers, as if the animal, like some athlete, was headed to the locker room for x-rays.

"Time to slaughter," said a man a few rows up.

We've been here three hours. A big man in a shirt that looks like a Rorschach Test walks towards us. He is familiar; he was at Click's earlier. He can't possibly be hungry, I think, but he's eating a corn dog. He stops, obstructing our view. It doesn't matter. I've had enough. The events, and there are still four to go, are maddeningly similar--more roping, more tackling, more jerking of animals, more cowboys being thrown to the ground.

Football, baseball, and basketball unfold like novels: fourth quarter interceptions, ninth-inning home runs, 3-pointers at the buzzer; rodeo is a collection of short stories in search of a narrative: defiant steers, weekend cowboys chasing dreams, young girls with pageant smiles vying for the trailer, a debate over whether it's sport or animal abuse, small Oklahoma towns in the dead of summer.

"You ready to go?" I ask.

Melissa gets up before I finish the question.

Earlier in the evening, former Pawnee Bill Rodeo Queens threw promotional items into the stands. We caught a sparkly pink ball with a "Sonic" logo.

"Got the ball?"

"Got it."

We thank the woman behind us who has been nice enough to swat bugs and mosquitoes and other flying evil from our backs all evening.

"You leaving already?" she asks.

Behind the stands, we see a girl with an autographed photo of Dakota Missildine, Miss Rodeo USA 2010. We pass the Christian Rodeo Fellowship trailer, the root beer concession stand, and then maneuver our way through men and women and children in cowboy hats and Wranglers. We stop to watch the cows and steers and bulls, lying in a giant holding area, waiting to play the part of the Washington Generals, and then walk to the exit, stepping over and between six piles of freshly deposited dung that inexplicably lead to the parking lot.

# A BEAVER'S TALE

*by Van Eden*

"Ruth line two."

Ruth and her two sons are leasing my house while I'm off doing other things. That's the good news; the bad news is Ruth never calls with good news.

"There's a big ol' beaver in the creek," says Ruth. "She's huge. The boys are excited."

I think about how excited the boys will be when a big ol' tree crushes their house in the middle of the night. The house has been smashed to pieces before by an industrious beaver. I live in midtown, precariously on an elbow of the North Fork of Crow Creek. I've lived here twenty-five years. In the blink of an eye a beaver can take down a tree so big it'll slice through your world like it was butter. Every morning I wonder what it's going to be that goes wrong today. If you don't wake up with these thoughts, you don't live in midtown. A beaver attack was not on my morning's threat estimation list.

"Tell the boys to keep an eye on it and I'll be right there."

I hang up and begin manically leafing through the yellow pages. Nothing under Beaver Extraction. Nothing under Gnawing. Dang. Finally, under pest control of all places, I spot an ad emphasizing humane wildlife control. Did you know there are as many advertisements for Pest Control companies as there are for lawyers; I'll bet there's even a pest control company for lawyers. I call the humane guy, get a machine—dang—leave a muddled message, then begin riffling around for someone less humane to call. Times have changed when it comes to people and wildlife. Back when, the accepted way to scupper a beaver was simply to shoot it. Bang, problem solved. Now, probably thanks to the Obama administration and the liberal democrats in Congress, the process is trickier. Then miracle of miracles, Ned Bruha returns my call.

"We've been after this beaver," Ned tells me.

I immediately liked Ned's basso profundo voice, his safari-like swagger. Later, I learned Ned came to his calling in life naturally. Before heading off for the Middle East to defend our country against weapons of mass destruction, Ned had grown up on a farm in Wisconsin with parents who wouldn't let him watch TV—hard to believe anyone's parents could be this benighted—so, as a result, he spent his deprived childhood outdoors learning the ways of all kinds of critters and varmints.

"She's been terrorizing this neighborhood, causing folks all kinds of trouble," Ned adds. Every chimerical monster is a she for some reason.

While Ned is explaining my options, I begin to think about my situation. What does all this mean to me? A property owner harboring in his backyard the most wanted beaver in town. What I didn't yet know was that this beaver was about to become—and soon—the most famous beaver on the planet.

The walk down my sandstone driveway is a long, bumpy one. People are always falling down on it. I lost a girlfriend once this way; wasn't sympathetic enough, and once, a friend sprained his ankle on it but was kind enough not to sue. When I reach the bridge, the cell rings. I'm giving this guy his own ringtone; probably the William Tell Overture.

"Mr. Eden? It's Ned Bruha."

"Ned, please call me Van. Hey, I'm on the bridge looking at the creek but don't see any—Whoa, my euonymus is gone!" It wasn't literally gone; it had just been reduced to a pile of giant toothpicks.

"Ruth tells me she [not Ruth] was swimming back and forth across the creek a few minutes ago and then disappeared into the creek bank."

Ned says, "I'd like to get an Animal Planet film crew over there."

"Hey, what an idea, Ned," I reply. You don't expect a pest control guy to be so funny. "Animal Planet is my favorite channel, but I never watch it."

It takes some talking, but Ned finally convinces me this was not a joke, that he has a series coming out on Animal Planet, that he's known as the Skunk Whisperer, and that with my consent he can bring a film crew to Tulsa to film the capture of my beaver. If Ned whispers to skunks, god knows what he does to beavers. A few minutes after this conversation, while still in a state of disbelief, staring at the creek, the phone rings again. It was Wendy from Animal Planet, calling from her office in Soho.

"Ned tells me we're on our way to Tulsa, that you've got a famous beaver in your creek that we need to shoot?

"Shoot? No, no."

"Film. We'll need releases, you and your tenant. Problem?"

"Uh. Not a problem. No problems on this end, Wendy."

The weekend flies by, like always. Other than a couple of emails from Ruth, diplomatically communicating her growing sense of nervousness about the situation, nothing much happens on the beaver front. Now it's Tuesday. I've moved on to other crises and have pretty much kept this story to myself, as none of my friends have anything resembling what you would think of as listening skills. If you can't say what you have to say in ten seconds, forget it, no one cares. They simply would not be capable of registering the hugeness of an Animal Planet film crew showing up in my backyard. I figure I'll just wait until I can say, "I called a pest control company and a couple of days later a crew from Animal Planet showed up."

"Mr. Eden. Ned Bruha. Can you meet me over at your creek in about thirty minutes? I want to discuss your extraction options."

As I drive up I see a spectacle of cars and trucks in front of my house, and groups of people milling around with cameras and strange pieces of equipment. I meet Ned. He's wearing Bermuda shorts, with black tennis shoes, black socks, and a big straw cowboy hat pulled down to his ears. The over-all impression is Ace Ventura meets Daniel Boone. I meet Wendy. Wendy's last name should be Wow, Winsome Wendy Wow. I meet everybody. We walk down the driveway, cameras rolling, and Ned explains my options. Basically, there's the humane expensive plan, the less humane expensive plan, and the least humane expensive plan.

Ned walks right into the creek, shoes and socks and all, with all the ease of someone walking across the street; waders, I guess, would be bad TV. Ned explains to the camera and the wild-eyed children who had gathered around that an angry beaver with young to protect can quickly chomp your hand off. Ruth winces. Wielding a camera specially designed to film sleeping beavers, Ned begins exploring the burrows.

Ned's expression is intense. Without taking his eyes off the viewer, "Whew, judging by the size of these burrows, what we have here," he tells the camera, "are two large families of beaver. At this time of day they'll be holed up way back in there"

If you're waiting for Ned to put a headlock on an angry beaver you're going to be disappointed with this ending. That may happen eventually, but not before the deadline of this piece. After a great deal of soul-searching, I choose option two, the less humane, expensive plan. We'll dig some holes to open up some skylights in their burrows, put some bio-friendly chemicals around, paint some trees, all designed to shoo the beavers up or down the creek, so my neighbors can get to know Mr. Bruha. Where are all these beavers going to go after they've humanely been given the bums out of all our hollers and swales, Burger King?

Ned reaches into the water and pulls out a handful of sticks that look suspiciously like pieces of my euonymus. He taps the pointed ends with his finger, and with a big grin tells the camera,

"These are for snacking." ◣

# POET ISSUES

*by Carol Johnson*

I have an almost pathological fear of poets. Well, not *all* poets.

I developed my phobia in a graduate poetry writing class. The visiting poet—a lovely Irishman named Richard Murphy—upon hearing my first poem, told me gently but firmly that my poetry displayed a certain lack of, well, "talent" was I believe the word he used. He saw no remedy but a return to that lower art: fiction. Clearly, my poem's magnificent *dreadfulness* caused him some alarm at what I might do if left alone with a rhyming dictionary and a pen. Although this was a traumatic experience, I was flattered when Murphy told another student that, while that student's attempt at a sonnet was appalling, he had yet to encounter anyone whose work approached the shocking awfulness of mine. I was awestruck, I guess, and why not? Murphy's words raised my lack of poetic ability to a level all its own.

Since then, I've met many poets, many of them during the *Nimrod* Hardman Awards, an assembly held in Tulsa each October, featuring the winners, runners-up and judges of the literary contest. Poets I've met in this intimate setting are generally considerate, accommodating, generous and even charming. Fran Ringold, twice Oklahoma's poet laureate and longtime executive editor of *Nimrod*, is one of the most engaging, at times profane, and consequently likable people I know. Mark Doty is kindness incarnate. Ted Kooser's avuncular nature is endearing. And

Billy Collins—labeled "too accessible" by those representing the tunnel-at-the-end-of the-light faction—enthralled a tough Tulsa audience for hours.

Nevertheless, affable poets I've encountered are far outnumbered by those who, well, who aren't affable. One whose name I'll keep to myself was as well known for his ill humor as his poetry. His whining tortured dogs in a four-block radius: "I can't drink this waaater. It came from a *taaap*. Oh! The bacteria. (Shudder) And I still have a headaaache. Probably brought on by dehydraaaation. No, I can't take that. I specifically said *Aleve*. I *know* I said it started with an *A*. Nothing about d-v-i-l. Of course I'm not taking it."

By now the muscles in my neck were clenched as tightly as my knees (over-anxious bladder, what can I say). Finally, after he'd removed all doubt about my intelligence and competence, he turned to another volunteer/victim.

"Is that *Aleve*? You have saved my life." He patted the new volunteer's arm. "And some water? In the square bottle. From real springs, not some river in Arkansas?" His withering glance sent me sprinting to the nearest restroom, wishing I had a bucket of pig's blood to dump over him. Let him make a villanelle out of *that*.

In short, I have fetched, ferried, carried and copied, retrieved eyeglasses, coats and cheap, but beloved, pens for poets like him, and believe me, that catalog of grievances begins at the baggage claim and ends, at least for me, when that airplane door hits him in the rondeau on the way out of town. So, last fall, I was terrified when I learned that my primary charge for the awards weekend was an internationally known, award-winning poet. I swooned. I really did. I thought I was going to have to lie down. Over the next few days I practiced a self-assured smile and mastered a standing position in which my thighs were not obviously clenched. When pick-up day arrived, I wouldn't say I was confident, but I felt reasonably certain that urination, driving and speaking would not happen simultaneously.

I stood in the airport with a large sign bearing the poet's last name (let's call her Jane), scanning the crowd nervously. When you're standing in an airport, everybody looks like a lost writer. Try it if you don't believe me. However, Jane walked straight to me, smiling broadly and looking as if Tulsa was the one place in the entire world she wanted to visit.

"You must be Carol!"

As indeed I was, we lugged her bag to the car and heaved it into my trunk. While we situated ourselves in the front seat, I patted my GPS. "This little gadget is going to save us a lot of time."

Dubious, but I felt bound to say it. The previous year, my author and I spent 20 minutes looking for the airport exit I'd driven through about a billion times. Once on the freeway, nothing looked familiar. That doesn't mean I hadn't seen it. It's just that most trees, wild flower, and whatnot bear an amazing resemblance to one another. Seriously. Trees are green and brown and flowers are other colors. And I certainly *do* have a sense of direction. Sun rises in the east, sets in the west. The moon is purposefully arbitrary. How is anybody supposed to keep up with that?

Long story short, my author and I reached an exit that didn't look familiar (like most of them).

"Over there? On the right?" my passenger said.

I looked.

"Your other right, Hon," she said gently.

Sure enough. Downtown. Probably exactly where it had always been. I delivered her to her hotel in less than five minutes.

I've earned my reputation for missing such looming structures such as the Crowne Plaza Hotel. Anthony Doerr, one of the nicest writers I've chauffeured, is probably convinced I'm a congenital idiot since I circled that hotel three times before being persuaded to unlock the doors and let him out. I'm sure he would have hung in there had it not been the fourth time in two days that I had come for him, and each time sailed serenely past the circular drive, populated with a dozen valets and doormen, even as my GPS squawked, "Destination on right. Recalculating . . . make a U-turn when possible."

So, as I touted to Jane the time-saving attributes of my GPS, I felt like one of those people who tell new parents how beautiful their child is, but can't find a single feature on the infant that is even remotely normal.

She patted my hand. "Oh honey, that's marvelous, but I've got to make a stop."

"Oh." Did I mention I don't like surprises? "What do you need?"

"A drugstore."

"Oh!" It so happened I knew the route—not a *direct* route, mind you, but a route, nevertheless—to several drugstores, even without a GPS. "Big? Small? Compounding pharmacy?"

Jane studied the landscape. "I need something a bit hard to find."

"Like what?"

"Oh, I'll just tell you straight up." She turned to me. "Feminine lubricant. I need lubricant. Where I'm from—those people seem to think women are just endlessly—let's say juicy. An absolute delusion on their part. We are *not* perpetually—well, you get my meaning."

"No. I mean yes." Feminine lubricant. Didn't see that one coming. I knew what it was. In theory. Because, you know, we do have sex in Oklahoma. Maybe Baptists and Pentecostals don't, lest somebody mistake it for dancing. But I'm a Congregationalist. We do have sex. I hear.

"It's called 'Me, Again,' and it's fabulous. Truly. It's like it says. 'Me, Again.'"

Its fabulous nature was not a conversation I felt up to, being close to hyperventilating.

"All righty then." My breath stuck in my chest, and I took an immediate wrong turn getting back on the highway.

Walgreen's was first, but I could have predicted that they wouldn't carry it. Frankly, I don't believe Walgreen's approves of women having sex. At least not good sex. A man can buy Viagra and that stuff that makes Bob smile really BIG on the TV commercials. And about 86 different condoms, some of which are boasted to be so thin you could read the Oxford English

Dictionary through them. They're made of lamb skin. Lamb skin! No wonder the lambs are silent. But go in there one time searching for a specific female lubricant and you do get a reputation. I'm pretty sure I'm on a list there.

Next was Drug Warehouse. The pharmacy tech pointed us toward the aisle that held hand lotion, petroleum jelly and similar items. The thing about Vaseline (besides the fact that you're sliding off your chair for weeks afterward because it's not water soluble) is that in the dark, the container feels an awful lot like a Mentholatum jar. You don't want to make that mistake. Not that I have. I hear things.

At any rate, we struck out at the first four drugstores we tried. At the following pharmacy, we were met by a young man about 20 with a nametag that read "Jared." I wanted to go around him, help ourselves. Want in one hand, spit in the other, my mother always said.

Jane smiled. "I'm looking for a particular feminine lubrication product."

Jared looked as if he knew what she meant but wished he didn't. "Wrinkle cream?"

Jane and I both burst into laughter and the more we laughed, the redder Jared's ears became. "Wrinkle cream," Jane gasped. "Wrinkle cream!"

Even through the laughter, my alarm escalated at the color of Jared's ears. I poked Jane in the arm. "You're embarrassing him," I whispered.

"I'm sorry." She wiped tears from her eyes. "Jared, I'm looking for a feminine—lubricant. It's called *Me, Again*, and it might be near the condoms."

Jared's ears had returned to normal, but his gaze couldn't meet either of ours. He pointed. "Aisle 7," he said. He seemed to be having a bit of trouble speaking.

Aisle 7's first offering was a plethora of flavored lubricants. I stopped. There was blueberry and peppermint and strawberry, probably tasty, but if lubricants were geared for more oral purposes, then why not lubricants with fluoride or teeth-whitening options? There's a million dollar idea for you. And stop looking at my teeth. They're naturally white.

"Bingo!" Jane cried, her eyes on a treasure trove of "Me, Again." Sweeping up as many of the containers as she could carry, she nodded at the shelf. "Can you get the last few?"

As we headed for the checkout, Jared, now at the register, saw us and hastily abandoned the area. A teen-aged girl glowered at him, then shrugged and began ringing up our purchases. Jane tossed a couple of *Snickers* on the counter with the rest of the merchandise.

In the car, she grinned. "Mission accomplished. An adventure, too." She tossed me a candy bar. "Chocolate for your troubles."

"You think there's a poem in this?" I asked, starting the car.

"Already percolating." She poked me. "And how about a story?"

"You never know." I returned the smile. The sweet taste of chocolate warmed me, and I backed from the space. In the growing dusk, I turned left out of the parking lot, and, after a few blocks, sighed and scanned the street for a likely place to make a U-turn. ◢

# INDEX

# ACKNOWLEDGEMENTS

SPECIAL THANKS TO THOSE WHOSE ASSISTANCE
HELPED MAKE THIS ANTHOLOGY POSSIBLE:

COURTNEY CAMPBELL, CECILIA WHITEHURST,
KATHRYN PARKMAN, AND CLAIRE SPEARS.

CPSIA information can be obtained
at www.ICGtesting.com
Printed in the USA
FSOW02n1816111116
27202FS